Dictionary of Confusable Words

Dictionary of Confusable Words

Adrian Room

Acquisition Director
Anne-Lucie Norton

FITZROY DEARBORN PUBLISHERS
CHICAGO • LONDON

428.003
Die

FITZROY DEARBORN PUBLISHERS
919 North Michigan Avenue — Suite 760
Chicago, IL 60611
U.S.A.

or

FITZROY DEARBORN PUBLISHERS
310 Regent Street
London W1R 5AJ
England

Library of Congress and British Library
Cataloging-in-Publication Data are available.

ISBN 1-57958-271-0

First published in the USA and UK 2000

Cover design by Peter Aristedes, Chicago Advertising and Design
Interior design and typeset by Print Means Inc., New York

For more information about Fitzroy Dearborn Publishers, see:
www.fitzroydearborn.com

Contents

Introduction

The English language has several words that are not only similar in meaning but similar in spelling or pronunciation. As a result, we are liable to use the wrong word in place of the right one and to regard all words of this type with uncertainty or suspicion. When is an *attack* an *assault*, for example, or a *discrepancy* a *disparity*? If you *debate* something, do you also *deliberate* it? If you do something *purposely*, do you also do it *purposefully*?

There is no doubt that abstract words cause much of the trouble. Many of them share a central element or 'core' that is differentiated only by a prefix or a suffix. An *accident* is thus not always the same as an *incident*, and something is done *successfully* today may be done *successively* tomorrow.

Most of these annoyances come in pairs, so that we wonder about the precise difference between *bedlam* and *babel*, *exotic* and *erotic*, *frown* and *scowl*, or *rigorous* and *vigorous*. There are also pairs of words that are quite different in spelling but sufficiently close in meaning to cause confusion. When is a *field* a *meadow*, or a *heath* a *moor*?

Confusing words can come in larger families than pairs. *Consist*, *comprise*, *constitute* and *compose*, for instance, are a fearsome foursome of words with similar forms and meanings. Sometimes the words are much less academic. Everyday examples of tantalizingly similar yet different words are such quartets as *giggle*, *snigger*, *snicker* and *titter*. Again, and back with the pairs, it can be a familiar phrase consisting of words linked by *and* that makes one wonder. How about *hustle* and *bustle*, for instance, or *stress* and *strain*?

Some confusing pairs of words are actually opposites. Although they have a common element which gives their linking sense, they also have contrasting elements which need to be differentiated. Examples are *prescribe* and *proscribe*, *upstage* and *downstage*, and *explicit* and *implicit*.

The vagaries of English spelling are a contributing factor to much of the confusion. Where the senses are widely different or very familiar there may be no problem. We hardly need to be told the difference between *fort* and *fought*, or *night* and *knight*. But often there is enough of a common association (or misassociation) to make us hesitate. Is it *vale* we want, or *veil*? These may be finicky points, but they can still cause hesitation.

In some instances it is the technical terms that cause the problem. We live in an increasingly scientific and technological world, and much of the vocabulary becomes familiar in everyday speech and certainly in the media. So we need to sort out *Celsius* and *centigrade*, *convex* and *concave*, *hypothermia* and *hyperthermia*, for example. At the other end of the usage scale, there are colloquial and slang terms to be distinguished. If something is a whole new *ball game*, is it in the same *ballpark*? Is a *slag* the same as a *slut*? If you *slaver*, do you *slobber*?

Confusable words are as old as the language. In the earliest example we have of the admittedly rather recondite word *macrocosm*, in an early 15th-century work by the monk and poet John Lydgate, the word appears consistently as *microcosm*, the exact opposite. Either Lydgate got it wrong or else his scribe did. We can tell the error because of the way the word is used. Today, in our time, we see evidence of similar confusion wherever words are spoken or written. An advertisement for the post of librarian placed by the British Library, no less, in the *Times Literary Supplement* of 21 January 1994, specifies that the successful applicant is expected to 'maintain and develop it's Information Service' and 'must not be adverse to working under pressure.' A few months later, a narrative text placed on billboards nationwide in Britain by the sponsors of the London Marathon spoke of the 'hoards of people' taking part. (See *microcosm*, *it's*, and *horde* in the present book.)

The book aims to clear up the confusion in such cases. In over 1100 entries, the meaning of around 3000 individual words are given (except where it would be insulting to do so), the difference between them is explained, and an illustrative example or quotation showing the correct usage is provided. Words occurring as the second or subsequent in a group are cross-referenced to their head word in the appropriate alphabetical place. As a bonus, the entries include some familiar proper names that are sometimes confused, such as *Liberia* and *Libya* (countries), *Monterey* and *Monterrey* (towns) and *Lloyds* and *Lloyd's* (financial institutions).

Confused? Be confused no longer, with this handy book as your user-friendly guide.

Adrian Room

A

abbreviation/acronym An *abbreviation* is any short form of a word, name or phrase: 'Many companies have a name that is an official abbreviation of their earlier name, so that International Business Machines is now IBM.' An *acronym* is an *abbreviation* that can be pronounced as a word or name: 'AIDS is an acronym for Acquired Immune Deficiency Syndrome.'

abdicate/abrogate/arrogate/derogate To *abdicate* is to renounce formally, especially a monarch the throne: 'Edward VIII abdicated in order to mary a divorcee.' 'She abdicated her rights to a pension.' To *abrogate* a law is to cancel or annul it: 'The old law on selling liquor on Sunday has been abrogated.' To *arrogate* a thing is to claim it presumptuously or without right: 'he arrogated special privileges for the staff.' To *derogate* a thing is to lessen or detract from it in some way: 'It would derogate from the park's attraction to compare it to a playground.'

ability *see* capability

abjure/adjure To *abjure* something is to renounce it or abstain from it, with the implication that this is done publicly: 'Members of the sect were required to abjure all alcoholic drink.' To *adjure* someone to do something is to request him or her solemnly to do it: 'The judge adjured the witness to tell the truth frankly.'

abrogate *see* abdicate

abstemious *see* abstinent

abstention/abstinence *Abstention* is the act of abstaining, especially when withholding one's vote at an election: 'There were 101 votes for, 57 against, and four abstentions.' *Abstinence* is also the act of abstaining, but from something that the abstainer regards as harmful: 'he maintained that abstinence from alcohol made a lifestyle that was not only healthier but cheaper.' *See also* abstinent.

abstinence *see* abstention

abstinent/abstemious *Abstinent* relates to abstaining or holding back from something, especially food and (alcoholic) drink: 'He holds that it is good for the body to be abstinent from time to time.' *Abstemious* means not taking too much food and (alcoholic) drink: 'His abstemious habits do not prevent him from enjoying parties.'

abstractedly/abstractly To do something *abstractedly* is to do it absent-mindedly, when thinking of something else: 'Beth paused from her letter, and stared abstractedly out the window.' To do something *abstractly* is to do it in the abstract, without reference to anything else: 'Considered abstractly, the proposal seems an excellent one.'

abstractly *see* abstractedly

abstruse *see* obscure

abuse/misuse To *abuse* something is to use it badly or wrongly: 'The banker abused the confidence of his costumers.' To *misuse* a thing is to use it in a way for which is was not intended, whether wrongly or not: '*A horse misused upon the road/Call to Heaven for human blood*' (William Blake).

academic/academical In general, *academic* relates to learning or scholarship, while *academical* has to do with an academy or place of learning: 'The school has an excellent academic record,' 'The question is merely academic,' 'The Royal Belfast Academical Institution is one of Northern Ireland's larger public schools.'

academical *see* academic

accede/concede To *accede* to something is to agree to it; to *concede* something is to accept it grudgingly or reluctantly: 'I accede to your request' (I accept it), 'I concede your superiority' (I have to admit you are better).

accent/accentuate To *accent* a word or syllable is to pronounce it more prominently, usually to clarify the meaning: 'That's the cause of all this crime,' he said, accenting the word "crime".' To *accentuate* something is to emphasize it generally, particular when it is something abstract: '*You've got to ac-cent-tchu-ate the positive/Elim-my-nate the negative*' (Johnny Mercer).

accent *see* dialect

accentuate *see* accent

accept/except To *accept* something or someone is to take it or him: to *except* it or him is to exclude it or him: 'Credit cards are accepted' (you can use them to pay), 'Credit cards are excepted' (you'll have to pay by cash or check).

acceptance/acceptation *Acceptance* relates to the accepting or approving of something: 'The agreement met with general acceptance.' *Acceptation* relates to the interpretation of a word or doctrine: 'In the acceptation of the government, "war" came to mean "self-defense", so that the War Department became the Department of Defense.'

acceptation *see* acceptance

access/accession *Access* is the act or process of gaining entry or admission (or admittance) to something: 'No access to storerooms: use the side door.' *Accession* is mostly used of a king or queen coming to the throne: 'Queen Elizabeth's accession was in 1952.' It can also be used of an item added to the stock of a library or museum: 'Latest accessions are shelved separately.'

accessary *see* accessory

accession *see* access

accessory/accessary *Accessory* is the normal spelling of the word to mean something extra or additional: 'The vacuum cleaner had several accessory parts.' In the legal sense, however, the spelling *accessary* is sometimes found: 'She was charged with being an accessary to the crime' (she had taken part in it).

accident/incident An *accident* is a mishap, mistake or disaster: 'The accident left three people injured,' 'The boys broke the goalpost by accident.' An *incident* is anything from a local 'heated argument' to an *accident* in the language of professional people who have to deal with it, such as police or firefighters: 'The meeting passed without incident,' 'Ambulances were called to a serious incident on the highway.'

accidental *see* incidental

accord/accordance If a thing is in *accord* with something else, it is in agreement with it: 'The contract is in full accord with company policy' (it agrees with it). If a thing is in *accordance* with something else, it obeys or follows it: 'The contract was drawn up in accordance with your instructions' (as you directed).

accord/account To do something of your own *accord* is to do it voluntarily, without prompting: 'The children straightened the room of their own accord.' To do something on your own *account* is to do it with some sort of risk, usually for your own benefit: 'He started a business on his own account.

accordance *see* accord

account/bill/invoice/statement In business, an *account* is a record of money, goods or services received and given: 'Some people settle their credit accounts monthly.' A *bill* is a note of charges for goods or services, usually on a single occasion: 'The bill for drinks was much more than we thought it would be.' An *invoice* is a list of goods and services provided, together with their cost, and may also act as a *bill*: 'Please return this invoice with your payment.' A *statement* is a formal *account* for a set period, usually a month: 'My bank statement says I am overdrawn.'

account *see* accord

accumulative/cumulative *Accumulative* relates to something that accumulates or gets greater by being gradually added to: 'The funds were earning accumulative interest.' *Cumulative* means basically the same, but often implies that the additions are not gradual but in successive separate stages: 'The old woman was suffering from the cumulative effect of a number of illnesses.'

acerbic *see* acid

achievement/exploit/feat An *achievement* is an accomplishment that involved the overcoming of a disadvantage or difficulty: 'It is an achievement to pass your driving test after only ten lessons.' An *exploit* is a brave, risky or cunning *achievement*: 'The war heroes were invited to talk about their exploits.' A *feat* is a difficult or 'showy' *achievement*: 'Jeff's greatest feat was to cycle up Pike's Peak.'

acid/acrid/acerbic *Acid* is used for something that has a bitter or sharp taste, or for something severe or sarcastic: 'I could taste the acid flavor of the lemon,' 'The teacher had an acid wit which not everyone appreciated.' *Acrid* is used for a strongly bitter smell or taste, or for something bad-tempered or caustic: 'Our eyes were smarting from the acrid fumes,' 'There was an acrid encounter between the two sides.' *Acerbic* is used for a speech or manner that is harsh or sharp: 'I can't stand his acerbic remarks.'

acquirement/acquisition An *acquirement* is a skill or quality that has been gained: 'Knowledge of word processing is a standard acquirement for most jobs.' An *acquisition* is a physical object that has been gained: 'Jack was admiring his latest acquisition, an 18th-century map of Scotland.'

acquisition *see* acquirement

acrid *see* acid

acronym *see* abbreviation

acrophobia/agoraphobia *Acrophobia* is fear of heights; *agoraphobia* is fear of open spaces. The two terms are often loosely used to denote apprehension about the respective locations: 'I suffer from acrophobia, and I am scared stiff of bridges,' 'She said she was prone to agoraphobia, and sometimes got panicky in crowds.'

act/action In general, an *act* is a deed, while an *action* is the process of doing it: 'It was an act of mercy to put the wounded bird out of its misery,' 'Her quick action stopped the child falling.' However, there is little difference in such sentences as: 'It was a very foolish act,' 'It was a very generous action.'

action *see* act

activate/actuate To *activate* something is to set it working or make it ready for use: 'The recorder is easy to activate: you just press this button.' To *actuate* something is to make it move or operate: 'This switch actuates the drive mechanism.' It is also to stimulate a person to do something: 'The old woman was actuated to steal because she was so hungry.'

actuate *see* activate

acuity *see* acumen

acumen/acuity *Acumen* is the ability to understand or appreciate things quickly and clearly: 'To become a congressman it helps to have political acumen.' *Acuity* is sharpness or keenness of thought or of the senses: 'The hawk has great acuity of sight.'

acute *see* chronic

adapt *see* adopt

adherence/adhesion Both words relate to 'sticking to' something, but *adherence* implies a strict observance, while *adhesion* usually indicates support: 'Most Muslims observe a strict adherence to the laws of Islam,' 'Many politicians were ready to declare their adhesion to the party.' *Adhesion* is also used literally, while *adherence* rarely is: 'Super-glue is well known for its special qualities of adhesion.'

adhesion *see* adherence

adjacent/adjoining If one thing is *adjacent* to another, it is next to it without necessarily making physical contact: 'The parking lot was adjacent to the sports stadium.' An *adjoining* object, however, has a common point of contact with another: 'The offices are to the left, with a parking garage adjoining.'

adjoining *see* adjacent

adjure *see* abjure

administer/administrate Both verbs can be used in the sense of managing or controlling something, though *administer* is more common: 'It is the job of judges to administer the law, but there are also other people who administrate, such as politicians and bishops.' To *administer* has the further sense, which *administrate* does not have, of giving something formally: 'The nurse administered the drugs nd medicine twice daily.'

administrate *see* administer

admission/admittance *Admission* is the right to enter a place, typically because one is a member or has paid an entrance fee: 'Admission to the exhibition is by invitation only.' *Admittance* is the physical act of entering a place, whether by right or not: 'No admittance except on business.'

admission *see* confession

admittance *see* admission

ado *see* to-do

adopt/adapt To *adopt* someone or something is to make him or it one's own: 'The childless couple adopted a baby girl,' 'The swimmer adopted a new style.' To *adapt* something is to alter it for a particular purpose: 'The bathtub was adapted to make its use easier for the elderly,' 'The novel was adapted for the TV version of the story.' On occasion it is possible to *adopt and adapt* something: 'A number of English words were adopted and adapted from the French' (they were borrowed from French and altered to conform to English sense or pronunciation).

adopted/adoptive The words are distinguished with regard to children that have been adopted (see **adopt**). *Adopted* is used for the children, and *adoptive* for the adults who have adopted them: 'She is an adopted child,' 'He never really took to his adoptive father.'

adoptive *see* adopted

advance/advancement The *advance* of something is its progress: 'The rapid advance of science and technology affects almost everyone.' The *advancement* of something is its promotion or encouragement: 'The society's objective is the advancement of research into anorexia.'

advancement *see* advance

advantage/vantage An *advantage* is a condition or circumstance that give you superiority or success: 'If you go abroad, it is an advantage to speak the language.' A *vantage* is a position that gives some kind of *advantage*: 'The cliff top afforded an excellent point of vantage for observing the yacht race.'

adventuresome *see* adventurous

adventurous/adventuresome/venturesome/venturous An *adventurous* person is one who seeks adventure or 'challenges': 'Jackie's quite adventurous: last year she cycled across India.' An *adventuresome* person is one who likes adventures but takes risks: 'Johnny's an *adventuresome* fellow: he likes exploring old tin mines.' A *venturesome* person is even rasher or bolder: 'Some novelists have heroes who are impossibly venturesome.' *Venturous* means the same, but is often applied to the deed rather than the doer: 'The prisoner made a venturous bid to escape.'

adverse *see* averse

aesthetic/ascetic *Aesthetic* relates to what is beautiful or artistic: 'The architect designed the shopping mall with both aesthetic and practical considerations in mind.' *Ascetic* relates to abstinence from worldly pleasure or 'creature comforts', often with the aim of spiritual gain: 'As a non-smoker and teetotaller he leads a very ascetic life.'

a few *see* few

affect/effect To *affect* something is to have an *effect* on it: 'Smoking can affect your health.' To *effect* something is to make it happen: 'The doctor's treatment effected an immediate improvement in the patient's health.'

affectation *see* affection

affection/affectation An *affection* is fondness for someone or something: 'I remember our times together with great affection.' An *affectation* is a display of unnatural behavior or speaking: 'Actors sometimes indulge in affectation to enhance their roles.'

afflicted *see* inflicted

affront/effrontery An *affront* us a deliberate insult; *effrontery* is impertinence: 'His remarks were an affront to all law-abiding citizens,' 'He had the effrontery to suggest I was mistaken.'

aggression/aggressiveness *Aggression* is a show of anger or hostility: 'Eve was always full of aggression as a child,' 'The prime minister warned against any act of aggression against their Arab neighbors.' *Aggressiveness* can also mean this, but can equally imply forcefulness and self-assertiveness: 'The sales staff were advised to display confidence and aggressiveness in approaching potential customers.'

aggressiveness *see* aggression

agnostic/atheist An *agnostic* is someone who holds that it is impossible to know whether there is a God or not. An *atheist* holds that there is no God: 'The word *agnostic* was invented by the 19th-century biologist T.H. Huxley,' '*By night an atheist half believes a God*' (Edward Young).

agoraphobia *see* acrophobia

aid/aide *Aid* is help or assistance; and *aide* is a helper or assistant: 'aid workers with the UN forces in Bosnia aimed to bring food, medicines, and clothing to the local population,' 'The chief aides to the United States president were also present at the meeting.'

aide *see* aid

alarm/alarum The usual spelling of the word in all senses is *alarm.* However, the spelling *alarum* is still occasionally found in the set expression *alarums and excursions,* used of a local disturbance or conflict. This was originally a stage direction in Elizabethan plays for 'noises off' to indicate a skirmish or battle: '*A Field of Battle near Barnet. Alarums and Excursions. Enter King Edward bringing in Warwick, wounded*' (Shakespeare).

alarum *see* alarm

ale/beer In general, *ale* is strong or draft *beer*: 'Two pints of light ale, please,' 'CAMRA, the Campaign for Real Ale, was set up in 1971 to promote the brewing and drinking of genuine ale.' But the word also simply means *beer*, especially in 'olde worlde' contexts: 'he likes to sup his ale.'

alias/alibi An *alias* is a false name, not a false description or personation: 'His real name was John Smith but he ran his business under the alias of Joe Bloggs.' An *alibi* is properly a statement that a person was somewhere else at the time a crime was committed: 'His alibi was supported by his sister, who had been visiting him that evening.' It can also be used for a general excuse: 'My alibi is that the train was late.'

alibi *see* alias

allay/alleviate/assuage To *allay* something is to make it less or get rid of it altogether: 'She allayed my fears by saying that she also had heard nothing,' 'I want to allay any doubts you may have about this.' To *alleviate* is to relieve something unpleasant or painful by making it less severe: 'The ointment soon alleviated the discomfort,' 'Volunteer workers did their best to alleviate the situation.' To *assuage* is similar but is mainly used of unpleasant emotions or bodily sensations: 'I tried to assuage the old man's terror,' 'The crew were desperate to assuage their fearful thirst.'

alleviate *see* allay

Allies/Axis In the Second World War, the *Allies* were the countries that fought against the *Axis*, i.e. Britain, the USA, the Soviet Union, France, China and Poland against Germany, Italy and Japan: 'The forces of the Allies outnumbered those of the Axis.'

allocate/allot To *allocate* something is to set aside or 'earmark' part of something for a particular purpose: 'Doctors were allocated parking spaces near the hospital entrances.' To *allot* something is to give it on the understanding that it is restricted or shared in some way: 'Each speaker was allotted a maximum of 10 minutes.'

allot *see* allocate

allude/refer To *allude* to someone or something is to mention him or it briefly or indirectly: 'When you said someone was unreliable, to whom exactly were you alluding?' To *refer* to a person or thing is to mention him or it generally or directly: 'To whom are you referring?'

allure *see* lure

alternately/alternatively *Alternately* means one after the other, of two people or things: 'The marksmen fired alternately at the target.' *Alternatively* means one instead of the other, also of two: 'white would suit you, or alternatively black.'

alternatively *see* alternately

although/though *Although* is generally felt to be stronger than *though*: 'She insisted on writing, although I advised her not to' (she ignored my advice), 'She insisted on writing, though I advised her not to' (she went ahead anyway).

amatory *see* amorous

amazed/astonished/astounded/dumbfounded If you are *amazed* you are very surprised or delighted at something: 'The skater's agility amazed me.' If you are *astonished* you are surprised at something, not necessarily pleasantly: 'The waiter's ignorance about the menu astonished me.' If you are *astounded* you are so surprised you are almost lost for words: 'Your impudence astounds me.' If you are *dumbfounded* you may even be struck dumb with shock or surprise: 'When Sally said she was going to marry Harry after all, I was dumbfounded.'

ambiguous/ambivalent If something is *ambiguous* it has more than one possible meaning, and so is obscure or difficult to understand: 'When I asked Stuart if he condemned my action, he gave me an ambiguous answer,' 'The message was perfectly clear and not the least ambiguous.' If a person is *ambivalent* he or she has an uncertain attitude or feeling toward someone or something: 'The French are ambivalent about royalty: they abolished their own monarchy but are very interested in the British royal family.'

ambivalent *see* ambiguous

amend/emend To *amend* something is to alter it, usually for the better: 'The referee amended certain rules to make it easier for the new players.' To *emend* something is to correct it, especially a printed text: 'The writer emended the awkward ending to the story so that it read better.'

amiable/amicable An *amiable* person or manner is one that is friendly: 'Joseph is a very amiable young man: he'd do anything to help anyone.' *Amicable* refers to something done with goodwill: 'The neighbors had an amicable agreement about who should cut the hedge.'

amicable *see* amiable

amid/among *Amid* (or *amidst*) properly applies to things that cannot be separated or counted: 'We stood amid the ruins of the building,' 'The cows stood peacefully amid the tall grass.' *Among* (or *amongst*) properly applies to things that *can* be separated or counted: 'We stood among the trees,' 'I found the letter among a pile of bills.' The words are often used interchangeably, however.

amok *see* berserk

among *see* amid

amoral *see* immoral

amorous/amatory *Amorous* usually relates to sexual love: 'She was tired of his amorous advances.' *Amatory* usually relates to love in the abstract, although it could imply eroticism, especially in literature: '*When amatory poets sing their loves/In liquid lines*' (Byron).

anarchism *see* anarchy

anarchy/anarchism *Anarchy* is the state of absence of government or control in society, or of lawlessness generally: 'After the revolution there was a period of anarchy.' *Anarchism* is the political theory that laws and government should be abolished: 'Some Russian revolution-aries put their theories of anarchism into practice.'

anger/rage/fury/indignation *Anger* is a strong feeling of annoyance, often with a desire for revenge: 'The residents expressed their anger at the felling of the oak tree.' *Rage* is a violent outburst of *anger*: 'Peter flew into a rage at the sight of his ruined car.' *Fury* is a *rage* that may well be out of control: 'Debbie was so cross with the boy that in her fury she smacked him.' *Indignation* is a more measured and 'moral' expression of annoyance: 'The priest wrote to express his indignation at the thefts from his church.'

announce/pronounce/proclaim To *announce* something is to state it publicly and fairly formally: 'The head teacher announced that the next day would be a holiday.' To *pronounce* is to state something solemnly or with authority, also usually in public: 'The art expert pronounced the picture to be a forgery.' To *proclaim* something is to *announce* it importantly and to a wide audience: 'The government proclaimed the country's independence.'

annual/perennial An *annual* event or occurrence is one that happens every year: 'The children were excited about the annual school field trip.' A *perennial* event or process lasts throughout the year or even over many years: 'The stream was a perennial source of fish and fresh water.'

antagonist/protagonist An *antagonist* is an opponent or adversary: 'The Leader of the Opposition proved himself a worthy antagonist of the Prime Minister in the parliamentary debate.' A *protagonist* is a leading character in a play or a leader in any enterprise or cause: 'The protagonist in *Hamlet* is one of Shakespeare's most complex and controversial characters,' 'The speaker was a protagonist of the superiority of the Western way of life.'

Antarctic *see* Arctic

antedate/postdate To *antedate* something is to date it earlier than the day when it is written or should be dated: 'He sent me an antedated check' (written on the 10th but dated the 5th). To *postdate* something is to date it later than it is written: 'I sent him a postdated check' (written on the 10th but dated the 20th, so that he couldn't cash it until that date).

anticipate/expect To *anticipate* something is to *expect* it and prepare for it: 'I don't anticipate any trouble' (I don't think there will be any, and I haven't prepared myself for it). If you *expect* someone or something, you do not need to prepare for him or her or it: 'I'm expecting her any minute now,' 'I was expecting a phone call.'

antiquated *see* antique

antique/antiquated As applied to furniture, ornaments and domestic items generally, something *antique* is old and valuable, while something *antiquated* is (usually) old-fashioned and obsolete: 'The old shop had some genuine antique pieces but also some very ordinary objects, such as an antiquated vacuum cleaner.'

anxiety *see* apprehension

aphorism *see* maxim

appraise/apprise To *appraise* is to evaluate or assess: 'The project was appraised as being viable.' To *apprise* is to inform: 'We were apprised of the committee's decision.'

apprehend/comprehend In the sense of understanding, to *apprehend* something is to perceive or appreciate its essential quality or nature, or to grasp its meaning or significance: 'Who can apprehend the true nature of beauty?' 'I'm not sure I apprehend you right.' To *comprehend* something is to understand it completely, with the implication that mental effort is required to do so: 'I can't comprehend the motives for her action.'

apprehension/anxiety *Apprehension* is a state of nervous uncertainty: 'Jack regarded his visit to the dentist with apprehension.' *Anxiety* usually implies a more protracted or 'emotional' state of *apprehension*: 'Deborah was sick with anxiety as she waited for the news of her son.'

apprise *see* appraise

appropriate/expropriate To *appropriate* something is to take it as one's own, especially without permission or illegally: 'The secretary was accused of appropriating club funds.' To *expropriate* something is also to do this, but the word emphasizes the illegal aspect of the action: 'The dancer expropriated the costume for her own use.' Otherwise the verb is used for the action of taking something such as property from its private owner for public use without making any payment: 'The farmer's land was expropriated by the Department of Defense for army exercises.'

a priori/prima facie *A priori* (Latin for 'from the previous') is used for something concluded from assumption rather than known facts: 'To say the electorate is impatient simply because the government has been in power so long is an a priori conclusion which cannot be supported.' *Prima facie* (Latin for 'at first sight') is used for something concluded despite lacking full evidence or proof: 'If you have been defamed, you have a prima facie case for bringing action of libel,' 'The director of education recommended the teacher be suspended because he had found prima facie evidence of gross misconduct.'

Arab/Arabian/Arabic As adjectives, *Arab* is used mainly of the Arabs and their modern countries, *Arabian* of Arabia (the peninsula between the Red Sea and the Persian Gulf), and *Arabic* of the languages and literature of the Arabs: 'The Arab nations now include countries outside the natural limits of the Arabian Peninsula, and the Arabic language has adopted many forms in those countries.'

Arabian *see* Arab

Arabic *see* Arab

arbiter/arbitrator An *arbiter* is someone who has the power to decide what will be done or accepted in a particular area or activity: 'The arbiters of fashion influence not just what we wear but also the way the sexes see each other.' An *arbitrator* is a person appointed to arbitrate (see below).

arbitrate/mediate To *arbitrate* is to hear evidence impartially from two sides and make a decision: 'An official was sent to arbitrate in the dispute between management and unions.' To *mediate* is to act as a go-between in a dispute by talking to each side separately in an attempt to bring them together in a mutually acceptable agreement: 'A friend of both men did his best to mediate in their quarrel.'

arbitrator *see* arbiter

arcane *see* arch

arch/arcane *Arch* means sly or knowing: 'When I said I might be late, Jim gave me an arch look.' *Arcane* means mysterious or obscure: 'The video manual had an arcane reference to a "skip search facility."'

Arctic/Antarctic The *Arctic* is the region of the North Pole: 'Polar bears are found in the Arctic, not the Antarctic.' The *Antarctic* is the region of the South Pole, so called as it is *anti* or opposite the *Arctic*: 'Vaughan Williams based his *Sinfonia Antarctica* on music he wrote for the film *Scott of the Antarctic*.'

arise *see* rise

arouse *see* rouse

arrogate *see* abdicate

art/science The *art* of photography, or the *science* of photography? The general distinction is: 'Science knows, but art does.' Since many *arts* depend on *science* (for example music), the best way of differentiating is to say that something is a *science* if it is theoretical, but an *art* if those theories are put into practice, especially skilfully or imaginatively: 'medicine was long regarded as an art before it became a science.'

arthritis *see* rheumatism

artist/artiste An *artist* is anyone engaged in the fine or performing arts, such as a painter, sculptor, actor or entertainer: 'Rembrandt remains a popular artist.' An *artiste* is usually a singer or dancer, or else a person skilled in a special craft: 'The hotel chef has trained professionally and is a real artiste.'

artiste *see* artist

ascendancy/ascendant *Ascendancy* denotes a superior position over others: 'Martina Navratilova gained general ascendancy over rival tennis champions." *Ascendant* denotes the rising in power to such a position: 'Her career was clearly in the ascendant.'

ascendant *see* ascendancy

ascetic *see* aesthetic

Asian/Asiatic The terms were at one time interchangeable for anyone or anything from Asia. *Asian* is now generally applied to people and their languages, and *Asiatic* to things: 'He has an Asian girlfriend,' 'The Asiatic plains and deserts are awesome in their vastness.'

Asiatic *see* Asian

assail *see* assault

assassin/murderer/killer An *assassin* is someone who kills for a political or (less often) social or religious reason: 'The supposed assassin of President Kennedy was Lee Harvey Oswald.' A *murderer* is someone who has been convicted of murder: 'The weapon used by the murderer was found in a nearby ditch.' A *killer,* at any rate in media usage, is someone who kills for any motive at all: 'Killer strikes again.'

assault/assail To *assault* a person or thing is to make a violent or shocking attack on him or her or it: 'The old man was assaulted and robbed in the park.' To *assail* someone or something is an attack that may well be figurative rather than physical: 'The runner was assailed by doubts as she lined up for the race.'

assault *see* attack

assent/consent *Assent* is agreement to a proposal, especially when readily given: 'Tina asked if she could pat the horse, and the rider nodded his assent.' *Consent* is agreement made after a due consideration or 'weighing up': 'My boss was not too happy about my request but finally gave his consent.'

assert/asseverate/aver To *assert* something is to declare it to be so: 'John has always asserted that Americans are generous hosts.' To *asseverate* is to *assert* something solemnly or emphatically: 'The accused men asseverated that they had never been near the place.' To *aver* something is to *assert* that it is true: 'She averred that she was entirely innocent of the accusation.'

assertion/assertiveness An *assertion* is a positive statement that something is true: 'I have my doubts about some of his assertions.' *Assertiveness* is the state of asserting something (see assert above), or saying it confidently: 'Assertiveness is often necessary in business in order to succeed.'

assertiveness *see* assertion

asseverate *see* assert

assiduous/sedulous An *assiduous* person is one who carries out work or a task with dedication and perseverance: 'The athlete was assiduous in her daily training and never missed a session.' A *sedulous* person is one who takes great care and trouble over something: 'The employees are not all as sedulous in their duties as Tim is.'

assignation *see* assignment

assignment/assignation An *assignment* is a task or piece of work allotted to a person or group of people: 'The secretary's first assignment was to learn how to work the fax machine.' An *assignation* is the actual arranging of an *assignment* or an appointment at a particular time and place, in particular a secret meeting of lovers: 'The assignation given the dog handlers proved harder than they expected.'

assuage *see* allay

assume *see* presume

assure/ensure/insure To *assure* something is to make certain it will happen: 'Victory is assured for the younger, fitter boxer as he has the advantage.' To *ensure* something is to take steps to make sure that something happens: 'Seat belts should ensure that you will be unhurt in an accident.' To *insure* something is to take precautions against something undesirable happening: 'The concertgoers insured against disappointment by buying their tickets early.'

astonished *see* amazed

astounded *see* amazed

astrology *see* astronomy

astronaut/cosmonaut As the terms were generally used, an *astronaut* was a spaceman or woman from any country except the Soviet Union, while a *cosmonaut* was specifically Soviet. Today all space travellers are *astronauts*, even Russians: 'In the 1960s, American astronauts and Soviet cosmonauts vied with each other in the space race.'

astronomy/astrology *Astronomy* is the scientific study of the stars and other celestial bodies; *astrology* is the quasi-scientific study of the stars and planets and their supposed influence on human life and destiny: 'For astronomy you may need a telescope; for astrology you need a horoscope.'

at *see* in

atheist *see* agnostic

attack/assault An *attack* on someone or something is a forceful act directed against him or it, whether literally or figuratively: 'The President was increasingly under attack that year.' An *assault* is a specifically hostile *attack*: 'George tried to win his case by constant assaults on his former colleague's reputation.'

attendant/attender An *attendant* provides a service to people: 'She worked for a while as a cloakroom attendant.' An *attender* is someone who attends something: 'He was a regular attender at church.'

attender *see* attendant

attorney/lawyer Strictly speaking, an *attorney* is a person, usually but not necessarily a *lawyer*, who acts for someone else in business or legal matters. A *lawyer* is thus a person trained and qualified in legal matters: 'In the United States, a lawyer representing someone in a court of law is officially known as an attorney-at-law.'

augury/auspice An *augury* is a sign or omen of something to come, whether good or bad: 'Red skies in the morning are often an augury of bad weather.' An *auspice* is almost always a good omen: 'Red skies at night can be an auspice of fine weather.'

aura/aurora An *aura* (literally 'breeze') is the characteristic atmosphere that someone or something has: 'The college exuded an aura of respectability,' 'Henrietta had an attractive aura of mischief about her.' An *aurora* (literally 'dawn') is a display of colored lights in the sky near the North Pole: 'The aurora borealis is more commonly known as the northern lights.'

aural/oral Anything *aural* relates to the ear and so to hearing: 'The doctor arranged an aural examination for his patient,' 'Many teachers work with both aural and written material.' Anything *oral* relates to the mouth and so to speaking: 'The French exam was in two parts; first written, then oral,' 'Many of the stories were passed down by oral tradition, and had never been written down before.'

aurora *see* aura

auspice *see* augury

auspicious/propitious If something is *auspicious* it promises well for the future: 'Clare's new term got off to an auspicious start.' If it is *propitious* it is favorable *now* as well as boding well for the future: 'It was hardly a propitious time to launch a new business,' 'Luckily the weather was propitious, and we were soon on our way.'

authoritarian *see* authoritative

authoritative/authoritarian An *authoritative* manner is that of a person who speaks, writes or acts with authority: 'Her authoritative reply to our questions gave us confidence.' An *authoritarian* manner is that of someone who subjects others, or would like to, to his or her authority: 'His speech was unpleasantly authoritarian in tone.'

autumn/autumnal As an adjective, *autumn* relates to something pertaining directly to autumn: 'The autumn term begins on 1st September,' 'He loved the gold and yellow of the autumn leaves.' *Autumnal* is used for something that has the characteristics of autumn but that is not directly associated with it: 'There was an autumnal chill in the air this morning, although it's only August.'

autumnal *see* autumn

avenge/revenge To *avenge* oneself is to obtain redress or vindication for a wrong against one, usually according to accepted traditions or rules, but not necessarily lawfully: 'The thief avenged himself by stealing his accuser's wallet.' To *revenge* oneself is to 'get one's own back' similarly, but the wrong may be imaginary or exaggerated: 'He said he would revenge himself on anyone who criticized him.'

aver *see* assert

averse/adverse A person who is *averse* to something does not like it or is not keen on it: 'He is not averse to a drink now and then.' A thing that is *adverse* to someone or something is hostile or harmful to him or it: 'Many campaigners saw the election result as adverse to the cause of democracy.'

avid/rabid *Avid* implies an almost greedy keenness: 'He was an avid collector of old coins.' *Rabid* is used for a feeling or emotion so intense that it is almost pathological or morbid: 'She formed a rabid dislike for her new neighbors.'

avocation *see* vocation

avoid/evade/elude To *avoid* a person or thing is to take action in such a way that one need not encounter or experience him or her or it: 'Sam avoids flying for fear of an accident.' To *evade* a person or thing is to escape him or her or it, or 'get out of it', usually by cunning: 'When I asked the mayor about the new tax, he evaded my question' (but he could not *avoid* it). To *elude* a person or thing is also to escape by cunning, but may equally be for some undefined reason: 'The prisoner managed to elude the police,' 'Her name eludes me for the moment.'

avow/vouch To *avow* something is to admit or declare it publicly: 'He avowed his determination to get his own back,' 'She avowed herself to be a loyal supporter of the party.' To *vouch* for someone or something is to produce evidence in support of him or her or it: 'I can vouch for her honesty,' 'Can you vouch for the truth of that?'

await *see* wait

awake *see* wake

awaken *see* wake

award *see* reward

awesome/awful *Awesome* is used for someone or something that inspires or displays awe or is usually impressive: 'The mountain was an awesome sight.' *Awful* formerly had a similar meaning ('full of awe'), especially when relating to something fearful or terrible, but now means little more than 'very great.' Something of the former sense remains in sentences such as: 'There was an awful noise outside last night.'

awful *see* awesome

axiom *see* maxim

Axis *see* Allies

B

babble/blather/gabble/rabbit To *babble* is to talk incoherently, incessantly or injudiciously: 'I asked him why he was late, and he babbled something in response,' 'The teacher found it hard to stop the children babbling all the time,' 'John babbled out the secrets of his many affairs,' To *blather* (or *blether*) is to talk foolishly: 'Stop your blathering and tell me what really happened.' To *gabble* is to talk rapidly and indistinctly: 'The actor gabbled his words, making it difficult to understand what he was saying.' To *rabbit* is to chatter or talk inconsequentially: 'The girls were rabbiting on about some new rock star.'

babel *see* babble

babysitter *see* childminder

back/rear The *back* of something is the opposite of its front, whether inside or out: 'There are two free seats at the back of the bus.' The *rear* of something is its hind part or section, often as viewed from outside: 'We arrived just in time to see the rear of the train disappearing round the bend.'

badinage *see* banter

bail/bale To *bail* someone out is to provide cash to get him/her out of prison, or more generally to help him/her out of a difficult situation, especially a financial one: 'I had to borrow $500 to bail John out,' 'If you hadn't bailed me out last year, I don't know what I would have done.' To *bail* water out is to scoop it out with a bucket or other container: 'We bailed out the water that was coming into the boat.' To *bale* out is to jump from an aircraft: 'The pilot had to bale out when the engine failed.' However, *bail* is also used in this last sense, especially in United States: 'The pilot bailed out.'

baited *see* bated

bale *see* bail

baleful/baneful Something that is *baleful,* such as a look or glance, is menacing or hurtful: 'The sergeant cast a baleful eye over the new recruits.' Something that is *baneful* is harmful or even fatal: 'The doctor warned his patients about what he called "the baneful effect of alcohol."'

ball game/ballpark The two expressions have colloquial senses that can be confusing: 'It's a whole new ball game' (circumstances have changed completely), 'You're just not in the right ballpark' (you're way out).

ballpark *see* ball game

balmy/barmy *Balmy* is used in all senses of the word, whether applied to gentle air or to something fragrant or soothing, or as the colloquial word meaning 'foolish.' This second sense usually has the spelling *barmy*, however: 'It was a still and balmy evening,' 'Why did you do that? You must be barmy!' *'People here must have gone balmy'* (J.B. Priestley).

baloney *see* blarney

baluster *see* banister

ban/bar A *ban* is a prohibition, often a permanent one: 'There is a ban against parking in this street.' A *bar* is a qualified or temporary *ban* or a restriction of some kind: 'There is a bar on people under eighteen entering,' 'His height was a bar to his acceptance.'

baneful *see* baleful

banister/baluster A *banister* is one of the upright rails supporting the handrail of a staircase: 'Most children like to slide down the banisters if they get a chance.' A *baluster* is one of the short pillars supporting the rail or stone coping round a balcony, terrace or the like: 'Many balusters are narrow at the top and bottom, and swell out in the middle.'

banter/badinage *Banter* is a good-natured tease: 'The banter in the bar continued loud and long that evening.' *Badinage* is similar, but usually lighter and more 'cerebral': 'The students engaged in a few minutes' nervous badinage before the exam.'

bar/barrier A *bar* is an expected or reasonable obstruction or prohibition on something: 'Age need not be a bar to promotion these days.' A *barrier* is an unexpected and unwelcome *bar*, and one usually difficult or even impossible to overcome: 'There was a tangible barrier of distrust between the boss and his employees.'

bar *see* ban

barbarian *see* barbarous

barbaric *see* barbarous

barbarous/barbaric/barbarian *Barbarous* behavior is primitive or cruel: 'The prisoners often had to put up with barbarous treatment in the camps.' *Barbaric* behavior is uncivilized or unrestrained: 'The football fans made a barbaric din throughout the game.' *Barbarian* is close to both these, especially when applied to something now normally regarded as civilized or cultured: 'The barbarian tribes indulged in rites that today would shock most of us.'

barmy *see* balmy

baron/baronet In Great Britain a *baron* is a member of the lowest rank of the peerage. A *baronet* ranks below him (but above a knight): 'Barons are called "Lord," but baronets are called "Sir".'

baronet *see* baron

barrier *see* bar

base/basis The *base* of something is its fundamental part, whether literal or figurative: 'Ron built his garden shed on a concrete base,' 'The discovery served as a base for further research.' A *basis* may also be literal, but is very frequently figurative, and by implication is the starting point for something more complex: 'The basis of the Spanish drink sangria is red wine and fruit juice,' 'I found it hard to understand the basis of the speaker's argument.'

basin *see* bowl

basis *see* base

bated/baited *Bated* is related to *abated,* so means 'lessened': 'We waited with bated breath to see who had won.' *Baited* means 'enticed' or 'tormented': 'The mousetrap was baited with cheese,' 'The class baited the new teacher, trying to make him lose his temper.'

bath/bathe To *bath* is to give a bath to someone: 'It was time to bath the baby again.' To *bathe* is either to swim in the sea (or a river) or to apply liquid to part of the body to soothe it: 'That afternoon we bathed three times,' 'They bathed her eyes whenever they were sore.'

bathe *see* bath

bathos *see* pathos

bay window/bow window A *bay window* projects outwards from a room in either a curve or with three straight sides: 'She liked to sit in the bay window, watching the world go by.' A *bow window* is a curved *bay window:* 'Bow windows are a distinctive feature of many 18th-century buildings.'

beast/brute A person who is a *beast* is unkind or thoughtless: 'Jamie rode his bike over the new lawn and ruined it, the little beast.' A *brute* is a cruel or violent person, and usually 'heavily' so: 'Her husband was a real brute, especially when he was drunk.'

becomes *see* behooves

bedlam/babel *Bedlam* is uncontrolled or confused noise or activity: 'It was absolute bedlam at the market, with people shouting and shoving everywhere.' *Babel* is usually a confusion of noises and voices only: 'There was such babel at the meeting that the chairperson had a job to make himself heard.'

beer *see* ale

beginning/start The *beginning* of something is its general commencement, often only vaguely defined: 'We usually visit her at the beginning of the month.' The *start* of something is its initial opening, often precisely defined or understood: 'The start of the movie was delayed half an hour.'

begrudge/grudge To *begrudge* something is to give it unwillingly or envy someone its possession: 'I don't begrudge the school fees, they're worth it,' 'Julie begrudged Molly her new car.' To *grudge* has the same two senses but less strongly or more generally so: 'Jim grudged the time it took to walk to work,' 'I don't grudge him his luck: he deserves it.'

behooves/becomes *Behooves,* always preceded by 'it', is used for something that is right or necessary: 'It ill behooves you to speak thus of your grandparents' (you should not speak of them like that). *Becomes* is used for something that is fitting, appropriate or (especially for clothes) well suited: 'It ill becomes you to speak thus of your grandparents' (it is not the sort of way I expect you to speak about them),' 'Amanda's new outfit certainly becomes her.'

belabor *see* labor

bellicose *see* belligerent

belligerent/bellicose If something or someone is *belligerent,* he or she or it is aggressive or hostile: 'There's no need to speak in such a belligerent tone.' *Bellicose* is similar but stronger, implying a readiness to fight or use physical violence: 'The drunk approached the policeman in a bellicose manner.'

belly *see* billow

beneficent *see* benevolent

benevolent/beneficent *Benevolent* means wishing well: 'The manager addressed his staff with a benevolent smile' *Beneficent* means doing good: 'The old lady left her local church $500, a beneficent gesture.'

benign/benignant If a person or thing is *benign,* he or she or it is kindly or gentle: 'He gave the child a benign smile,' 'The benign influence of the spring sunshine began to work its magic.' *Benignant* means virtually the same, but is a loftier word, and can imply a patronizing or condescending attitude: 'The professor gave the students a benignant glance at this point.' *Compare* malign

benignant *see* benign

bereaved/bereft The words are related, but are now used in quite distinct senses. *Bereaved* is used for a person who has been deprived of someone, often a relative, through his/her death; *bereft* is used for a person who has been deprived of anything at all: 'The bereaved family are still in a state of shock,' 'I was quite bereft of speech' (I couldn't speak), *'Of friends, of hope, of all bereft'* (William Cowper).

bereft *see* bereaved

berserk/amok To go *berserk* is to behave crazily or violently: 'When the trainer saw his team lose, he went berserk.' To run *amok* is to lose control and run about wildly like someone in a murderous frenzy: 'The crowd ran amok when the singer appeared, and the police could scarcely control them.'

beside/besides *Beside* means next to; *besides* means in addition to; 'There was no one beside Jane' (there was no one next to her), 'There was no one besides Jane' (she was the only one there).

besides *see* beside

biannual/biennial A *biannual* event happens twice a year: 'We make a biannual visit to the in-laws: once at Christmas and again in the summer.' A *biennial* event happens every two years: 'The school was due for its biennial inspection.' (A *biennial* plant lasts two years.)

biennial *see* biannual

bill *see* account

billion *see* million

billow/belly To *billow* is to swell out and collapse or subside in waves or repeated motions: 'The curtains billowed in the breeze,' 'Thick clouds of smoke were billowing from the chimney.' To *belly,* usually applied to something large, is to swell out and stay swollen: 'The sails of the yacht were bellying in the wind.'

bisect *see* dissect

blanch *see* blench

blare *see* blast

blarney/baloney *Blarney* is a wheedling or flattering talk: 'Let's have none of your blarney now.' *Baloney* (or *boloney*) is foolish or meaningless talk: That's absolute baloney; you don't know what you're talking about.'

blast/blare/bray As applied to a noise or sound, a *blast* is loud and piercing, implying a hearty blow, as typically in a battle or hunt: '*O, for a blast of that dead horn*' (Walter Scott). A *blare* is both loud and raucous, as typically of trumpets or other brass instruments: 'The band blared out a march.' A *bray* is similar, but implying a discordant musical phrase: '*And the brass will crash,/ And the trumpets bray,/And they'll cut a dash/On their wedding day*' (W.S. Gilbert).

blatant/flagrant A *blatant* offense or injustice is a glaring or obvious one: 'She said she was out, but that's a blatant lie as I saw her through the window.' A *flagrant* offense is similar but stronger, implying a deliberate flouting of a law or code of behavior: 'The judge's verdict was thought to be a flagrant miscarriage of justice.'

blather *see* babble

blench/blanch To *blench* is to go pale through fear or some strong emotion: 'The nurse blenched when she saw the first victim.' To *blanch* is similar, but is often used of the part of the body that turns pale: 'His cheeks blanched in horror.'

blessed/blissful As applied to something pleasurable or enjoyable, *blessed* implies a change from what was unpleasant to what is now pleasant, while *blissful* has a connotation of gentleness and peacefulness: 'At last she could enjoy a few minutes of blessed peace and quiet,' *'But still the hands of mem'ry weave/The blissful dreams of long ago'* (George Cooper). *Bless* and *bliss* are in fact unrelated in origin.

blink *see* wink

blissful *see* blessed

bloater *see* kipper

bloc *see* block

block/bloc *Block* is used in many familiar senses, from a large piece of material to an obstacle. *Bloc* (the French form of it) is used solely for a group of people or countries with a common interest: 'The culture block between East and West began to dissolve after the collapse of many Communist bloc countries.'

blond/blonde As applied to fair-haired people, *blond* is normally used of males, and *blonde* of females: 'Her boyfriend is a dishy blond Australian,' 'Is she a blonde or a brunette?'

blonde *see* blond

bloom/blossom To *bloom* is to come into flower, literally or figuratively: 'The cherry tree bloomed late this year.' To *blossom* is to be in full flower, with a promise of fruit or ripeness to come: *'Blossoming boughs of April in laughter shake'* (Robert Bridges), 'Juliet is blossoming into a fine actress.'

blossom *see* bloom

blush/flush To *blush* is to redden with embarrassment or some other emotion: 'When I told him that I admired his work, he actually blushed.' To *flush* is similar but stronger, implying a sudden or involuntary reddening, and one not necessarily due to an emotion: 'The driver flushed up violently when the policeman asked to see his license,' 'Her cheeks were flushed from the exercise.'

blusterous *see* boisterous

boat/ship A *boat* is usually small, propelled by oars, paddles, sail or power (motor), and used for short distances, as up rivers or across bays: *'Speed, bonny boat, like a bird on the wing'* (R.L. Stevenson). A *ship* is usually large, propelled by sail or power (engine) only, and used for long distances, as across seas or oceans: *'Where lies the land to which the ship would go?/Far, far ahead, is all her seamen know'* (A.H. Clough). Loosely, however, *boat* can be used of a *ship,* especially a passenger liner or ferry: 'When does the next boat leave for Calais?'

bodge *see* botch

boil/broil To *boil* food is to cook it in boiling water; to *broil* food is to cook it by grilling it: 'We had boiled potatoes with broiled chicken.' Figuratively the words are closer: 'It was boiling in the sun' (it was very hot), 'We were broiling in the sun' (we were very hot and 'cooking' in it).

boisterous/blusterous *Boisterous* means noisy and lively, often playfully so, with an implied lack of restraint or control: 'The grandparents found the children's behavior too boisterous for their liking.' *Blusterous* means not only noisy but loud and bullying: 'Our next-door neighbor was helpful but his blusterous manner put us off.'

bon mot/mot juste A *bon mot* (French, 'good word') is a witty or clever saying: 'Oscar Wilde was famous for his bons mots.' A *mot juste* (French, 'right word') is a word or phrase that fits the context or occasion exactly: 'The writer was especially pleased when she was able to hit upon the *mot juste,*' 'I would hardly think "winsome" *le mot juste* for someone as boorish as he is.'

booty *see* loot

border/boundary/frontier The *border* of something is its edge or margin: 'You can literally walk across the border from France to Germany.' A *boundary* is the limit of an area, its well-defined *border,* with the implication that the region the other side is different in some way: 'The stream formed the boundary between the two estates.' A *frontier* is the *border* or limit of a country or other extensive region, its *boundary,* the crossing of which is achieved with a special permit or with difficulty: 'We reached the frontier at dawn and waited for the customs post to open.'

born/borne Both verbs derive from a verb *bear. Born* relates to giving birth: 'She was born in August.' *Borne* relates to any other kind of carrying or bearing: 'The seeds of the dandelion are borne by the wind,' 'He dies yesterday after an illness bravely borne,' 'It was borne in on me how close they had been together.'

borne *see* born

bosom/breast *Bosom* denotes not only a woman's breasts but the clothing over them: 'The mother held the child to her bosom' (to her body), 'The mother held the child to her breast' (to feed it). But *bosom* and *breast* overlap in many senses, not least when they relate to a source of emotions: '*Love, in my bosom, like a bee/Doth suck his sweet;/Now with his wings he plays with me,/Now with his feet./Within mine eyes he makes his nest,/His bed amid my tender breast*' (Robert Greene).

botch/bodge To *botch* something is to spoil it by poor or clumsy work: 'That patio's a real botched job, isn't it?' To *bodge* something is similar, although the word often implies that the work has been done temporarily or inexpertly rather than actually spoiled: 'I rather bodged that repair; I'll do it again properly if I have time.'

bough *see* branch

boundary *see* border

bowl/basin A *bowl* is usually deep and round: 'Who left the salad bowl in the sink?' A *basin* may be deep or shallow, and is often narrower at the bottom than at the top: 'First pour half a quart of milk into the basin.'

bow window *see* bay window

boycott/embargo With reference to trade or commerce, a *boycott* is a refusal to handle or buy goods, while an *embargo* is a restriction against trade, especially a ban on the import or export of goods: 'There was a boycott on imports from France' (people wouldn't handle them), 'There was an embargo on imports from France' (they were restricted or banned altogether).

brake *see* break

branch/bough A *branch* is any limb of a tree or a bush: 'The branches of the tree brushed out faces as we ran under it.' A *bough* is a big or heavy limb, with its own *branches:* 'The bough broke with a sharp crack.'

bravado *see* bravery

bravery/bravado/bravura *Bravery* is courage or fortitude in general: 'Some soldiers were decorated for their bravery in battle.' *Bravado* is an act of daring: 'Frank jumped into the icy water in a show of bravado.' *Bravura* is the bold performance or attempted performance of some difficult feat: 'The player's brilliant passing was sheer bravura.'

bravura *see* bravery

bray *see* blast

breach/breech *Breach* relates to *break* in some sense: 'It was clear that there had been a serious breach of confidence,' 'The tank made a breach in the wall.' *Breech* relates to the lower or bottom part of someone or something: 'The baby was born by a breech delivery' (feet and buttock first, instead of head first, as more usual), 'If you "break" a rifle, you open its breech by snapping the barrel away from the butt.'

break/brake *Break* has several meanings as a verb, including to separate things into pieces, to stop something, or to transgress a law. To *brake* is to slow down or stop: 'In order to break speed in the car, you have to brake.'

breast *see* bosom

breech *see* breach

brim *see* rim

Britain/Great Britain/British Isles *Britain* is the short name of *Great Britain*, which is England, Scotland and Wales, as part of country officially designed the United Kingdom of Great Britain and Northern Ireland. The *British Isles* are the whole of the United Kingdom and the island of Ireland, including the Republic: 'The British Isles are a geographical unit, while Britain is a political one.'

British Isles *see* Britain

broach/brooch Although now quite different in meaning, the words are related by a common reference to a pointed object (French *broche* is 'spit,' the pointed rod on which meat is roasted). To *broach* something is thus to pierce it in some sense: 'I broached the matter of payment' (I introduced it), 'Let's broach another bottle' (let's open one). A *brooch* is an ornament with a clasp, worn on clothes: 'I bought mother a new brooch for her birthday.'

brochure/pamphlet/leaflet A *brochure* is usually a commercial publication, advertising something: 'The travel agent gave us lots of brochures to choose a vacation from.' A *pamphlet* is a small publication, of a few pages only or even of a single page, on some specialized subject: 'The stereo had a pamphlet explaining how to operate it.' A *leaflet* is a single, often folded, page or sheet advertising or announcing something: 'The charity workers put leaflets in all the mail boxes.'

broil *see* boil

brooch *see* broach

brush *see* bush

brute *see* beast

bud/burgeon To *bud* is to begin to grow: 'The apple-tree budded and blossomed unusually early that year,' 'It was good to see signs of his budding confidence.' To *burgeon* is to be in the early stages of growth, especially when it is marked or rapid: 'The avenues of burgeoning trees were a sure sign that spring had arrived,' 'When I next saw Helen, she had burgeoned into a lively teenager.'

bug/tap In the world of espionage or surveillance, a *bug* is a listening device concealed in a building, car or the like, while a *tap* is a device attached to a telephone so as to pick up conversations on the line: 'The embassy officials were unaware of the bug in the washroom,' 'Clicks during the phone conversation suggested there might be a tap.'

burgeon *see* bud

burst/bust In their commonest sense, to *burst* is to break something violently, often by applying internal pressure, while to *bust* something, as used colloquially, is to break it in any sense: 'Emma burst the balloon, 'I dropped the mirror and bust it.' The verbs are also used without a direct noun, when they have the main sense of *burst*: 'If I eat any more I'll burst,' 'She was busting to tell him the news.' However, *bust* is less common as a phrasal verb (with a preposition), except in American usage: 'The men burst into the room,' '*June is bustin' out all over*' (Oscar Hammerstein II).

bush/shrub/scrub/brush A *bush* is a small, low tree with dense foliage: 'The cats liked to prowl in the bushes at the bottom of the garden.' A *shrub* is similar, but usually larger and not so dense: 'The rhododendron, with its clusters of flowers, is one of the most colorful of shrubs.' *Scrub* is a collective term for *shrubs* or stunted trees growing wild, especially in an arid area: 'The tourists made their weary way through miles of scrub.' *Brush* is similar, but denser and thornier, as typically in North America and Australia: 'We couldn't walk through the brush or even drive through it.'

business/busyness *Business* is the doing or carrying out of something: 'He made it his business to find out,' 'It is the business of the city council to provide public services.' *Busyness* is the state of being busy: 'The squirrel is well know for its busyness; it is always bustling about.'

bust *see* burst

bustle/hustle To *bustle* is to be busy and active: 'Whenever I called on the old woman, she was bustling about in the kitchen.' To *hustle* is to move hastily or roughly, or make someone move thus: 'The newcomers hustled through the audience to the stage,' 'The farmer hustled the dog into its kennel.'

C

cad/card Both words refer to a particular type of person. A *cad* is a boor or 'bounder', someone who is 'not a gentleman' in behavior or attitude: 'Only a cad would leave his guests to pay the check.' A *card* is a witty or original person, a 'character': '"*He's a cheery old card," grunted Harry to Jack/As they slogged up to Arras with rifle and pack*' (Sigfried Sassoon).

cafe/cafeteria A *cafe* is usually smallish with either self-service or staff service; a *cafeteria* is more of a restaurant but is almost always self-service: 'We had coffee in the cafe, and a couple of hours later lunched in the cafeteria.'

cafeteria *see* cafe

callous/callus The words are related in their common derivation from Latin *callum,* 'hardened skin'. However, *callous* is an adjective, meaning 'hard' in the sense of being cruelly insensitive, while *callus* is a noun as a term for an area of hard skin on the feet or hands: 'He gave a callous laugh when she told him about her callus.'

callow *see* shallow

callus *see* callous

candelabra *see* chandelier

cannon *see* canon

canon/cannon Both words are related to *cane*. The use of a cane as a measuring rod gave *canon* in the sense of 'rule', 'standard', and from that the sense of 'priest' (who lives under a church rule). The cane as a tube gave *cannon* as a gun or piece of artillery. The word takes no plural s: '*Cannon to the right of them,/Cannon to the left of them,/Cannon in front of them/Volley'd and thunder'd*' (Tennyson).

canopy/panoply A *canopy* is an overhead covering, usually a literal one: 'The trees served as a welcome canopy from the boiling sun.' A *panoply* is a complete covering, especially one that is impressive, and often figurative: 'The bride smiled, secure in her panoply of love and attention.' (The word often has a religious or spiritual connotation, especially of the biblical 'whole armor of God.')

canvas/canvass The words have a common origin but have developed quite different senses. *Canvas* is both the coarse cloth used for making tents and sails, and also the cloth that artists paint on: 'His canvas gradually became a painting of a sailing boat under full canvas.' To *canvass* is to solicit support from voters before an election: 'On the eve of the election, the party workers went out canvassing.'

canvass *see* canvas

capability/capacity/ability The *capability* for something is the actual potential to do it: 'She has the capability to pass the exam if she tries.' The *capacity* for something is the power or reserve to do it when necessary: 'He has a real capacity for work, and spends long hours studying.' The *ability* for something is the power or competence to do it, whether put to use or not: 'The ability to learn languages often depends on an interest in words and meanings.'

capacity *see* capability

capital/capitol A *capital* is the town or city that is a country's seat of government: 'Berlin is now again the capital of Germany.' A *capitol* is a statehouse in the United States, i.e. the building that houses the state's legislature: 'One of America's best known buildings is the Capitol, the meeting place of the Congress of the United States of America in Washington, D.C., the American capital.'

capital punishment *see* corporal punishment

capitol *see* capital

carcass *see* corpse

card *see* cad

careen *see* career

career/careen To *career* is to go rapidly or even dangerously: 'I held the strap tight as the taxi careered down the steep hill.' To *careen* is to sway or tilt dangerously to one side: 'The amusement park train careened first to one side then to the other as it hurtled round the track.'

carefree/careless In their most common usages, *carefree* means 'free of care' and *careless* 'showing no care': 'The children ran barefoot and carefree over the sand,' 'That was a very careless mistake.' But *careless* can also means 'having no care', and so be close to *carefree*: '*Lest you think he could never recapture/The first fine careless rapture!*' (Robert Browning).

careless *see* carefree

caricature *see* cartoon

carousal/carousel Both are to do with fun and laughter. A *carousal* is a noisy drinking party, and a *carousel* a roundabout or merry-go-round: '*Sounds of carousal came, and song*' (Southey), 'The carousel is always a popular attraction at a county fair.'

carousel *see* carousal

carp *see* cavil

cartoon/caricature A *cartoon* is a stylized and usually amusing drawing or series of drawings: 'Children and animals are favorite subjects for cartoons.' A *caricature* is a drawing of a person that exaggerates some feature or characteristic by way of satire or simply for amusement: 'The actor, with his bald head and bushy moustache, was an artist's dream as a caricature.'

cast/caste A *cast* is a company of actors; a *caste* is a Hindu social class: 'The cast had a number of unknown actors,' 'Americans often find it difficult to understand the caste system.' The two words are unrelated, though *caste* is of the same origin as *chaste.*

caste *see* cast

caster/castor As applied to the sugar sprinkle and the swivelling wheel of furniture, the word can have either spelling: 'Caster sugar is finely ground white sugar,' 'It can be difficult to move a bed if it is not on castors.' *Castor* oil, however, has only the one spelling: 'How about a nice dose of castor oil?'

castigate *see* chastise

castor *see* caster

cataclysm *see* catastrophe

catastrophe/cataclysm A *catastrophe* is a spectacular disaster or accident, literal or figurative: 'It was a catastrophe when I lost my money and credit cards.' A *cataclysm* is a violent upheaval, especially a military, political or social one, with the implication that it was also disastrous: 'Many people regard the Second World War as the greatest cataclysm of the 20th century.'

catch phrase/cliché A *catch phrase* is a phrase or sentence popularized by a particular person or group of people, such as a media personality or commercial company: 'The American TV cop Telly Savalis introduced the catch phrase "Who loves ya, baby?".' A *cliché* is a trite, hackneyed word or phrase: 'A cliché commonly heard from officials when giving interviews is "at this moment in time".' *Catch phrases* are often ephemeral; *clichés* tend to live longer.

catholic/Catholic In lower case, *catholic* is used for something general or universal: 'She has very catholic tastes.' With a capital letter, it refers to the Roman Catholic Church: 'The Catholic population is smaller than the Protestant.' Even in a religious context, and with a capital letter (as used in a former style of English), *catholic* may still mean universal: *'And I believe one Catholick and Apostolic Church'* (Book of Common Prayer: Nicene Creed).

Catholic *see* catholic

cave/cavern A *cave* is a place hollowed out of rocks or firm soil, typically underground or by the sea: 'Fingal's Cave is a large cave on the island of Staffa with basalt pillars at its entrance.' A *cavern* is a large *cave,* especially one formed by water underground: *'Sand-strewn caverns, cool and deep'* (Matthew Arnold).

cavern *see* cave

cavil/carp To *cavil* is to raise irritating or trivial objections: 'He caviled when I proposed a trip to London, saying the journey bored him.' To *carp* is to find fault, often pettily and unreasonably: 'The music critic carped at the conductor's flamboyant style.'

celebrant/celebrator A *celebrant* is a clergyman leading a communion service or mass: 'The celebrant was Reverend Peter Stone.' A *celebrator* is someone celebrating: 'The celebrators kept the party going until three in the morning.'

celebrator *see* celebrant

Celsius/centigrade The two temperature scales are one and the same, and both differ from Fahrenheit: 'The Celsius scale was invented by the Swedish scientist Anders Celsius. It is called centigrade because it measures 100 degrees between the freezing and boiling points of water.'

cement *see* concrete

censor/censure To *censor* something is the ban or suppress it, often on moral grounds: 'The publisher censored part of the play because of its bad language.' To *censure* something is to criticize it or find fault with it: 'The tennis player was censured for her unsporting behavior on court.'

censure *see* censor

census/consensus A *census* is an official counting of numbers or statistics: 'A census of the population in the United States is taken every ten years.' A *consensus* is a general or widespread agreement by a number of people on something: 'The consensus is that we should wait for a while.'

center/middle *Center* is normally used for a position or location that is especially significant or important: 'There was a vase in the center of the table, (where everyone could see it),' 'The post office is in the town center' (where most of its commercial activities are concentrated). *Middle* implies a mere location equidistant from others: 'He drove in the middle of the road' (not on the right-hand side), 'There was a vase in the middle of the table' (not to one side).

ceremonial/ceremonious If something is *ceremonial,* it is proper for a ceremony: 'The victory was marked by a ceremonial parade,' 'The best china was brought out only on ceremonial occasions.' If it is *ceremonious* it is done with great ceremony, that is, extremely politely or formally: 'He gave my wife a ceremonious bow, as if she were a princess.'

ceremonious *see* ceremonial

certainty/certitude *Certainty* is the (objective) state of being certain: 'I can say that with absolute certainty.' *Certitude* is a (subjective) feeling of certainty: 'The certitude with which the government official expressed his views was not shared by all of his colleagues.'

certitude *see* certainty

cessation *see* cession

cession/cessation *Cession* is to do with yielding or giving up something (ceding it), but *cessation* with stopping (ceasing): 'The cession of the territory by the enemy led to a cessation of hostilities.'

chafe/chaff To *chafe* is to irritate or be annoyed: 'Nancy's shoes were chafing,' 'The passengers were chafing at the long delay.' To *chaff* someone is to tease him or her: 'The trainee was chaffed about his girlish locks.'

chaff *see* chafe

chandelier/candelabra A *chandelier* is an ornamental hanging light with several branches for bulbs or candles: 'Some churches are lit by one or more chandeliers.' A *candelabra* is an ornamental (but not hanging) branched holder for candles or lights: 'The dinner table was lit by a fine central candelabra.'

charted *see* chartered

chartered/charted *Chartered* relates to a charter, such as an agreement or contract for the hire of a ship or plane; *charted* relates to a region, such as a sea, that has had a chart made of it: 'The chartered plane flew over the uncharted waters of the lake.'

chary *see* wary

chasten *see* chastise

chastise/chasten/castigate To *chastise* someone is to punish him or her, often by beating: 'The angry father chastised his son with a slipper on his backside.' To *chasten* someone is to make him or her feel ashamed, usually by correcting them or punishing them: 'When he said it was all my fault, I felt really chastened.' To *castigate* a person is to scold or punish him severely: 'The coach castigated the team for its poor performance.'

chat/chatter To *chat* is to have a pleasant and usually fairly trivial conversation: 'The two old ladies were chatting over their tea.' To *chatter* is to do the same, but with the suggestion that the conversation is lively or 'gossipy': 'The children were chattering at the bus stop.'

chatter *see* chat

cheerful/cheery *Cheerful* relates mainly to mood: 'He gave me a cheerful smile,' 'You're looking cheerful this morning!' *Cheery* relates more to manner: 'She gave me a cheery wave,' 'He called a cheery greeting.' (You can be *cheery* when you are not *cheerful*.)

cheery *see* cheerful

cherish *see* nurse

cherubic *see* chubby

chicken/hen A *chicken* is the bird regarded as potential meat: 'It's time to feed the chickens' (to fatten them for the table). A *hen* is the bird regarded for its eggs: 'It's time to feed the hens' (so that they lay well). In practice, however, the two words are often used indiscriminately.

childish/childlike *Childish* relates to something typical of a child, especially in a derogatory sense when applied to an adult: 'Shouts of childish laughter rang in the park,' 'For goodness' sake, grow up and stop being so childish!' *Childlike* is more positive and pertains to qualities associated with the ideal child, such as innocence, trust, charm and beauty: 'He had an almost childlike trust in the goodwill of his friends.'

childlike *see* childish

childminder/babysitter Generally speaking, a *childminder* is a person who looks after young children in the daytime while the parents are at work, while a *babysitter* looks after them in the evening when the parents are out: 'Lisa had been a babysitter when at school and was now a qualified childminder.'

chime *see* peal

chiropodist/chiropractor A *chiropodist* treats people's feet, while a *chiropractor* manipulates people's joints, especially the spine: 'If you have corns, go to a chiropodist, 'Chiropractors believe that disease is caused by an abnormal function in the nervous system.'

chiropractor *see* chiropodist

choir/chorus A *choir* is a regular body of singers which may or may not have soloists: 'The church choir sang in the town square at Christmas.' A *chorus,* which is usually larger, is a body of singers who take part in a choral work, often with an orchestra, and who usually have soloists: 'The climax of Beethoven's Ninth Symphony is when the chorus sings Schiller's *Ode to Joy* in the last movement.'

choose *see* pick

chop/cutlet A *chop* is a thick slice of meet that is cut from the loin (the side or back) and that usually includes a rib: 'Would you like a lamb chop for supper?' A *cutlet* is also a thick slice of meat, but is cut from the neck or any part of the animal and usually includes no bone: 'I've bought a couple of lamb cutlets.'

chord *see* cord

chortle *see* chuckle

chorus *see* choir

chronic/acute A *chronic* illness or disease is a long-standing or protracted one: 'She suffers from chronic arthritis.' An *acute* illness is a short but sharp one: 'Our boss is off work with an acute attack of the flu.'

chubby/cherubic/seraphic *Chubby,* of a person, means plump and with a round and possibly babyish face: 'I opened the door to find a chubby little boy on the step.' *Cherubic,* literally like a cherub, means innocent-looking: 'The small girl's cherubic expression belied her tempers and tantrums.' *Seraphic,* literally 'like a seraph', means blissful-looking: 'The vicar walked up the path with a seraphic smile on his face.'

chuckle/chortle To *chuckle* is to laugh quietly, often to oneself: 'He chuckled when I said he was the world's worst letter-writer.' To *chortle* is to *chuckle* gleefully: 'When the Secretary of the Treasury explained that the tax affected him, too, his listeners chortled long and loud.' (The word was invented by Lewis Carroll as a blend of *chuckle* and *snort.*)

chum *see* crony

chute *see* shoot

cite *see* quote

citizen/denizen A *citizen* is the permanent or native inhabitant of a country or city, usually regarded as having particular rights and responsibilities: '*The first requisite of a good citizen in this Republic of ours is that he shall be able and willing to pull his weight*' (Theodore Roosevelt). A *denizen* is either a person permanently resident in a foreign country, and enjoying there many of the rights of its own *citizens,* or else a plant or animal living somewhere where it is not native: 'The denizens of the zoo included two elephants and three tigers.' The word can also be used generally of any resident or inhabitant, whether native or not.

civic *see* civil

civil/civic/civilian *Civil* relates to *citizen,* with all that it implies: 'It is your civil duty to protect your neighbors.' *Civic* relates to a city, as well as its *citizens*: 'The town's local government offices are all at the Civic Center.' *Civilian* is used for someone or something that is not military: 'Civilian life is not always easier than life in the army.' *Civil* also has the non-military sense, and is used for something non-legal or non-ecclesiastical: 'They didn't get married in church but had a civil ceremony at a registry office.'

civilian *see* civil

clad/clothed Both words relate to having clothes on or being dressed, although *clad* is more common after an adverb and to apply to things, not people: 'The players were thinly clad but did not seem to notice the cold,' 'The ivy-clad walls were a picturesque sight.' *Clothed* is common in most other cases: 'She was clothed entirely in black,' 'It is the duty of a government to see that people are properly housed, clothed, fed and educated.'

claque *see* clique

classic/classical Something is *classic* if it is the first or finest of its kind, or is regarded as standard: 'This book is the classic authority on beekeeping.' *Classical* also has this sense, but implies a link with the culture of Greece and Rome: 'The statue had a classical simplicity and beauty.'

classical *see* classic

clean/cleanse To *clean* something is to remove its dirt and impurities: 'Not everyone cleans his teeth twice daily.' To *cleanse* something is also to do this, but implies that the dirt was defiling, and the process therefore purging or purifying. The word is also used figuratively: '*O cleanse thou me from my secret faults*' (Book of Common Prayer). *See also* cleanness

cleanliness *see* cleanness

cleanness/cleanliness *Cleanness* is the state of being clean (usually of things); *cleanliness* is the state of keeping clean (usually of people and animals): 'The sparkling cleanness of the crockery and cutlery made dinner a delight,' 'Cats are noted for their natural cleanliness.'

cleanse *see* clean

clench *see* clinch

clerihew *see* limerick

cliché *see* catch phrase

client/customer In the commercial world, a *client* is usually someone who receives professional advice, from a lawyer or accountant, while a *customer* is someone who buys something in a store (by giving it his or her custom): 'Many of the lawyer's clients were house purchasers,' 'Customers are requested to retain their receipts as proof of purchase.'

climate/clime The *climate* of a place is its regular weather conditions: 'I wished we lived in a warmer climate.' *Clime* means the same, but refers to the place or region itself. The word is invariably used in the plural and is now regarded as facetious or poetic: 'He said he was seeking warmer climes for his holiday this year,' *'She walked in beauty, like the night/Of cloudless climes and starry skies'* (Byron).

clime *see* climate

clinch/clench To *clinch* something is to hold it firm, literally by hammering sideways the top half of a protruding nail: 'The cabinetmaker clinched the corners of the frame.' To *clench* is to close two things tightly together: 'He clenched his teeth in anger.'

clique/claque A *clique* is a small and exclusive group of people with a common cause or shared interests: 'The political party included a clique of young activists.' A *claque* was originally a group of people hired to applaud in theater, and so came to denote a group of fawning admirers: 'The senator had a claque of devoted local party workers.'

clothed *see* clad

clue/cue A *clue* gives guidance to the solving of a mystery or problem, without actually being the key to it: 'When I heard she had left her husband, that gave me the clue to her recent request.' A *cue* is a signal or reminder to do something already agreed: 'You go ahead; I'll take my cue from you.'

coarse/crude If a person or things are *coarse* they are unrefined or uncultured: 'Steve made some coarse remark about the meal, saying even pigs ate better.' If they are *crude* they are *coarse* in an offensive or even sexually explicit way: 'I was shocked when Lucy made some crude joke about her fiancé.'

comfy/cosy *Comfy,* short for *comfortable,* is used for something soft and pleasant, especially clothes or furniture: 'You sit here, in this comfy chair.' *Cosy* is used for something warm and snug, or something intimate or friendly: 'We sat in a cosy corner by the fire and had a cosy little chat.'

comic/comical *Comic* is used for something intended to be amusing (though it may not be); 'Phil then sang one of his comic songs.' *Comical* is used for something amusing (though not necessarily intended to be): 'The toddler pulled a comical face when he dropped his mug.'

comical *see* comic

comment/commentate To *comment* on something is to give one's views or opinion on it: 'I'm afraid I couldn't possibly comment on that.' To *commentate* on something is to give a running report or commentary on it, especially as a broadcast at a sporting event: 'After retiring from professional tennis, Virginia Wade took to a career commentating on the championships at Wimbledon.'

commentate *see* comment

commissar *see* commissioner

commissionaire *see* commissioner

commissioner/commissionaire/commissar A *commissioner* is the title of various public officials: 'He has been a commissioner with the City Water Board for a number of years.' A *commissionaire* is a uniformed attendant at the entrance to a public building such as a hotel or theater: 'The commissionaire offered to get us a taxi.' A *commissar* was the head of a government department or an army officer responsible for political instruction in the former USSR: 'In 1946 the government commissars were renamed ministers.'

commute/compound To *commute* a punishment or sentence is to change it for a less severe one: 'His life sentence was commuted to ten years' imprisonment.' To *compound* a crime or offense is to agree, for a consideration or by private arrangement, not to prosecute or punish the person who carried it out: 'The debtors asked his creditors if they would agree to compound his liabilities so that he could avoid bankruptcy.'

compact *see* contract

comparable/compatible If two things or people are *comparable,* they are similar: 'Although the sisters went to different schools, their exam results were consistently comparable.' If things or people are *compatible,* they are mutually suited, and can exist or work together: 'This computer is compatible with most other models and can 'talk" to them,' 'The couple split up because they were not at all compatible.'

compatible *see* comparable

compel/impel To *compel* someone to do something is to force him or her to do it: 'We can't compel you to take part, but you can if you like,' 'I felt compelled to report his behavior.' To *impel* someone to do something is to make him or her feel obliged or moved to do it: 'Your frank account impels me to admit that I admire your honesty,' 'The singer received such rapturous applause that she felt impelled to give an encore.'

competition/contest A *competition* is a sporting venture of some kind in which a winner is selected (or is apparent) from two or more entrants: 'There was a competition to see who would blow the biggest bubble.' A *contest* is similar, but is usually more formal and implies a 'trial of strength' between opposing teams, sides or forces: 'The second round of the contest was won by the Japanese.'

compile *see* compose

complacent/complaisant/compliant *Complacent* refers to a feeling of self-satisfaction: 'Grace left for home with a complacent smile; she knew she had done a good day's work.' *Complaisant* refers to a willingness to comply or oblige: *'The girl was complaisant enough to make the bearers stop'* (Jonathan Swift). *Compliant* refers to an actual complying or obliging, whether willingly or not: 'All the countries were compliant with the royal will.'

complaisant *see* complacent

complement/compliment To *complement* something is to suit it or complete it (*see* supplement); to *compliment* someone is to praise him or her or approve of him or her : 'For a performance to succeed, the audience should complement the performers' (they should match their enthusiasm and involvement); 'For a performance to succeed, the audience should compliment the performers' (they should applaud them).

complement *see* supplement

complex *see* complicated

compliant *see* complacent

complicated/complex A *complicated* task is one involving many stages or actions, but that may not overall be particularly difficult: 'It was a complicated business getting the cow out of the ditch.' A *complex* task also involves many stages but is difficult or intricate as well: 'The preparation of annual accounts is a complex job, requiring many drafts and much cross-checking.'

compliment *see* complement

compose/compile/concoct To *compose* something is to work it or arrange it in such a way as to make a finished product: 'The angry house-owner composed a letter to his congressman.' To *compile* something is to put its various parts or components in an order of some kind: 'Ann compiled a list of videos she had seen.' To *concoct* something is to *compose* it hastily or contrivedly: 'Gerald concocted some story about the train's being late.'

compose *see* consist

compound *see* commute

comprehend *see* apprehend

comprehensible/comprehensive If something is *comprehensible,* it can be understood, and one can comprehend it (*see* apprehend): 'The account was comprehensible' (it could be understood). If a thing is *comprehensive,* it includes all or most things: 'The account was comprehensive' (it included everything).

comprehensive *see* comprehensible

comprise *see* consist

compulsive/impulsive/impetuous A *compulsive* action is one done involuntarily: 'He was so nervous that he gave a compulsive laugh whenever she spoke to him.' An *impulsive* action is done on the spur of the moment, without hesitation, often as a consequence of a "gut feeling" that it is right: 'She gave him an impulsive kiss.' An *impetuous* action is a rash or impulsive one, often performed with some vigor: 'He gave an impetuous flick of his hand to motion the beggar away.'

concave/convex Anything *concave* curves inwards; anything *convex* curves outwards: 'Much of the coast of Australia is concave, whereas the coast of most other large islands is convex.'

concede *see* accede

conciliate *see* reconcile

concoct *see* compose

concrete/cement The two are not the same. *Concrete* is made by mixing *cement,* its binding agent, with water and by adding sand, gravel, crushed rock and the like: 'The paving stones on the path were all broken, so we replaced them with concrete,' 'In concrete used for buildings and in civil engineering the binding agent is usually Portland cement.'

condition/precondition A *condition* is a requirement for something: 'It is a condition of this course that you take the tests regularly.' A *precondition* is a *condition* needed in advance: 'It is a precondition of this course that you already know something about the subject.'

condole/console To *condole* with somebody is to express sympathy with him or her ; to *console* someone is to *give* him or her sympathy or comfort him or her: 'When her mother died, I first condoled with her on her loss, then did my best to console her.'

confer *see* collude

confession/admission A *confession* is a personal acknowledgment, however hesitant, of something wrong, that one has done: 'I have a confession to make; I forgot to mail your letter.' An *admission* is similar, but implies a readiness to 'own up' and a resolve not to repeat the offense: 'On his own admission he was rarely on time for work.'

confine/contain To *confine* something is to keep it within its proper bounds: 'The speaker confined herself to just a few words.' To *contain* something is to stop it from breaking its bounds, with the implication that if not so checked, it will do so: 'The firemen struggled to contain the blaze.'

congenial/genial If someone is *congenial,* they are agreeable company, because they share one's own interests or temperament: 'My fellow travellers were congenial companions, and the journey passed quickly.' If someone is *genial,* he or she is generally pleasant and sociable: 'The salesman welcomed me with a genial smile and asked if he could help.'

connive *see* collude

connote *see* denote

consent *see* assent

consequent/subsequent *Consequent* is used for something that follows as a result of something else: 'Peter's illness and consequent lengthy absence from school were a serious setback to his studies.' *Subsequent* is used for something that simply follows in due course: 'The textile workers discussed the new pay offer at a subsequent meeting.'

conserve/preserve To *conserve* something is to keep it and protect it in its original state, i.e. from the past to the present: 'The architect said the building could be conserved.' To *preserve* something is to keep it and protect it for subsequent use, i.e. from the present to the future: 'Regular exercise will preserve your health.'

consist/comprise/constitute/compose To *consist* of something is to be made up of it: 'The program consisted of two short plays.' To *comprise* something has the same meaning, often implying that the whole is regarded from the point of view of its individual parts: 'The program comprises two short plays' (they were chosen to make it up). To *constitute* something is to form a whole, especially of dissimilar components: 'Wealth and health do not necessarily constitute happiness.' To *compose* means the same, but implies that the components have something in common: 'Water is composed of hydrogen and oxygen.'

consistent/persistent Something is *consistent* if it is done repeatedly in the same manner: 'Why can't you be consistent? You keep changing your mind.' Something is *persistent* if it is repeated, constantly recurring—deliberately so if done by humans: 'The persistent rain kept us indoors,' 'Terry has a persistent habit of arriving late.'

console *see* condole

conspire *see* collude

constant *see* continual

constitute *see* consist

constraint/restraint Both nouns have to do with being limited, but whereas *constraint* relates to an abstract or at any rate undesirable restriction, *restraint* can refer to either physical or abstract force:

'There are no constraints on your choice of color,' 'Mental patients were formerly kept under conditions of restraint,' 'The manager was keen to impose restraints on pay settlements.'

contagious *see* infectious

contain *see* confine

contemporaneous *see* contemporary

contemporary/contemporaneous *Contemporary* relates to something happening, or people living, at the same time as something else, whether in the past or the present: 'Dickens was contemporary with Thackery,' 'Many people find contemporary poetry difficult.' *Contemporaneous* means much the same, but is mostly used of things rather than people: 'The burial mounds nearby were believed to be contemporaneous with the stones.'

contemptible/contemptuous A person is *contemptible* if he or she is despised or held in contempt for some reason: 'Stealing that money was a contemptible thing to do.' *Contemptuous* means that the person expresses contempt for someone or something else: 'When I said I was sorry, he simply gave me a contemptuous look.'

contemptuous *see* contemptible

contest *see* competition

continual/continuous/constant Something is *continual* if it happens repeatedly: 'Our holiday was ruined by the continual rain' (it rained often but not all the time). It is *continuous* if it goes on without a break: 'Our holiday was ruined by the continuous rain' (it rained all the time). If something is *constant,* it happens many times in the same manner: 'Ruth suffered from constant colds as a child.'

continuous *see* continual

contract/compact A *contract* is a formal agreement for something, such as a performance or a particular piece of work: 'The comedian's contract ran for the summer season only.' A *compact* can be the same, but is more often simply a mutual agreement of some kind: 'The pen pals made a compact that they would correspond once a month.'

contrary/converse It a thing is *contrary,* it either differs or disagrees: 'I took the contrary view, that we should go by train rather than drive.' If something is *converse,* it is the opposite: 'I held the converse view, that railroads should be privatized, not nationalized.' *See also* converse.

contravene/controvert To *contravene* something is to be contrary to it or in conflict with it: 'You must be careful not to contravene the law when abroad,' 'Your explanation contravenes my own theory.' To *controvert* is to deny the truth of something: 'Whatever you say, you can't controvert the facts.'

controvert *see* contravene

converse/reverse Both words can refer to an opposite, but in different ways: 'He says he is rich, but I believe the converse to be true' (i.e., that he is poor), 'He says he is rich, but I would have said the reverse' (i.e., that he is not).

converse *see* contrary

convex *see* concave

cooperate/collaborate To *cooperate* is to help another person to do something, sometimes unwillingly: 'The prisoner was reluctant to cooperate.' To *collaborate* is the same, but implies that the help is willingly given, sometimes for the bad: 'Writer and artist collaborated to produce a most attractive book,' 'The older citizens were reluctant to collaborate with the enemy.'

cord/chord A *cord* is strong string or something resembling it: 'I'll tie the door back with this cord,' 'The choirmaster was testing the soloist's vocal cords.' A *chord* has various specialized senses, such as a straight line in mathematics or a simultaneous sounding of musical notes. (It can also be used to refer to vocal *chords.*) Figuratively, it has the musical sense when referring to an emotional response: 'The mother's TV appeal struck a deep chord with many viewers.'

co-respondent *see* correspondent

corollary *see* correlation

corporal/corporeal *Corporal* is to do with the body: 'Corporal punishment is now mostly a thing of the past.' *Corporeal* is used for something that is intended for the body or that has a bodily substance: 'Hospitals not only treat patients but attend to their corporeal needs,' (i.e., provide them with food and drink), 'Ghosts do not have a corporeal existence.'

corporal punishment/capital punishment *Corporal punishment* is physical punishment such as beating: 'Corporal punishment is banned by law in all schools.' *Capital punishment* is the death penalty, involving execution by hanging or some other means: 'Capital punishment was abolished in Great Britain in 1965 for all crimes except treason.'

corporeal *see* corporal

corpse/carcass A *corpse* is the dead body of a human, or less often of an animal: 'The battlefield was strewn with corpses.' A *carcass* (or *carcase*) is the dead body of an animal, especially one slaughtered as food: 'Veal carcasses have very little fat.'

correlation/corollary The *correlation* of two things is the mutual or reciprocal relationship between them: 'Dieticians recorded the correlation between the patients' ages and their weight.' A *corollary* is the natural consequence of something, its logical result: 'Once the art of writing had been established, the science of printing was likely to follow as a corollary.'

correspondent/co-respondent A *correspondent* is a person one writes to regularly: 'My pen pal and I have been correspondents since we were teenagers.' A *co-respondent* is (or was) a person (usually a man) accused of committing adultery in a divorce case, the other person (usually a woman) being the respondent: 'He was cited a co-respondent.'

corrode *see* erode

cosmonaut *see* astronaut

cosset *see* coddle

cosy *see* comfy

council/counsel A *council* is a body of people who meet for discussion or consultation: 'The church council meets once a month.' *Counsel* is advice: *Take my counsel, happy man;/Act upon it, if you can!'* (W.S. Gilbert). The two senses are reflected in *councillor* for a member of a *council* and *counsellor* for an official adviser.

counsel *see* council

coup de force *see* coup de grâce

coup de grâce/coup de force/tour de force A *coup de grâce* (French, 'stroke of grace') was originally the stoke with which a condemned person or wounded prisoner was "put out of their misery," so that it is now the term for a final blow, or whatever puts an end to something: 'Expulsion from college gave the coup de grâce to his career as a teacher.' A *coup de force* ('stroke of force') is a sudden, violent action: 'The workers decided their demands could be met only by some kind of coup de force, such as an all-out strike.' A *tour de force* ('feat of force') is an outstanding achievement of some kind: 'The author's latest novel is a real tour de force, the finest work she has yet produced.'

crape/crepe *Crape* is a black silk or cotton material with a wrinkled surface: 'Mourners formerly wore crape armbands.' *Crepe* (or *crêpe*) is a light thin material with a wrinkled surface: 'Margaret looked elegant in her white silk crepe-de-Chine blouse.'

crass *see* gross

credence/credit To give *credence* to something is to believe it: 'I find it hard to give credence to his explanation' (I don't believe it). To give *credit* to something is to believe *in* it: 'I don't give any credit to that theory' (I don't trust it).

credible/creditable/credulous *Credible* is used for something that can be believed: 'It seems hardly credible that last week we were still abroad.' *Creditable* is used for something that deserves praise or credit: 'The gymnast gave a highly creditable performance.' *Credulous* is used for a person who is gullible or all too readily believes things: 'He was a credulous child, and thought the stories they told him were true.'

credit *see* credence

creditable *see* credible

credulous *see* credible

crepe *see* crape

crevasse *see* crevice

crevice/crevasse A *crevice* is a narrow opening in something such as a wall or a rock: 'The birds had built their nests in the crevices of the cliff.' A *crevasse* is a deep open crack in the ice of a glacier: 'The polar explorers had to negotiate several crevasses.'

criticism/critique In the literary or artistic sense, *criticism* is the judgment of literature and works of art: 'The reviewer's criticism of the play was regarded by some as too generous.' A *critique* is a critical analysis of something: 'The writer's next work was a critique of the Roman Catholic Church.'

critique *see* criticism

crony/chum A *crony* is a friend or colleague you have known some time and who shares your tastes: 'He is dining with some crony of his tomorrow.' A *chum* is a close friend: 'Who's your new chum?' *Chum* can be used to address someone, often ironically: 'Look, chum, I'm doing the talking.' *Crony* cannot, however.

crumpled/rumpled If something is *crumpled* it is creased or wrinkled: 'When I got off the bus, my new coat was all crumpled.' The same applies if it is *rumpled,* but to a lesser extent, so that the folds can perhaps be smoothed out: 'She smoothed the rumpled sheet on the bed.'

cue *see* clue

cultivated *see* cultured

cultured/cultivated Both words relate to culture in the sense of education or refinement. *Cultured* refers specifically to education and to an appreciation of the arts, however, while *cultivated* is used for refined behavior or speech: 'Cultured people do not necessarily speak in a cultivated accent.'

cumulative *see* accumulate

customer *see* client

cutlet *see* chop

cynical/skeptical A *cynical* person is one who sneers or mocks, especially about someone or something normally held in high esteem: 'Whenever my father visits the doctor, he makes some cynical remark about "seeing the quack".' A *skeptical* person is dubious or mistrustful: 'She seemed skeptical when I said we'd be back by noon.'

D

dally *see* delay

damp/moist If something is *damp* it is slightly wet: 'There was a damp patch on the wall.' If it is *moist* it is slightly *damp*: '*The lady wiped her moist cold brow*' (Coleridge). The difference is thus usually in the degree of wetness.

dapper/debonair A *dapper* person (who is usually small and male) is smart and neat: 'What a dapper little man her brother is!' A *debonair* person (who is also usually a man) is cheerful and self-assured: '*The Frenchman, easy, debonair, and brisk*' (Cowper).

Dark Ages/Middle Ages The *Dark Ages* is a now dated term for the period from the 5th century AD to about 1000 AD: 'The Dark Ages are so called as they formerly were regarded as unenlightened.' Occasionally, the same name is used for the *Middle Ages,* which extend from the 5th century to the 15th: 'The Middle Ages are so called as they fall between "ancient" and "modern" times.'

dash *see* rush

date *see* day

day/date With regard to the calendar, a particular *day* is one either in the week or in a month, while a *date* is the *day* of the month only: 'What day is it today? It's Tuesday,' 'What's the date today? It's the 28th,' 'Please indicate day or date of arrival' (i.e. day of the week and date of the month).

daze/dazzle To *daze* is to stun, literally or figuratively: 'The noise of the music left him dazed.' To *dazzle* is to blind temporarily or to amaze by being splendid: 'On turning the corner, she was dazzled by the sun,' 'The dancers put on a dazzling show of color and synchronized movement.'

dazzle *see* daze

deadly/deathly If something is *deadly* it is either literally fatal or, less commonly, suggests death: 'The insect is well known for its deadly sting,' 'She was deadly pale.' If something is *deathly* it may be literally fatal but is more likely to suggest a dead state: 'His face was deathly pale.'

deathly *see* deadly

debar/disbar To *debar* someone is to bar or exclude him or her from a place or prevent him or her from exercising a right: 'Women are still debarred from some London clubs,' 'People under 18 are debarred from voting.' To *disbar* someone means the same, but the word is used mainly in a legal context: 'The lawyer was disbarred' (expelled from the Bar).

debate/deliberate To *debate* is to discuss something or consider something: 'We debated whether to invite Sid.' To *deliberate* something is also to consider it, but with a greater degree of thought or at greater length: 'We deliberated whether to invite Sid or not and finally agreed not to.'

debonair *see* dapper

deceitful *see* deceptive

decent/decorous *Decent* implies that something or someone is morally correct and proper: 'You could do the decent thing and apologize.' *Decorous* has the same sense but relates more to outward appearance or behavior: 'If Brian was late for breakfast, his father maintained a decorous silence.'

deceptive/deceitful If something is *deceptive* it is misleading, not necessarily intentionally: 'The size of the house was deceptive; it was quite spacious inside.' If someone is *deceitful* he or she deliberately deceives: 'Spending that money without telling me was a deceitful thing to do.'

decided/decisive As an adjective, *decided* means unmistakable: 'There was at last a decided improvement in the weather after days of rain.' If a thing is *decisive* it is conclusive: 'Johnson played well enough to win a decisive victory over his opponent and so become champion.'

decisive *see* decided

décolleté *see* déshabillé

decorous *see* decent

decry/descry The similar but unrelated words have unrelated meanings. To *decry* something is to criticize or belittle it: 'He decried her attempts to rectify the situation.' To *descry* something it to catch sight of it, usually when it is far off. The word is formal and poetic: '*And now the herald lark/left his ground-nest, high tow'ring to descry/The morn's approach, and greet her with his song*' (Milton).

dedicated *see* devoted

deduce/deduct The two verbs were at one time synonymous, but are now quite distinct. To *deduce* is to conclude something on the basis of evidence: 'There was no light anywhere in the house, and I deduced he was not at home.' To *deduct* is to take away a part from a whole, such as an amount from a total: 'Income tax is normally deducted by the employer.'

deduct *see* deduce

defective/deficient if something is *defective* it is imperfect or faulty: 'The machine wouldn't operate because of the defective switch.' If something is *deficient* it is incomplete and lacks everything it should have: 'The stew was shown to be deficient in its meat content.'

deficient *see* defective

definite/definitive If something is *definite* it is certain or clear: 'There was a definite chill in the air,' 'I'll give you a definite answer tomorrow' (a straight one). If a thing is *definitive* it is final and authoritative: 'This is the definitive version of the story,' 'I'll give you a definitive answer tomorrow' (one that will settle it).

definitive *see* definite

delay/dally/dither To *delay* is to be slow or tardy, so that what happens take longer or is later than it should be: 'Don't delay, buy today!' To *dally* is to waste time or dawdle, by implication when one should be doing something: 'He just dallies away his time.' To *dither* is to hesitate or be indecisive: 'Stop dithering and make up your mind!'

delectable *see* delightful

delegate/relegate To *delegate* someone or something is to appoint him or it for a special purpose: 'Andy was delegated to act as guide,' 'Jean was delegated the task of booking the seats.' To *relegate* a person or thing is to assign him or it to a lower or less important position or to refer him or it to others: 'The team was relegated to the Third Division,' 'The French church authorities relegated the execution of Joan of Arc to the English secular powers.'

deliberate *see* debate

delicious *see* delightful

delightful/delicious/delectable A *delightful* person or thing is one that gives great pleasure: 'He was a delightful companion, charming and witty.' A *delicious* person or thing gives a sensual pleasure in a 'tasty' or palatable way: 'These apples are simply delicious,' 'What a delicious actress Celia is' (she is good to watch). A person or thing that is *delectable* is both *delightful* and *delicious*: 'The chocolates you sent me were quite delectable' (they gave pleasure and tasted good).

deliverance/delivery *Deliverance* refers to an act of delivering or freeing someone from danger, captivity and the like: 'The hostages prayed for an early deliverance from their captors.' *Delivery* is used for all other senses of delivering: 'There are two mail deliveries a day,' 'I admired the delivery of his speech,' 'The nurse helped with the delivery of the baby.'

delivery *see* deliverance

delusion/illusion A *delusion* is a belief that a thing is really other than it is: 'The patient was under the delusion that the potatoes they gave him were rocks' (they were obviously not). An *illusion* is a deception caused by a thing *appearing* to be other than it really is: 'She has the illusion that she is very musical' (she could be but she isn't).

demonstrate/remonstrate To *demonstrate* something is to show it clearly: 'The teacher demonstrated the way to set up the apparatus.' To *remonstrate* about something is to object to it by doing one's best to *demonstrate* that it is wrong or unacceptable: 'The men remonstrated with the owner of the bar when he said it was closing time.'

denizen *see* citizen

denote/connote To *denote* something is to indicate it directly: "A persistent aching of the joints can denote arthritis.' To *connote* something is to indicate it in addition or at a secondary level: 'The word "home" usually connotes comfort and security, as well as a place to live.'

dependant *see* dependent

dependent/dependant *Dependent* is the adjective, used for a person or thing that depends on someone or something; *dependant* is the noun, and is a person who relies on someone for financial support: 'Admission to college is dependent on entrance examination results,' 'Do you have any dependants?'

depository/repository A *depository* is a place where things are stored, especially furniture: 'When we moved, we had to leave half of our stuff in a depository while the new house was being decorated.' A *repository* can also be this, but is equally a place where things are kept because of their value or rarity: 'A section of the museum served as a repository for local archeological finds.'

depraved/deprived Someone who is *depraved* is morally bad or corrupt: 'He was utterly depraved, and had a bad influence on many of his colleagues.' Someone who is *deprived* lacks the normal benefits of food, clothing, housing and the like: 'The housing authority was particularly concerned about the number of deprived children living in high-rises.'

deprecate/depreciate To *deprecate* something is to disapprove of it: 'I deprecated the inclusion of gratuitous violence in TV drama.' To *depreciate* something is to belittle or disparage it: 'Why does he always depreciate my efforts to help?'

depreciate *see* deprecate

depression/repression As psychological conditions, *depression* is a feeling of gloom and despair, or the psychiatric disorder that involves these emotions: 'She was suffering from mental depression.' *Repression,* on the other hand, is the forcing of certain strong emotions and responses into the unconscious, resulting in abnormal behavior: 'His problem seemed to stem from sexual repression.'

deprived *see* depraved

derisive/derisory *Derisive* is used for something that conveys contempt: 'The driver answered the traffic cop with a derisive gesture.' *Derisory* is used for something that invites contempt or scorn: 'The workers were offered a derisory pay increase.'

derisory *see* derisive

derogate *see* abdicate

descry *see* decry

desert/dessert When stressed on the second syllable, *desert* means something that is deserved, especially in the plural: 'He got his just deserts,' *'According to their deserts will I judge them'* (Bible: Ezekiel 7.25). *Dessert* is the sweet course of a meal: 'We had a straightforward lunch, appetizer, entrée and dessert.'

deshabillé/décolleté The French words, sometimes written without their accents, refer to a state of revealing dress, *deshabillé* being a partially dressed state generally and *décolleté* specifically denoting a low neckline: 'She came to the door in deshabillé,' 'Queen Victoria prudishly disapproved of ladies appearing décolleté in society.'

desiderate *see* desire

designated *see* designed

designed/destined/designated A thing *designed* for something is intended for it: 'The fax machine was designed to speed up communication.' A thing or a person *destined* for something has a particular purpose or function ahead of it or him, whether *designed* or not: 'The Beatles were destined to be one of the most famous pop groups of all time.' A person or thing *designated* for something is selected or appointed for it: 'The officer was designated to look into the matter.'

desirable/desirous *Desirable* is used for a person or thing that is desired or worth having: 'Is not peace desirable?', *'She doted upon the Assyrians her neighbors, captains and rulers clothed most gloriously, horsemen riding upon horses, all of them desirable young men'* (Bible: Ezekiel 32.12). *Desirous* is a formal word that simply means 'desiring,' 'wanting,': 'Are not all nations basically desirous of peace?'

desire/desiderate To *desire* something is to want it or wish for it: 'Julie had all that her heart desired,' 'I desire your presence at the meeting.' To *desiderate* something is to *desire* it with a feeling of regret that one does not have it, or that one no longer has it: 'Mark felt that he would never enjoy the kind of life he desiderated.'

desirous *see* desirable

despair/desperation *Despair* is loss of hope: 'She gave up the struggle in despair.' *Desperation* is the state of being in *despair*: 'When I lost my wallet, I rang the police in desperation.'

desperation *see* despair

despoil *see* spoil

dessert *see* desert

destined *see* designed

detract *see* distract

deviate *see* digress

devoted/devout/dedicated *Devoted* implies a personal loyalty or interest and a desire for active involvement: 'Tom is absolutely devoted to his fishing.' *Devout* is similar, with an added implication of earnestness or 'worship': 'Brenda is a devout follower of all the latest macrobiotic diets.' *Dedicated* implies a *devoted* attachment to someone or something, but with a strong sense of duty and 'single-mindedness': 'As a boy, Gerald was a dedicated train-spotter.'

devout *see* devoted

diagnosis/prognosis Both words have medical uses, but in the general sense can be distinguished. A *diagnosis* is the identification of a condition or problem: 'Paul's diagnosis of the situation was that people were simply ignoring the advertisements.' A *prognosis* is a forecast: 'The economic prognosis this month is rather more favorable.'

dialect/accent A *dialect* is the form of a language that deviates from the norm, not only in vocabulary and grammar, but also in pronunciation: 'Tennyson wrote some poems in a Lincolnshire dialect.' An *accent* is a local or individual way of pronouncing a language: 'The professor had a marked foreign accent,' 'Some people know French quite well but speak it with an American accent.'

differentiate/distinguish To *differentiate* is to tell two or more things apart: 'It's quite easy to differentiate between a robin and a sparrow.' To *distinguish* is the same, but applies when the things concerned are similar or almost identical: 'The twins are so alike I can hardly distinguish between them.'

diffident *see* different

digress/diverge/deviate To *digress* is to wander off the track, literally or figuratively: 'A good teacher should resist the temptation to digress.' To *diverge* is to go in different directions, also literally or figuratively: 'We agree on most things, but in this instance our opinions diverge.' To *deviate* is to turn aside from a particular course, implying that one has left the true or proper direction: 'She was resolved not to deviate from her plan of action.'

dilate/dilute To *dilate* something is to make it wider or larger: 'The eye-drops dilated her pupils.' To *dilute* something is to make it thinner or weaker: 'The drink was so strong that we diluted it with water.'

dilute *see* dilate

dinner *see* lunch

disbar *see* debar

discerning/discriminating *Discerning* means having good taste, taking minor details into consideration as well as major facts: 'John prides himself on his discerning palate, especially when it comes to fish.' *Discriminating* means the same, but implies a process of selection and rejection before a final, careful choice is made: 'Discriminating buyers usually shop at the best stores and supermarkets.'

discomfiture *see* discomfort

discomfort/discomfiture *Discomfort* is pain, unease or embarrassment: 'Linda's sprained wrist caused her continuous discomfort,' 'I had to face the discomfort of telling them myself.' *Discomfiture* is also embarrassment, but on the whole slighter or briefer than that expressed by *discomfort*: 'He laughed at my momentary discomfiture.'

discreet/discrete *Discreet* relates to modesty or reserve, otherwise discretion: 'We must be discreet about this in case he suspects something.' *Discrete* is used for things that have been separated into distinct parts: 'The coroner's task was to reconcile the discrete events that lead to the death.'

discrepancy/disparity A *discrepancy* is a conflict between facts or figures that should have been compatible: 'There is a discrepancy between the amount on the invoice and the quantity of good supplied.' A *disparity* is similar, but emphasizes the difference or inequality: 'Despite the disparity in their ages, their marriage is a very happy one.'

discrete *see* discreet

discriminating *see* discerning

disease *see* illness

disguise *see* guise

disinterested/uninterested If you are *disinterested* in something you are impartial and do not take sides: 'A disinterested observer of the scene would have wondered what all the fuss was about.' If you are *uninterested* you have no interests at all: 'The player was uninterested in the public reaction to his remark.'

disparity *see* discrepancy

dispel *see* disperse

dispersal *see* disposal

disperse/dispel/dissipate To *disperse* something is to make it go in different directions: 'The police dispersed the crowd.' To *dispel* something is to drive it away: 'He could not dispel his apprehension about the meeting.' To *dissipate* something is to make it disappear by breaking it up; 'The aircraft dissipated the clouds by dispersing dry ice into the atmosphere.'

dispersion *see* disposal

disposal/dispersal/dispersion/disposition *Disposal* is getting rid of something: 'The safe disposal of nuclear waste is a key issue.' *Dispersal* is the scattering or spreading of things or people: 'We were relieved to see the eventual dispersal of the rioters.' *Dispersion* basically means the same, but has various specialized applications: ''The dispersion of the Jews after the Babylonian and Roman conquest of Palestine is known as the Disapora.' *Disposition* is the arrangement or positioning of something, especially military forces: 'The agents discovered the disposition of the Soviet fleet.' *See also* disperse.

disposition *see* disposal

dissect/bisect To *dissect* something is to cut it into pieces and analyze it: 'The pathologist dissected the body,' 'The new film was dissected by the critic.' (The word begins with *dis-*, 'apart', not *di-*, 'two'). To *bisect* something is to cut it into two: 'The path bisected the park.'

dissension *see* dissent

dissent/dissension *Dissent* is the opposite of assent, so refers to a difference of opinion: 'Some Russian dissidents were not afraid to voice their dissent from Communist party policy.' *Dissension* is angry or heated disagreement: 'The manager's proposal was the cause of much dissension among the workforce.' *See also* dissenting

dissentient *see* dissenting

dissenting/dissident/dissentient *Dissenting* means disagreeing: 'There was only one dissenting vote when we took a show of hands.' *Dissident* means the same, but implies a stronger or more personally felt disagreement, especially with the authorities: 'There were many dissent writers in Soviet Russia keen to make their opinion felt.' *Dissentient* also means the same, but emphasizes the difference between those who disagree and the majority: 'The Democrats became the dissentient voices of American politics in the 1980s.'

dissident *see* dissenting

dissipate *see* disperse

dissipated *see* dissolute

dissolute/dissipated A *dissolute* person or life is a debauched one: 'He was a true playboy, and led a dissolute existence until his money ran out.' A *dissipated* person or life is similar, but the word hints at pleasures themselves: 'Charles II has gone down in history as a dissipated king, notorious for his many mistresses.'

distinct/distinctive *Distinct* is used for something clearly apparent or obvious: 'There has been distinct improvement in the weather this month.' *Distinctive* is used for something that can be distinguished in some way or that stands out by being different: 'The singer had a distinctive voice that won her many fans.'

distinctive *see* distinct

distinguish *see* differentiate

distract/detract To *distract* someone is to draw his or her attention away from something: 'Don't let the children distract you,' 'The music distracted me from my reading.' To *detract* from something is to make it seem less important or valuable: 'The constant packing and unpacking detracted from the enjoyment of our holiday,' 'The loudness of the music detracted from the originality of its composition.'

distracted *see* distraught

distrait *see* distraught

distraught/distressed/distracted/distrait A *distraught* person usually behaves irrationally when affected by a deep emotion such as grief or fear: 'The distraught mother looked for her missing child everywhere.' A *distressed* person is very upset at the result of some affecting experience: 'Many of the hostages were in a distressed state when freed.' A *distracted* person is often one who is mentally confused or even insane, albeit only temporarily: 'The poor woman was quite distracted and keep murmuring the same words over and over again.' A person who is *distrait* is absent-minded (i.e., *ab*stracted rather than *dis*strated): 'My fellow guest appeared gloomy and distrait, and I wondered what was troubling him.'

distressed *see* distraught

distrust/mistrust *Distrust* implies absence of trust: 'He has an innate distrust of foreigners.' *Mistrust,* the weaker word, implies a hesitation to trust: 'She lacked confidence, and mistrusted her own judgment in such things.'

disturbed/perturbed A *disturbed* person is agitated by something, often physically: 'When I heard the news I was extremely disturbed' (I was sick with anxiety). Someone who is *perturbed* is worried by something, usually mentally: 'What you say perturbs me; I thought we had agreed on what to do.'

dither *see* delay

diverge *see* digress

divers *see* diverse

diverse/divers *Diverse* is used for things that are different or varied: 'There were diverse opinions about the matter.' *Divers,* an old-fashioned or literary word, means that there are simply various things or a number of them: *'And he healed many that were sick of divers diseases'* (Bible: Mark 1.34).

doctrine/dogma *Doctrine* is a set of beliefs; *dogma* is a set of beliefs put forward by an authority to be accepted as a matter of faith: 'Christian doctrine today is no longer the dogma that is was in the early years of the Church.'

doddering/doting A *doddering* old man is one who trembles or shakes or walks unsteadily: 'The actor's portrayal of the king as a doddering old monarch was both comic and touching.' A *doting* old man is one who is senile, or who wanders in his mind. The word more commonly has the sense of being foolishly fond of someone, however, as old people can be: 'He really doted on her, and wanted to leave her his money!'

dogma *see* doctrine

Domesday/doomsday *Domesday* is the usual spelling for the *Domesday* Book, while *Doomsday* is Judgment Day and *doomsday* is this same word in a general sense: 'The Domesday Book was probably so called as there was no appeal against it, any more than there was against Doomsday,' 'This work will take me till doomsday.'

dominate/domineer To *dominate* is to have a superior position or greater authority, so that one influences or controls others: 'The chairman dominated the meeting, hardly letting anyone else have their say.' To *domineer* is to assert one's authority over others, usually imperiously or arrogantly: 'I strongly object to his domineering tone.'

domineer *see* dominate

Dominica/Dominican Republic *Dominica* and the *Dominican Republic* are both in the West Indies: 'Dominica is a small island in the southeastern West Indies; the Dominican Republic, to the west, occupies the eastern half of the large island of Hispaniola, sharing it with Haiti.'

Dominican Republic *see* Dominica

doomsday *see* Domesday

doting *see* doddering

doubtful/dubious If something is *doubtful* it is uncertain, and one needs to know more about it: 'The weather looks doubtful' (it may rain, but it may not). If a thing is *dubious* it raises or causes doubt: 'He gave a dubious reply when I asked him about it,' 'Christine had the rather dubious privilege of staying behind to keep an eye on things.'

doubtless/undoubtedly/indubitably The words express various degrees of concession or willingness to agree on the part of the speaker, as noted in the following examples: 'You are doubtless right' (you may well be, though I do not want to admit it), 'You are undoubtedly right' (you almost certainly are, as I would agree), 'You are indubitably right' (you definitely are, and I readily concede as much).

douse/souse/dowse To *douse* something is to extinguish it: 'We doused the blaze with buckets of water,' 'Hey, douse that light!' To *souse* something is to drench it: 'The firefighters soused the oildrums with jets of water.' To *dowse* is to search for water underground by using a special divining rod: 'A dowsing party soon established the presence of water of an underground stream.' However, *douse* can also be spelled *dowse* in the first sense.

dove *see* pigeon

dower/dowry Although both words can now mean the same, a *dower* is properly a widow's life share in her husband's property, while a *dowry* is the money or property brought by a woman to her husband when she marries: 'The old man deprived his wife of her rightful dower by a special clause in his will,' 'In his speech, the groom said that his bride's dowry, her brains and her beauty, was worth far more to him than any amount of money.'

downstage *see* upstage

downtown/uptown In American usage, the *downtown* area of a city is the center, and the *uptown* the outer or residential districts: 'They lived in downtown Chicago, where they had moved from uptown Philadelphia.' In New York City, the usage is more particular. The area south of 14th Street in Manhattan is referred to as *downtown,* the area north of 59th street is *uptown,* the area between is *midtown.* In addition, New Yorkers use the term *downtown* to mean south, *uptown* to mean north: 'I am going uptown to see my sister' (she lives north of where I live).

dowry *see* dower

dowse *see* douse

doze/drowse/snooze To *doze* is to sleep fitfully or lightly, typically in the daytime or on first waking in the morning: 'He dozed for most of the train journey.' To *drowse* is to be close to sleep, as in the evening or when very tired: *'Good things of day begin to droop and drowse/ Whiles night's black agents their preys do rouse'* (Shakespeare). To *snooze* is to sleep lightly and briefly, especially when most people are usually awake: 'The club was full of elderly gentlemen snoozing after their lunch.'

drab/dreary If something is *drab* it is faded or shabby: 'Our first task was to paint over the old, drab wallpaper.' Something that is *dreary* is mournful or depressing: 'The station announcer had a very dreary voice.'

draft/draught A *draft* is either a preliminary written version of something or a body of people selected for a special purpose: 'The lawyer had prepared a draft of the letter he intended to send.' A *draught* is a current of air or a swallowing of liquid: 'There's a terrible draught here.' In American usage, draught is usually also spelled 'draft.'

dramatist/playwright Both words are used for a person who writes plays. However, a *dramatist* is often thought of as a 'classic' or serious writer (of drama), while a playwright is often a modern writer, or someone who writes a lighter type of play: 'The French dramatist Racine is famous for his tragedies,' 'The British playwright Alan Ayckbourn is well known for his comedies.'

draught *see* draft

dreary *see* drab

drip/drop A *drip* is in general an unwanted *drop*: 'We put a basin under the leaking pipe to catch the drips,' 'These nose drops should help your stuffiness.' However, the verb *drip* is used for a falling of *drops*, hence the *drip* that is the medical device: 'They put her on a drip.'

drop *see* drip

drowse *see* doze

drunk/drunken As applied to an inebriated person, *drunk* normally follows the person so afflicted, and *drunken* immediately precedes him or her, especially if the state is a regular one: 'She was drunk,' 'A drunken partygoer staggered across the road,' 'He aimed to get drunk,' 'She divorced her drunken husband.'

drunken *see* drunk

dual/duel *Dual* is an adjective relating to anything of which there are two; *duel* is a noun, and is the formal fight or contest between two people: 'A public path and a stretch of grass separated the house from the dual evils of highway and factory,' 'The men arranged to meet in a duel at down.' (The two words are not related, and *duel* actually comes from Latin *duellum*, a form of *bellum*, 'war.')

dubious *see* doubtful

duel *see* dual

dumbfounded *see* amazed

dysfunction *see* malfunction

E

eatable/edible *Eatable* is used for something that is in a fit state to be eaten: 'The school lunches were sometimes barely eatable.' *Edible* can also be used in this way, but is frequently reserved for something that can basically be eaten or serve as food: 'Are these berries edible?'

eccentric/erratic *Eccentric* is used for someone or something markedly unusual, deviating from an accepted norm: 'He had an eccentric taste in drinks: sherry mixed with evaporated milk was just one of them.' *Erratic* is used for a person or thing that is inconsistent or unpredictable: 'Sam was an erratic driver, suddenly speeding up then slowing down without warning.'

éclat/élan *Éclat* relates to a brilliance of some kind: 'The pianist performed the piece with great éclat.' *Élan* refers to a combination of style and energy: 'We all admired the tremendous élan with which she threw herself into the routine.' The respective French words mean literally 'flash' and 'dash.'

eclectic *see* esoteric

economic/economical *Economic* pertains to economy (or to the economy), or to something that is profitable: 'Business leaders looked eagerly for signs of an economic recovery,' 'It's not really economic to run buses on all the routes.' *Economical* relates to a person or thing that economizes, or is not wasteful: 'She is economical by nature and keeps a regular note of her expenses.'

economical *see* economic

Ecuador/Equatorial Guinea *Ecuador* is a country in northwest South America; *Equatorial Guinea* is a country in West Africa; 'Ecuador and Equatorial Guinea are so named as they are on or close to the Equator.' *See also* Guinea.

edible *see* eatable

edification *see* education

education/edification *Education* is instruction or the imparting of knowledge: 'Our trip abroad was a real education: we'd no idea they lived like that.' *Edification* is enlightenment of a moral or spiritual kind: 'I am not telling you this simply for your edification, but because it is something you need to know.'

e're/ere These old-fashioned and poetic words may be misunderstood in literature of their period, especially as their spelling are sometimes interchanged. *E're* means 'ever,' while *ere* means 'before': '*And my desires, like fell and cruel hounds,/E're since pursue me*' (Shakespeare), '*The nobleman saith unto him, Sir, come down ere my child die*' (Bible: John 4.49).

effect *see* affect

effective/effectual/efficacious/efficient If something is *effective* it has an noticeable effect: 'The actor made a most effective entrance.' If it is *effectual* it produces a particular effect, usually the one intended: 'We took effectual steps to redress the situation.' If a thing is *efficacious* it has the power or potential to produce a particular effect: 'These tablets are efficacious against malaria.' If a thing is *efficient* it works well: 'Josie did a very efficient job with the lawns.'

effectual *see* effective

effeminate/effete *Effeminate,* as used of a man, means not manly, in other words womanish: 'Adam has a slightly effeminate way of walking.' *Effete* is now also used in this sense, but more exactly means feeble or even decadent because over-refined: 'The uniform of long blue coat, yellow stockings and black buckled shoes gave the boys a rather effete appearance.'

effete *see* effeminate

efficacious *see* effective

effrontery *see* affront

e.g./i.e. The abbreviation *e.g.* (from Latin *exempli gratia,* 'for sake of an example') indicates that one or more examples follows of what has been mentioned in general terms: 'It could be cheaper by public transportation, e.g. by train or bus.' The abbreviation *i.e.* (from Latin *id est,* 'that is') indicates that an explanation follows of what has just been mentioned: 'Gratuities are discretionary, i.e. you don't have to leave a tip if you don't want to.'

egoist/egotist There is a considerable overlap between the words, but a difference exists. An *egoist* is someone who is self-centered or selfish, often without realizing it: 'He's a proper egoist, never thinking to inquire about the needs or wishes of anyone else.' An *egotist* is an arrogant or conceited person, always talking about himself: 'She's a real egotist, always on about what she has done or is planning to do.'

egotist *see* egoist

élan *see* éclat

elapse/lapse As used of time, to *elapse* is simply to pass, but to *lapse* is to pass away, or near its end: 'Two years elapsed before we next met.' 'Our time was lapsing fast,' *She knew that the moments were fleetly lapsing away'* (Nathaniel Hawthorne).

elated *see* elevated

elder/older *Elder* is used in family or professional relationships: 'His elder brother was an elder partner in the business.' *Older* is used in a general sense: 'She is not much older than me.'

elect/elite The *elect* are the people selected as the best or most suitable for something: 'Admission to this sports club is only for the elect.' The *elite* are the people in a group or class who are regarded as superior, for example in wealth, breeding, talent, or a combination of these: 'At one time, private schools were mainly for sons of the elite.'

electric/electrical *Electric* is used for something that works by electricity: 'Most houses have electric light,' 'He switched to an electric razor quite late in life.' *Electrical* is used for something concerned generally with electricity: 'He set up business as an electrical engineer,' 'The office copier developed an electrical fault.'

electrical *see* electric

elegance *see* eloquence

elemental *see* elementary

elementary/elemental *Elementary* refers to something basic or primary: 'Many Americans have only an elementary knowledge of a foreign language.' *Elemental* relates to elements of some kind, usually in the natural or scientific world: 'The explorers were successful in capturing on video something of the elemental beauty of the region.'

elevated/elated If something is *elated* it is literally or figuratively raised: 'The walkers reached a more elevated position,' 'Some classical writers are famous for their elevated writing and for their lofty noble style.' A person who is *elated* is in high spirit or buoyant mood: 'When I was offered the appointment, I was absolutely elated.'

elite *see* elect

elope *see* escape

eloquence/elegance *Eloquence* is the use of expressive language, especially when persuading people of something: 'The eloquence of the guest speaker was most impressive.' *Elegance* is the state of being tasteful and stylish, otherwise elegant: 'The novel's descriptive passages have an elegance that make them a joy to read.'

El Salvador *see* Salvador

elude *see* avoid

embargo *see* boycott

emend *see* amend

emigrant *see* immigrant

émigré *see* immigrant

eminent/imminent Both words are based on Latin *minere*, 'to jut out', but their meanings are now quite different. *Eminent* means famous, outstanding (literally 'standing out'), while *imminent* means about to happen, impending (literally 'standing over'): 'The arrival of the eminent visitor was imminent.'

Emmy/Grammy/Tony All three are annual American awards. The *Emmy* is awarded by the Academy of Television Arts and Sciences for achievement in television; the *Grammy* is awarded (in the form of a gold-plated gramophone record) by the National Academy of Recording Arts and Sciences for achievement in recording, and the *Tony,* named after the actress Antoinette Perry, is Broadway's award for achievement in the theater: 'Kirstie Alley won an Emmy for her part in *Cheers;* Quincy Jones won a Grammy for his album *Back on the Block;* and Nigel Hawthorne won a Tony for his leading role in *Shadowlands.*'

emotional/emotive *Emotional* is used for something that expresses emotion or that is affected by emotion: 'He read us an emotional account of his loss,' 'There's no need to be so emotional: crying like that won't help matters.' *Emotive* is used for something that has the potential to affect the emotions, but may not necessarily do so: 'Abortion tends to be a very emotive subject.'

emotive *see* emotional

empathy *see* sympathy

en bloc/en masse The literal French meanings of the respective phrases are 'in a block' and 'in a mass.' Both mean 'all together', but *en block* implies a unity and *en masse* a quantity: 'The union members left the meeting en block,' 'Children can be delightful on their own, but en masse they can be little horrors.'

encumber/lumber To *encumber* someone with something is to burden him or her with it so that he or she is hampered: 'He had been to the stores and was encumbered with parcels when I met him.' To *lumber* a person with something is to 'saddle' him or her with it, the implication being that a tedious task or chore is involved: 'When my neighbor was away last week, I was lumbered with feeding her cat.'

endemic/epidemic An *endemic* disease is one regularly found in a particular place or region: 'Malaria is endemic in the tropics.' An *epidemic* disease, or simply an *epidemic,* is one that spreads quickly in a region but that lasts only for a time: 'The flu is one of the commonest epidemic diseases.'

endowed/endued *Endowed* is used for people or things that have been provided with something, whether concrete or abstract: 'She was endowed with both wealth and beauty.' *Endued* is used only of abstract qualities: 'He was endued with a wisdom far beyond his years,' '*I thank God I am endued with such qualities*' (Elizabeth I).

endued *see* endowed

enervate/invigorate Because of a false association with such words as *elevate* and *energy, enervate* is often used to mean 'invigorate.' It actually means the opposite: to drain and weaken: 'The climate in hot countries can be depressing and enervating.' To *invigorate* someone or something thus means to give him or her or it vigor and energy: 'The freshness of the morning invigorated me as I walked.'

engine/motor An *engine* develops its own power, while a *motor* gets its power from an outside source: 'Early railway locomotives were basically steam engines on wheels,' 'The fan was operated by an electric motor.'

en masse *see* en bloc

enormity *see* enormousness

enormousness/enormity *Enormousness* relates to the state of being much larger than expected: 'She was stunned by the enormousness of the task of feeding everyone.' *Enormity* can also mean this, but properly refers to something that is outrageously or horrifyingly large, such as a crime: 'James was appalled at the enormity of the theft.'

enquiry *see* query

ensure *see* assure

enthralled *see* thrilled

entitled/titled As used of book titles and the like, *entitled* is normally used actively and *titled* passively: 'He entitled his novel "The Tree of Terror",' 'The poem was titled "Maids of the Mist".'

entomology/etymology These two subjects of popular interest have similar names but dissimilar meanings. *Entomology* is the study of insects (Greek *entomon*, 'insect'); *etymology* is the study of the origin and history of words (Greek *etymos*, 'true', 'real'): 'Both entomology and etymology can lead to flights of fancy if not scientifically studied.'

enviable *see* envious

envious/enviable If somebody is *envious* they experience envy: 'I am envious of your home computer: I could do with one too.' If a thing is *enviable* it causes envy: 'He has an enviable way with everyone, always ready with a word and a smile.'

envisage/envision To *envisage* something is to regard it as likely: 'I don't envisage any difficulty over your application,' 'The pensioners envisaged vacations abroad as well as at home.' To *envision,* as a loftier word, is to have aims or prospects for the future: 'Many of us find it hard to envision a world without was.'

envision *see* envisage

envy/jealousy *Envy* is the desire to have a particular thing that someone else has, especially when it is superior to what one has oneself: 'His comfortable house and spacious garden instantly aroused my keenest envy.' *Jealousy* is the desire to have a particular thing that another person has when one believes one has a right to it oneself. The feeling is thus accompanied by a sense of rivalry: 'All the boys seemed to be flirting with Laura, and Sophie experienced pangs of jealousy.'

epidemic *see* endemic

epigram/epigraph/epitaph/epithet An *epigram,* originally an inscription on a monument or statue, is now short, witty statement, especially one with two counterbalancing halves: 'Francis Bacon popularized the epigram: "If the hill will not come to Mahomet, Mahomet will go to the hill".' An *epigraph* is either an inscription on a monument or statue, or a motto or quotation as the beginning of a book: 'The epigraph of E.M. Forster's novel *Howards End* is "Only connect!".' An *epitaph* is an inscription on a tomb or grave: 'Dryden's epitaph on his wife was: "Here lies my wife: here let her lie!/Now she's at rest, and so am I".' An *epithet* is an adjective or phrase describing a person or thing: 'Richard Coeur de Lion earned the epithet 'Lionheart' because of his bravery.'

epigraph *see* epigram

epitaph *see* epigram

epithet *see* epigram

equable/equitable If a thing is *equable* it is unvarying in an agreeable way: 'The island of Malta has an equable climate, with stable temperatures for most of the year.' If it is *equitable* it is impartial or reasonable: 'The crew reached an equitable agreement: they would take turns to keep watch.'

Equatorial Guinea *see* Ecuador

equitable *see* equable

ere *see* e're

erode/corrode To *erode* something is to gradually eat away some part of it: 'The current of the river began to erode its banks.' To *corrode* something is to destroy the whole of it gradually: 'His feelings of envy began to corrode the pleasure he had in his work.'

erotic *see* exotic

erratic *see* eccentric

erupt/irrupt To *erupt* is literally to burst out, while the less common *irrupt* is literally to burst in: 'The gang erupted from the building unto the street when the police irrupted into it.'

escape/elope To *escape* is to get away from something, usually something dangerous or unpleasant: 'I managed to escape being trapped into his tedious conversation.' To *elope* is to get away secretly, to abscond: 'The lovers eloped on a moonless night,' 'The shop assistant appears to have eloped with the day's takings.'

esoteric/eclectic Something *esoteric* is designed for the select few or the initiated, with the implication that the thing in question is abstruse or obscure: 'James Joyce's esoteric use of language can deter the average reader.' If a thing is *eclectic* (an *esoteric* word), it implies that the best of something has been selected from a number of sources, or simply that a person has wide or catholic tastes: 'The concert was enjoyably eclectic, and included music from Bach to the Beatles.'

especially *see* specially

estimable/inestimable *Estimable* applies to someone worthy of great respect: 'He was generally regarded as an estimable man and a worthy husband.' *Inestimable* is used for something that is literally too great to be estimated, and that therefore is invaluable: 'I am most grateful for your inestimable contribution to the project.'

estimate/estimation An *estimate* is an approximate figure or idea that is arrived at by judging or estimating; *estimation* is judgment itself: 'I can give you a rough estimate of the cost,' 'She's gone up in my estimation.'

estimation *see* estimate

eternity *see* infinity

etymology *see* entomology

eugenics/genetics *Eugenics* is the science of the production of healthy children; *genetics,* more widely, is the scientific study of heredity: 'Eugenics centers on an area of study also covered by human genetics.'

evacuate *see* vacate

evade *see* avoid

evasion/evasiveness *Evasion* is used for a statement or excuse that someone makes in order to avoid answering a question: 'I kept asking him if he was firing me, but all I got was a series of evasions.' *Evasiveness* is the quality of being evasive: 'Some politicians are notorious for their evasiveness.'

evasiveness *see* evasion

evince/evoke To *evince* something is to exhibit or show that one has it: 'Mozart evinced an amazing talent for music as a young child.' To *evoke* something is to bring it to mind or actually cause it as a response: 'The music evoked memories of her days at school,' 'The pianist's fine performance evoked prolonged applause from the audience.'

evoke *see* evince

exacerbate/exasperate To *exacerbate* something is to make it worse or aggravate it: 'The patient exacerbated the disease by constant scratching,' 'Your delay in answering has only exacerbated the situation.' To *exasperate* someone is to irritate or annoy him or her: 'His habit of never tidying up afterwards really exasperated her.'

exalt/exult To *exalt* someone or something is to raise him or her in esteem or honor by praising him or her: 'Many of Churchill's contemporaries exalted him as a fine leader,' *"Tis not what man does which exalts him, but what man would do!'* (Robert Browning). To *exult* is to rejoice greatly: 'Roberta exulted at her first professional success,' *'Exult O shores, and ring O bells!'* (Walt Whitman).

example/sample/specimen An *example* of something is a simple instance of it, often a typical one: 'The office was a successful example of the open-plan style.' A *sample* is a small quantity of something, especially when offered for examination or evaluation: 'Please send me a sample of the cloth you mentioned.' A *specimen* is a typical *sample* of something in a specialized field, whether complete in itself or part of a whole: 'Here are some specimen pages, showing the layout of the text,' 'The doctor said he would need a specimen of urine.'

exasperate *see* exacerbate

exceed/excel To *exceed* is to surpass or go beyond something, whether good or bad: 'The cottage exceeded our wildest dreams,'

'The driver exceeded the speed limit.' To *excel* is to be outstanding, or to be better than anyone else or anything else: 'Alison excelled at tennis,' *'Love divine, all loves excelling'* (Charles Wesley). *See also* exceedingly.

exceedingly/excessively *Exceedingly* usually means very much, while *excessively* properly means *too* much: 'I am exceedingly grateful to you for your help,' 'I was excessively upset yesterday' (I was more upset than I need have been). However, some people use *excessively* as simply a stronger form of *exceedingly*: 'I was excessively annoyed when I heard the news' (I was not just annoyed but *extremely* annoyed). *See also* exceed.

excel *see* exceed

except/exempt To *except* a person or thing is to make an exception of him or her or it, to exclude him or her or it: 'Present company excepted.' To *exempt* someone or something is to free him or her or it from some obligation: 'Conscientious objectors were exempted from military service during the war,' 'Children's clothes are exempt from sales tax.'

except *see* accept

exceptionable *see* exceptional

exceptional/exceptionable *Exceptional* refers to something that forms an exception, usually with the implication that it is especially good or important: 'The book was of exceptional interest to those who had shared the writer's experiences,' 'Marian's gift for gardening is exceptional.' *Exceptionable* means that a thing is open to objection, that is, people take exception to it: 'We referred him to a child psychiatrist because of his continuing exceptionable behavior.'

excerpt *see* extract

excessively *see* exceedingly

excite/incite To *excite* someone is to work him or her or it into a state of emotion or action: 'Don't excite the dog; he'll never stop barking.' To *incite* someone is to provoke him or her to do something: 'The rebels incited the people to take up any weapons they could find.'

exclude/preclude To *exclude* someone or something is to stop him or her or it from entering or getting in; to *preclude* a person or thing is to prevent him or her or it from doing something in general: 'All children under the age of 16 were excluded from the contest' (they were not allowed to enter it), 'Lack of funds precluded further development' (they did not allow it to take place).

excoriate *see* excruciate

excruciate/excoriate/execrate To *excruciate* (literally 'crucify') is to torment or torture: 'She had an excruciating headache,' 'He gave an excruciatingly feeble excuse.' To *excoriate* (literally 'flay') is to censure someone vigorously: 'Many newspapers excoriated the prince for his failure to set an example.' To *execrate* (literally 'curse') is to deplore something or express one's extreme dislike for it: 'I execrate his underhand behavior.'

execrate *see* excruciate

exempt *see* except

exercise/exorcise To *exercise* is to use or practice the mind or body in some activity: 'Jogging exercises the body and often the mind as well.' To *exorcise* something is to drive it out, with particular reference to an evil spirit: 'The priest exorcised the house when the family claimed they had an active poltergeist.' The words are unrelated.

exhausting/exhaustive *Exhausting* is used for something that exhausts the person concerned: 'Her research was exhausting' (it wore her out). *Exhaustive* applies to something thorough or complete: 'Her research was exhaustive' (she went into every aspect of the subject).

exhaustive *see* exhausting

exorcise *see* exercise

exotic/erotic Something *exotic* has a strange allure or beauty, especially if has come from a foreign country: 'The Far East is still popularly regarded as one of the most exotic places to go for a vacation.' Something *erotic* also has a special and mysterious attraction, but a sexual one: 'The belly dance is well known for its erotic appeal.'

expect *see* anticipate

expedient/expeditious If a thing is *expedient* it is useful or helpful, though not necessarily morally justifiable: 'As we drove up to the house, we thought it expedient to turn off the headlights,' 'Many investors felt it would be expedient to sell the shares before the election rather than after.' If something is *expeditious* it is speedy and efficient: We appreciated our senator's expeditious response to our questions.'

expeditious *see* expedient

expertise *see* expertness

expertness/expertise *Expertness* is the quality of being an expert: 'I was impressed with the expertness of my companion's driving after only six months on the road.' *Expertise* is expert knowledge or skill, especially in a particular field: 'The pitcher's expertise in handling the ball made the rest of the team look like amateurs.'

explain/explicate To *explain* something is to make it clear or under-standable: 'Can you explain this joke to me?' 'She couldn't explain why she was late.' To *explicate* something is to *explain* it and analyze it: 'Philosophers often have to explicate complex concepts and theories,' 'The lecturer explicated the plot and plan of the novel.'

explicate *see* explain

explicit/implicit If something is *explicit* it is clear or unambiguous, and expressed directly: 'He gave them explicit instructions not to got out.' If a thing is *implicit* it is implied, and expressed only indirectly: 'I have implicit faith in her ability.' *See also* imply, explicitly.

explicitly/expressly *Explicitly* is used for something done or said care-fully and clearly: 'The girls were explicitly forbidden to go there' (it was made clear to them why they shouldn't). *Expressly* has a similar sense, but implies a warning rather than an explanation: 'To girls were expressly forbidden to go there' (it was made clear to them that they were not allowed to do so).

exploit *see* achievement

expressly *see* explicitly

expropriate *see* appropriate

extant/extinct The two adjectives are almost opposites. If something is *extant* it has survived and still exists; if something is *extinct* it has died out, and no longer exists: 'Sophocles wrote more than a hundred plays, but only seven tragedies are extant,' 'Many species of animals have become extinct.'

extempore/impromptu An *extempore* speech is one made with little or no preparation: 'The speaker then departed from his text to add a few extempore words.' An *impromptu* speech is one that is improvised and given 'off the cuff': "In her impromptu response to the award the actress begun by thanking her agent.'

extemporize/temporize To *extemporize* is to do something *extempore* (see above), without preparation: 'The pianist had no music so extemporized the singer's accompaniment.' To *temporize* is to gain time by stalling or being evasive: 'The businessman was reluctant to make a firm decision on the matter and temporized as long as he could.'

extended/extensive Something *extended* has been made larger or longer than the norm: 'We went on an extended tour of the French vineyards' (it took longer, and we went further). Something *extensive* is large in area: 'The guide took us on an extensive tour of the extensive grounds of the house.'

extensive *see* extended

exterior/external If something is exterior it is outside rather than inside: 'I painted the exterior walls of the house' (but not the ones inside). If something is *external* it belongs outside only, although there may be some connection with what is inside: 'The gables at either end of the roof were two attractive external features,' 'The ointment was for external use only.' *Compare* interior.

external *see* exterior

extinct *see* extant

extract/excerpt An *extract* is a quoted passage: 'The chairman read an extract from the forthcoming company report.' An *excerpt* is the same, but is a specially chosen passage: 'The video opened with excerpts from other recently released films.'

extract/extricate If you *extract* yourself from something, you get out of it: 'I extracted myself from the meeting and made my way outside.' If you *extricate* yourself, you do the same but with difficulty or ingenuity: 'I wondered how I was going to extricate myself from the mess I was in.'

extricate *see* extract

exult *see* exalt

F

facility *see* faculty

factitious *see* fictional

faculty/facility A *faculty* is one of the natural powers of the mind or body, or else the ability or capability to do something: 'Has he taken leave of his faculties?' 'She has a wonderful faculty for hard work.' A *facility* is either a provision for doing something, or a means of doing it, or else the ability to do something easily: 'Guests will be afforded every facility during their stay,' 'Tessa has an enviable facility for working with the handicapped.'

Faeroes/Fair Isle The *Faeroes,* or *Faeroe Islands,* are a group of Danish islands between Iceland and the Shetland Islands. *Fair Isle,* famous for its knitwear, is a Scottish island between the Shetlands and the Orkneys: 'Both the Faeroes and Fair Isle are named from a Scandinavian word meaning "sheep".'

failing *see* fault

Fair Isle *see* Faeroes

fairy/fay/fey As adjectives applied to people, *fairy* means 'fairylike,' especially implying petiteness or delicacy: 'her fine features and fairy figure were those of a supermodel.' *Fay* is an alternative spelling of *fey,* a word used for someone or something that has a strange, otherworldly quality: 'She gave me a fay look,' 'Despite its fey moments, the play overall is entirely enchanting.'

fallacious *see* fallible

fallible/fallacious *Fallible* is used for people or things that are liable to be wrong or misleading: 'Human nature is fallible,' 'That is not a fallible rule.' *Fallacious* applies to something that contains a fallacy, so is illogical or false: 'The judge was not deceived by the clearly fallacious argument of the accused.'

falsehood/falsity Both words can be used to mean a lie or untruth. More generally, *falsehood* is the quality of being untrue, while *falsity* is the state of being untrue: 'Falsehood is the opposite of truth,' 'Can't you see the falsity of your situation.'

falsity *see* falsehood

famished *see* ravishing

famous/infamous A *famous* person or deed is widely known and is usually good or praiseworthy: 'We saw a film about Captain Scott, the famous explorer.' An *infamous* person or deed is widely known and is bad or to be deplored: 'We saw a film about the infamous king Richard III.'

fanatical *see* frantic

fancy/whimsy/whim A *fancy* is a sudden idea or inspiration: 'We took a fancy to his suggestion,' 'I had a fancy that I was being followed.' A *whimsy* is an unconventional or absurd notion, whether sudden or long-lasting: 'He always wears that ridiculous beret: it's one of his whimsies.' A *whim* is similar, but is trivial or transitory, and perhaps irrational: 'What Rachel has for breakfast depends on the whim of the moment.'

Far East *see* Middle East

farther/further The two are to an extent interchangeable, though there are certain distinctions and established usages. *Farther* is used for something more distant or remote: 'Her house is on the farther bank of the river,' 'It's farther from Chicago to New York than from Detroit to Cleveland,' 'I ran farther than you did.' *Further* can be used for farther in all these examples, but not when it refers to something extra or additional: 'Are there any further questions?' 'Further, it has been brought to my attention that you left early,' 'Godfrey said he would enquire further about the matter.'

fashion/vogue/mode A *fashion* is the prevailing adoption of a certain manner of dress, speech, behavior or the like, especially when seen from a historical perspective: 'The fashions of the sixties made a comeback in the nineties.' A *style* relates to the particular way in which a *fashion* is realized or presented: 'The style then was for long skirts.' A *vogue* is a passing *fashion,* one prevalent for a short time: 'Rap talk became the vogue for a while.' A *mode* is either a general way of doing something or a current (rather than historical) *fashion* or *style* : 'Last year the fashion was to wear underwear as outerwear. Now the mode is to wear nightwear as daywear.' All four terms usually relate to dress.

fatal/fateful If something is *fatal* it causes death: 'His second heart attack was fatal,' 'Have you seen the gory film *Fatal Attraction*?' If it is *fateful* it is ominous or decisive, perhaps bringing death, but perhaps not: 'That day was to be the fateful one for her.' In popular speech, however, the two words are not differentiated.

fate/fortune Both words denote powers that affect people's lives and the course of events. *Fate* implies a fixed predetermined future or destiny, however, and is often bad or negative, whereas *fortune* implies an unpredictable future that depends on chance or luck, and that is often good or positive: 'I shall just have to resign myself to my fate,' 'She had the good fortune to catch him just as he was leaving.'

fateful *see* fatal

father-in-law *see* stepfather

fault/failing/foible A *fault,* as applied to human character, is an obvious flaw or imperfection: 'His main fault is his failure to see things from other people's point of view.' A *failing* is a less serious flaw of this type, or perhaps a temporary one: 'Impatience is inclined to be one of my failings, I'm afraid.' A *foible* is a harmless or idiosyncratic 'weakness': 'She has a foible for chocolates.'

faun *see* fawn

fawn/faun A *fawn* is a young deer, or the pale yellowish-brown color of its coat: 'A doe stepped into the clearing with her two fawns,' 'The raincoat in fawn was both smarter and cheaper.' A *faun* is a mythological creature who is half man, half goat: 'The Roman fauns were identified with the Greek satyrs.' (For the latter, *see* **satire**.)

fay *see* fairy

fearful/fearsome Both words have to do with fear or fright, but *fearful* can mean either 'frightening' or 'frightened', while the less common *fearsome* means 'frightening' alone: 'The car sped down the highway at a fearful rate,' 'I was fearful for what might happen,' 'The iron railings had fearsome spikes on them.'

fearsome *see* fearful

feat *see* achievement

feckless *see* reckless

feed *see* food

felonious *see* nefarious

female/feminine *Female* relates to the sex of living things in general and when applied to humans emphasizes the physical aspects of being a girl or woman: 'Height and weight requirements for female recruits were lower than those for males,' 'The female voice is higher than that of the male.' *Feminine* relates to the general characteristics of a girl or woman, even when applied to a boy or man: 'There was something touching about his almost feminine tenderness towards his charges.' *Compare* male.

feminine *see* female

ferment *see* foment

fervent/fervid Something *Fervent* is warm or passive: 'It is my fervent wish that we shall all meet again very soon.' *Fervid* has the same sense, but is a more literary word and carries something of a greater strength: 'The solider was welcomed home amid fervid excitement.'

fervid *see* fervent

festal *see* festive

festive/festal *Festive* relates to something that is appropriate for a feast or festival: 'We were all in festive mood.' *Festal* relates directly to the feast or festival itself: 'The Christmas dinner consisted of turkey, plum pudding, and other festal fare.'

few/a few *Few* means not many; *a few* means some (as distinct from none): 'Few of us knew the meaning of the word' (though one or two did), 'A few of us knew the meaning of the word' (the speaker was surprised that any of us did).

fey *see* fairy

fiancé/fiancée The second word is sometimes written as the first. However, the *fiancé* is the man (the bridegroom), while *fiancée* is the woman (the bride): 'She introduced her mother to her fiancé, and he then met both his fiancée's parents.' The words have the respective masculine and feminine French endings.

fiancée *see* fiancé

fiction/figment A *fiction* is an invented story: 'His account of his journey was pure fiction: he had never even been there.' A *figment* is a fantastic notion, one that is obviously unreal: 'The girl at the gate must have been a figment of my imagination.'

fictional/fictitious/factitious Something *fictional* is imaginary or invented: 'Some young children have a fictional friend that to them can seem very real.' Something *fictitious* is false: 'When arrested, the thief gave a fictitious name and address.' Something *factitious* is artificial rather than natural: 'I was surprised by the factitious elegance of his speech' (it was not natural to him).

fictitious *see* fictional

field/meadow A *field* usually has a specific purpose, often agricultural, and is often enclosed: 'The gate led into a cornfield.' A *meadow,* often unenclosed, is an area of grassland, used either for hay or grazing or simply as open common land by a river: 'We had a picnic in the meadows.' The word is also the more poetic of the two: '*Meadows trim with daisies pied*' (Milton).

figment *see* fiction

filled *see* full

financial/fiscal *Financial* has to do with money, while *fiscal* has to do with government money: 'Are you in any financial difficulty:' 'The spokesman explained the government's fiscal policy.' Sometimes the two words coincide in meaning: 'The British financial year is the tax year, and is the equivalent (though not in the calendar) to the American fiscal year.'

finicky/pernickety *Finicky* is used for things (less often people) that are unnecessarily fussy: 'The finicky rules of the place were rather irritating.' *Pernickety* means the same, but is used more of people: 'The pernickety old man was constantly grumbling about the state of the sidewalks.'

fir/pine Both trees have cones and needle-like leaves, but the *fir* has leaves placed singly on its shoots whereas the *pine* has leaves growing in pairs or larger numbers: 'The Scots fir is actually not a fir put a pine.'

fiscal *see* financial

flabby/flaccid As used of flesh, *flabby* means soft and loose, while *flaccid* means soft and limp: 'The nurse patted the old man's flabby cheek with one hand while holding his flaccid fingers in the other.'

flaccid *see* flabby

flagrant *see* blatant

flail *see* flay

flair/flare A *flair* is a gift or talent for something: 'Emma has a real flair for music.' A *flare* is a literal or figurative blaze or outburst of something: 'There was a flare and the gates opened,' 'He rose to his feet in a sudden flare of anger.'

flammable *see* inflammable

flare *see* flair

flaunt *see* flout

flavor/savor A *flavor* is used for something added to food or drink to give it a special taste or smell (or both): 'The cake had a strong flavor of almonds.' A *savor* is a thing's basic taste or (less often) smell: 'Food can lose much of its original savor when eaten cold.'

flay/flail To *flay* is literally to skin something, especially by whipping, and hence to criticize severely: 'The popular papers flayed the new rock opera.' To *flail* is literally to thresh grain by hitting it with a bar attached to a handle, and hence to lash or hit out in general: 'The boy could not swim and was flailing the water desperately.'

flee *see* fly

fleeting *see* flying

fleshly/fleshy Both adjectives relate to flesh, but *fleshly* relates to *the* flesh, that is the body, with its sensual and sexual connotations: *'Abstain from fleshly lusts, which war against the soul'* (Bible: 1 Peter 2.11). *Fleshy* thus usually relates to the physical qualities of flesh, such as its plumpness, softness or color: 'She had fleshy arms and even fleshier thighs,' 'There's nothing I like more than a nice fleshy peach.'

fleshy *see* flesh

flinch/wince To *flinch* is to shrink from something painful, or something that might be painful: 'The patient flinched when the dentist switched on his drill.' To *wince* is to start or recoil when actually experiencing pain or discomfort; 'He winced when I stood on his toe in the crush,' 'His efforts at poetry were making me wince.'

floor/story Although both words mean the same, and refer to a particular level section of a building, *floor* is mostly used for the interior of the apartment, and *story* for its exterior or its structure in general: 'We had an apartment on the third floor,' 'The new office block is six stories high.'

flotsam/jetsam Technically, *flotsam* is cargo or wreckage *floating* on the surface of the sea, while *jetsam* is cargo that has been thrown overboard (*jettisoned*) or washed up on the beach. However, the two words are linked to refer to homeless people: 'The government seemed to do little to help the flotsam and jetsam of society.'

flounder/founder To *founder* is to struggle in an attempt to control a situation: 'The swimmer began to flounder in the heavy seas,' 'My next question made him flounder.' To *founder* is to sink or collapse: 'The ship sprang a leak and started to founder,' 'The project foundered when we no longer had the funds to support it.'

flout/flaunt/vaunt To *flout* someone or something is to treat him or her or it with constant contempt and ignore him or her or it: 'The school's lack of discipline meant that many pupils flouted the rules.' To *flaunt* something is to parade it ostentatiously: 'He loved flaunting his knowledge on the subject.' To *vaunt* something is to boast about it, but not necessarily ostentatiously: 'She vaunted her prowess at skiing.'

flush *see* blush

fly/flee Both verbs mean to escape or run away from danger or a threat, but *fly* is used more in the present and *flee* almost always in the past: '"*Shall we fight or shall we fly?*"' (Tennyson), 'The men fled the bank after the robbery,' '*The boy stood on the burning deck/Whence all but he had fled*' (Felicia Hemans).

flying/fleeting *Flying* is used for something hasty or hurried: 'We paid a flying visit to the cathedral but couldn't stay long.' *Fleeting* is used for something brief: 'We caught a fleeting glimpse of the sea as we left the town.'

fob/foist To *fob* something off on someone (or *fob* someone off with something) is to trick or deceive him or her into buying or accepting something inferior: 'The dealer fobbed me off with a cheap imitation.' To *foist* a thing on someone is to make him or her accept something they don't want: 'He used to foist the routine task on his assistant.'

foible *see* fault

foist *see* fob

foment/ferment To *foment* is to stir up trouble or something undesirable: 'I don't want to foment any ill feelings.' To *ferment* is to stir up emotions or reactions, not necessarily bad ones: 'The race fermented considerable excitement among the spectators.'

food/feed *Food* is generally for humans, and *feed* for animals, especially livestock: 'Have we got enough food in?' 'Cattle feed is delivered regularly to farmers by corn and agricultural merchants.'

forbid/prohibit Both verbs mean to ban something, or not allow it, but it is people who mainly *forbid,* and things that chiefly *prohibit. Prohibit* is also more authoritative than *forbid*: 'I forbid you to see him,' 'The city council has prohibited ball games on this stretch of grass.'

forbidding/foreboding *Forbidding* is used for someone or something that looks threatening or dangerous: 'The heavy gates and high walls gave the house a forbidding appearance.' *Foreboding* is used for something that is a sign of what is to come, especially when it is unpleasant: 'We glanced at the darkening sky, foreboding a storm,' 'She had an angry face, foreboding another of her rows.'

forceful/forcible A *forceful* argument for or against something is an impressive one, but not necessarily a convincing one: 'Joe opened the debate with a forceful argument against the bypass.' A *forcible* argument is a strong and persuasive one: 'In reply, Mrs. Hanley countered with a forcible speech explaining why the bypass was necessary.'

forcible *see* forceful

foreboding *see* forbidding

forego/forgo Both spellings are used for the sense 'do without': 'We'll have to forego our coffee break,' 'The workers agreed to forgo their expected pay raise.' Only *forego* is possible in the sense 'go before,' 'precede': 'The foregoing details relate to first-time buyers only,' 'It looks like a foregone conclusion.'

foreword/preface A *foreword* is a short introduction to a book, usually written by someone other than the author: 'The foreword to John Fisher's *Funny Way to be a Hero* is by the popular singer Chesney Allen.' A *preface* is similar, but is usually by the author: 'Authors often use the preface to explain their aims in writing the book.'

forgo *see* forego

formally *see* formerly

formerly/formally The words are unrelated but sound exactly the same and often make sense even when one is misused in place of the other. *Formerly* means previously, earlier; *formally* means in a formal manner: 'Agreement was formerly given' (it was given earlier), 'Agreement was formally given' (it was given officially or in principle).

fort/fortress A *fortress* is a large *fort*: 'The wooden forts built by William the Conqueror to consolidate his conquest of England gave way to the castles and fortresses of medieval times.'

fortress *see* fort

fortuitous *see* fortunate

fortunate/fortuitous *Fortunate* means lucky, bringing good fortune: 'The encounter was a most fortunate one, as it enabled me to put my case to her' (I was lucky to meet her). *Fortuitous* means occurring by chance, with no implication of being favorable or unfavorable: 'A fortuitous meeting with her enabled me to put my case to her' (we happened to meet and I turned the encounter to my advantage). *See also* fate.

fortune *see* fate

founder *see* flounder

fragile/frail *Fragile* implies a liability to break because delicate: 'The china is very fragile,' 'I'm feeling rather fragile this morning.' *Frail* means feeble or weak: 'In recent years she has grown very frail.'

fragrance *see* perfume

frail *see* fragile

frantic/frenetic/fanatical/phrenetic *Frantic* implies a desperation and a wild striving: 'The poor animal was nearly frantic with pain,' 'Sue was nearly frantic when she heard the news.' *Frenetic* means frenzied: 'A morning of frenetic activity followed.' *Fanatical* is used for a keen and often illogical dedication or devotion: 'My grandfather was a fanatical believer in the value of fresh air.' *Phrenetic* means the same as *frenetic,* but its classical spelling gives it a particular association with religious fanaticism or mental derangement: 'He lashed out at everyone who came near him with an almost phrenetic violence.'

frenetic *see* frantic

frontier *see* border

frown/scowl To *frown* is to contract the eyebrows in displeasure, puzzlement, or thought: 'When I introduced myself he frowned for a moment.' To *scowl* is to make the same gesture but in a threatening, angry or sullen manner: 'When I sent the youth away, he scowled and muttered something under his breath.'

frowzy *see* fuggy

fruit/fruition In a figurative sense, *fruit* (or *fruits*) relates to the result or consequence of something: 'You should soon see the fruits of your hard work and patience.' *Fruition* is the realization or enjoyment of that consequence: 'Her plans at last came to fruition, and the business began to take off.'

fruition *see* fruit

fuggy/fusty/frowsty/frowzy *Fuggy* is used for a dense atmosphere inside an enclosed space: 'The bar was so fuggy with cigarette smoke that I could barely breathe.' *Fusty* implies a moldy or stale smell: 'The professor wore a fusty old gown.' *Frowsty* means the same, but suggests that the smell is unpleasant: 'The hostages were confined in damp and frowsty quarters.' *Frowzy* also means the same, but additionally implies that the place is dirty: 'We were offered a frowzy little room at the back of the hotel.'

full/filled To be *full* of something is to be replete with it, and unable to contain any more: 'The cupboard was full of old clothes,' ''Tuesday's child is full of grace' (nursery rhyme). To be *filled* with something is also to be *full* of it, but the word draws attention to the agent, the thing that fills: 'I am filled with envy,' 'They look like rosebuds filled with snow' (Thomas Campion).

funeral/funereal As used adjectivally, *funeral* relates directly to a funeral, while *funereal,* which is always an adjective, describes something done in the manner of a funeral: 'The funeral services was held on Saturday,' 'The cars moved at a funeral pace' (very slowly).

funereal *see* funeral

furor *see* fury

further *see* farther

fury/furor A *fury* is a great rage or show of anger, usually from a single person or body of people: 'He was in a real fury,' 'The union expressed its fury at the decision.' A *furor* is a public outburst or 'commotion' about something, usually but not always in protest: 'There was a furor when the government imposed even further taxes,' 'Her virtuoso performance to packed houses caused a furor.'

fury *see* anger

fusty *see* fuggy

G

gabble *see* babble

gad/gallivant To *gad* is to go out in search of enjoyment: 'He spent much of his time gadding about when he should have been working.' To *gallivant* is to do the same, though through its suggestion of *gallant,* the word suggests a more modish pursuit of pleasure, and one undertaken with a member of the opposite sex: 'She was convinced her husband was gallivanting around with the maid during her absence.'

Gaelic/Gallic *Gaelic* relates to the Celtic languages of the people of Scotland and Ireland; *Gallic* relates to the Gauls, the ancestors of the French, or to the French themselves: 'The Gaelic languages are closely related,' 'Our French hosts were Gallic charm personified.'

gallant *see* valiant

Gallic *see* Gaelic

gallivant *see* gad

gamble/gambol To *gamble* is to risk or chance something: 'He gambled away a lot of his money on the horses,' 'I wouldn't gamble on the weather staying fine.' To *gambol* is to frisk or leap about playfully: 'The little lambs were gambolling in the field,' 'After the wedding, the younger children were gambolling around the churchyard.'

gambol *see* gamble

gammon/ham *Gammon* is usually bacon from the hind leg or side of a pig: 'Gammon steaks often form a part of a mixed grill.' *Ham* also comes from the hind leg, but usually the upper part: 'What could be tastier than a ham sandwich?'

gamut/gauntlet A *gamut* is the range of extent of something: 'Her expectations ran the whole gamut of emotions, from intense apprehension to unrestrained and joyful longing.' In its figurative sense, *gauntlet,* after the verb *run*, refers to an ordeal: 'He knew he would have to run the gauntlet of criticism from his colleagues.'

gangly *see* gaunt

gargantuan *see* giant

garish *see* gaudy

gaudy/garish Something *garish* is ostentatiously bright and 'flashy': 'Edward was sporting one of his gaudy ties.' Something *garish* is crudely colorful: 'The doors and windows of the house were painted a garish green.'

gaunt/gawky/gangly *Gaunt* means bony and emaciated: 'I was shocked by her gaunt appearance after her illness.' *Gawky* means clumsy or ungainly: 'The door was opened by a gawky youth, who gave us a gruff welcome.' *Gangly* (or *gangling*) is used for a combined awkwardness and lankiness: 'The foal stood unsteadily by its mother on long gangly legs.'

gauntlet *see* gamut

gawky *see* gaunt

gem *see* jewel

genetics *see* eugenics

genial *see* congenial

genie *see* jinn

genius *see* jinn

genteel *see* gentle

gentle/genteel As used (rather datedly) of social standing, *gentle* relates to an aristocratic or upper-class background inherited by birth, while *genteel* refers more to 'breeding' and a style of living that aims to be socially superior: 'He came from old English family of gentle birth,' 'The old lady lived in genteel poverty' (she tried to lead an upper-class life but was too poor to do so).

gentleman/man Class differences apart, *gentleman* is the courteous way to refer to a *man,* especially an old one: 'Can I just serve this gentleman?' 'Elderly gentleman requires housekeeper,' 'Who's that man over there?' 'I asked the man if he would mind moving.' *Compare* lady, and *see also* gentle.

gesticulate *see* gesture

gesture/gesticulate To *gesture* is to move a part of the body such as the hands or head to emphasize or indicate something: '"Help yourself," he said, gesturing towards the table.' To *gesticulate* is to do so vigorously, usually with the arms: '"Wait for me!" she cried, gesticulating wildly.'

giant/gigantic/gargantuan *Giant* is used for anything very big: *'That's one small step for man, one giant leap for mankind'* (Neil Armstrong). (The quotation evokes the *giant* steps that the astronauts were able to take on the Moon.) *Gigantic* is used for something large and possibly awesome (as a *giant* is): *'Mr. Holmes, they were the footprints of a gigantic hound!'* (Conan Doyle). *Gargantuan,* from Rabelais' character *Gargantua,* with his huge capacity for food and drink, is often used of appetites, or at any rate of something gross: 'We were unable to do justice to the gargantuan meal.'

gibber/jabber To *gibber* is to talk rapidly and usually incoherently: 'What's he gibbering about?' To *jabber* is to do the same, although the words may make some sort of sense: 'He was jabbering on about the accident he'd seen.'

gibe/gybe/jibe To *gibe* someone, or at someone, is to mock him or her or jeer at him or her: 'They gibed him about the error.' To *gybe,* as applied to a sailing ship, is to shift direction: 'The yacht gybed suddenly to port.' Both verbs have the same alternative spelling *jibe.*

gigantic *see* giant

giggle/snigger/snicker/titter To *giggle* is to laugh nervously or foolishly: 'The girls giggled as they were called up onto the stage.' To *snigger* is to laugh at something improper, often half-stifling the laugh: 'He sniggered at the smutty joke.' To *snicker* is the same, but the words suggests the actual sound of the laugh: 'One or two people started snickering, and soon we were all laughing openly.' To *titter* is to give a suppressed laugh, especially at something not very amusing or in circumstances where a full laugh might be inappropriate: 'The congregation tittered at the minister's pleasantry in his sermon.'

gild *see* guild

gilt *see* guilt

glance/glimpse A *glance* is a brief or indirect look at someone or something: 'She gave me a meaningful glance,' 'Could I have a quick glance at your paper?' A *glimpse* is a very brief sight of something or someone: 'We caught a glimpse of the sea through the trees.'

gleam/glow/glimmer/glint A *gleam* is a faint or intermittent show of light: 'There was a gleam from under the door.' A *glow* is a warm, steady and usually reddish show of light: 'The bushes were clearly visible in the glow from the bonfire,' 'There was a glow on her cheeks after the walk.' A *glimmer* is a faint show of light: *'By the glimmer of the half-extinguished light, I saw the dull yellow eye of the creature open'* (Mary Shelley). A *glint* is a sudden small *gleam* or flash: 'I caught a glint of his glasses.'

glimmer *see* gleam

glimpse *see* glance

glint *see* gleam

glow *see* gleam

glower/lower/lour To *glower* is to stare angrily or sullenly: 'I could see him glowering throughout the ceremony.' To *lower* is to scowl or frown, or of the sky, to look threatening: 'The children's lowering faces showed keen disappointment,' *'It will be foul weather to day: for the sky is red and lowring [sic]'* (Bible: Matthew 16.3). *Lower* rhymes with *power,* and *lour* is simply an alternative form of it (one preferred by many).

gold/golden *Gold* relates to something actually made of gold: 'He gave her a gold ring,' 'Lucy found a gold coin in the field.' *Golden* relates to something that is the color of gold, or that is precious, as gold is: 'Before us lay fields of golden corn,' 'This is a golden opportunity to tell him.' However, *golden* also formerly had the literal sense, and this persists in some set expressions and in poetry: 'He thought the goose that laid the golden eggs,' *'Can Wisdom be put in a silver rod,/Or Love in a golden bowl?'* (William Blake).

golden *see* gold

gourmand/gourmet A *gourmand* is someone who is excessively fond of food and drink: 'He's a real gourmand, and never stints on his weekly shopping.' A *gourmet* is a connoisseur of food and drink: 'TV cookery expert Graham Kerr was nicknamed the "Galloping Gourmet" because he did everything very quickly.'

gourmet *see* gourmand

grab/grabble/grapple/grope To *grab* something is to seize or take it suddenly: 'She grabbed the letter from the table.' To *grabble* is to scratch or feel about for something: 'He was grabbling in the garden for his wallet.' To *grapple* is to come to grips with someone or something, literally or figuratively: 'The wrestler grappled with his opponent,' 'Mike grappled with the problem.' To *grope* is to feel one's way or search uncertainly: 'We groped along the dark passage,' 'She groped for words but could find nothing to say.'

grabble *see* grab

graceful/gracious A *graceful* person or thing show grace or elegance: 'The ballet dancer gave a graceful leap across the stage.' A *gracious* person or thing is kindly or indulgent, as typically aristocrats and royalty are or were said to be: 'Gracious living is not everybody's cup of tea,' *'God save our gracious Queen'* (British National Anthem). The word can be sued patronizingly or sarcastically: 'How incredibly decent of you to honor us with your gracious presence.'

gracious *see* graceful

Grammy *see* Emmy

Granada *see* Grenada

grand-/great- In family relationships, *grand-* is used for one's parents' parents and for one's children' children, while *great-* is used for one's grandparents' parents and one's grandchildren's children: 'My grandfather was born in San Francisco, and his father, my great-grandfather, in Sacramento.' For relatives by marriage one can use great- or grand-, but great- is always more common: 'He had a surprise visit from his great-niece,' 'She has kept in touch with her grandaunt.'

grandiloquence *see* magniloquence

grapple *see* grab

great- *see* grand-

Great Britain *see* Britain

Grecian *see* Greek

Greek/Grecian *Greek* relates to Greece in any sense: 'The largest of the Greek islands is Lesbos.' *Grecian* applies more to ancient Greece, its culture and people: 'The actor was proud of his Grecian profile,' 'Keats's *Ode to a Grecian Urn* describes the pastoral scenes illustrated on an ancient Greek urn.'

Grenada/Granada *Grenada* (rhyming with 'aider') is the Caribbean island: 'Grenada is the most southern of the Windward islands.' Granada (rhyming with 'ardor') is the Spanish city and province: 'As soon as we arrived in Granada we made our way to the Alhambra palace.'

grieve *see* mourn

grill/grille A *grill* is the electric device or gas burner that directs heat downwards in a stove; a *grille* is any other framework of bars, such as a grating over a window or other opening: 'We can heat it up quickly under the grill,' 'The counter clerk opened the grille to take the packages.' *Grille* is sometimes spelt *grill*, but the cooking device is never spelt *grille*.

grille *see* grill

grisly *see* gruesome

groan *see* moan

grope *see* grab

gross/crass Something *gross* is repulsively or excessively large: 'A man with a gross beer gut walked in,' 'Accepting that invitation was a gross error of judgment on your part.' *Crass* is also used for something excessive, but with an implication of foolishness or stupidity: 'Fancy giving him all that money; what a crass thing to do.'

gross *see* net

grudge *see* begrudge

gruesome/grisly *Gruesome* is used for something horrific or repugnant: 'The squashed bird was a gruesome sight.' *Grisly* is close in meaning, but can imply something fearful or grim: 'The skull lay there with a grisly grin.' Both words are used in a facetious or euphemistic sense:

'There was a gruesome line at the checkout,' 'We had rather a grisly journey: the train was packed and we had to stand all the way.'

Guadalupe/Guadaloupe *Gaudalupe* is a town in southwest Spain and a city, properly Guadalupe Hidalgo, in Mexico. *Guadeloupe* is a French island group possession in the Caribbean: 'Through religious associations, the Spanish town of Gaudalupe gave the name of both Guadalupe Hidalgo and Guadaloupe.'

Guadeloupe *see* Guadalupe

guarantee/warranty The two terms are interchangeable up to a point, although *guarantee* is a more general term than the legal-sounding *warranty*. As popularly used, a *guarantee* undertakes to repair or replace something bought, while a *warranty* declares that what has been bought is the property of the vendor and that it is serviceable and fit for use: 'The sales clerk stamped and dated the guarantee card when I bought the hair drier,' 'The salesman stamped and dated the warranty when I bought the second-hand car.'

Guiana *see* Guinea

guild/gild A *guild* is a society of people such as craftsmen; to *gild* something is to cover it with gold, or with something the color of gold: 'The local Townswomen's Guild is very active,' 'We bought some old picture frames with the aim of gilding them.' The two words are actually related, the common link being money (German *Geld*) in the form of gold. *See also* guilt.

guilt/gilt *Guilt* is the state or feeling of having done something wrong: 'The police established his guilt.' *Gilt* relates to something gold, whether metal, color or money: 'The old lady wore a gilt brooch.' This second *gilt* is related to guild (*see above*).

Guinea/Guiana/Guyana *Guinea* is a large region of West Africa where the countries of Guinea, Guinea-Bissau and Equatorial Guinea are now situated. *Guiana* is a region of northeast South America where the French overseas region of French Guiana and the country of *Guyana* (formerly British Guiana) are now located: 'Guineas were minted from gold exported from Guinea,' 'The Pacific island of New Guinea was so named by its Spanish discoverers, who thought its people resembled those of Guinea.'

guise/disguise Both words refer to the external appearance of someone or something. A *disguise* is always a false appearance, however, whereas *guise* may not be. *Guise,* too, is normally always qualified (identified): 'Thomas went to the dance in the guise of a Highlander,' 'Natalie came to the party in disguise.'

Guyana *see* Guinea

gybe *see* gibe

H

habitable/inhabitable/uninhabitable Something *habitable* can be lived in: 'The builders made the old cottage habitable.' *Inhabitable* means the same, but is used for a place or area, rather than a house or home: 'The rocky island was inhabitable only by birds.' *Uninhabitable* is used for a place that is not *habitable:* 'The rocky island was uninhabitable so far as human habitation was concerned.'

hag/harridan/harpy A *hag* is an ugly old woman (who is probably also bad-tempered), a *harridan* is a bad-tempered one (who may well also be ugly), and a *harpy* is a cruel, greedy and hard-hearted woman (not necessarily an old one): 'The old hag in there wouldn't serve me,' 'His wife is a real old harridan,' *'Was it my mother-in-law, the grasping, odious, abandoned, brazen harpy?'* (Thackeray).

hail/hale In their respective senses of 'greet' and 'healthy', *hail* and *hale* are related (with a common link in *whole*): 'The audience hailed the appearance of the new actor,' 'She was now within hailing distance, so I called her,' 'You're looking hale and hearty!' The *hail* that is frozen rain is another word altogether: 'The rain turned to hail, and the hail to sleet.'

hale *see* hail

handiwork/handwork *Handiwork* is work, often something artistic or complex, that has (literally) been carried out by hand. The implication is often that the work was done by human hands (or God) rather than by nature: 'We admired the gardener's handiwork, *'The heavens declare the glory of God; and the firmament sheweth his handywork [sic]'* (Bible: Psalm 19.1). *Handwork* is work done by hand rather than by machine: 'The embroidery was an example of her handwork.'

handwork *see* handiwork

harbinger *see* herald

harbor *see* port

harpy *see* hag

harridan *see* hag

harum-scarum *see* helter-skelter

healthful *see* healthy

healthy/healthful *Healthy* relates directly to health; *healthful* is used for something that is good for one's health: 'Healthful foods, such as those grown in the garden, can help maintain a healthy diet.'

hear/listen To *hear* someone or something is to perceive the sound that the person or thing makes: 'We heard the sound of approaching footsteps.' To *listen* to a person or thing is to make a conscious effort to *hear* him or her or it, especially with the aim of understanding or appreciating what is heard: 'She listened to the radio every evening.' In some older texts, however, *hear* has this sense: *'And David said to Saul, Wherefore hearest thou men's words?'* (Bible: 1 Samuel 24.9).

heath/moor A *heath* strictly speaking has heather growing on it, and is typically a large open stretch of country with sandy soil and scrubby vegetation, as typically found in Scotland (where heather itself is often known as *heath*): 'We rode in driving rain over the heath.' A *moor,* which may or may not have heather, is an elevated area of rough land, often with peaty soil, coarse grass and moss: 'The national parks of England include Exmoor, Dartmoor and the North Yorks Moors.'

heathen/pagan A *heathen* is a person who has not been introduced to a 'formal' religion such as Christianity or Judaism, and who is thus regraded as a barbarian: *'The heathen in his blindness/Bows down to wood and stone'* (Bishop Heber). A *pagan* is a person who either worships a *heathen* god or deity or who has no religion at all: 'The Druids worshipped pagan gods.' A *pagan* belief is generally regarded as more advanced or 'enlightened' than a *heathen* one.

heaved/hove Both these words are past forms of the verb *heave,* though *hove* is now only found in a nautical sense, or in an expression adopted from that context: 'We heaved the furniture onto the van,' 'A ship hove into sight' (appeared), 'The ferry hove to outside the harbor' (stopped without anchoring), 'As we rounded the bent, a pub hove into view and we hove to for lunch.'

heel over/keel over To *heel over* is to lean over, tilt or list, as will a ship when unevenly loaded or standing on dry land: 'The truck heeled over as it sped round the bend.' To *keel over* is to collapse suddenly and fall on one's back. The term properly applies to a ship that has capsized so that its keel is uppermost: 'The animals were seriously affected by the disease, and many had already keeled over.'

helter-skelter/harum-scarum/hurry-scurry/higgledy-piggledy   *Helter-skelter* is used for a haphazard or hasty flight or dispersal: 'As soon as the games were over, the children ran helter-skelter from the field.' *Harum-scarum* implies a wild or reckless action (not necessarily a motion): 'His conduct is all harum-scarum, with no attempt at organization.' *Hurry-scurry* applies to something both hasty and disorderly: '*The victor ox scoured down the street/The mob fled hurry-scurry*' (Coleridge). *Higgledy-piggledy* is used for things in a mess or 'pickle': Karen's clothes were all higgledy-piggledy on the floor.'

hen *see* chicken

herald/harbinger In a figurative sense, a *herald* is a person or thing that announces something: '*hark, the herald angels sing*' (John Wesley). A *harbinger* is a person or thing that is a sign of something to come: 'Primroses are harbingers of spring.' The two senses can overlap, since a *herald,* in the act of appearing, is also a *harbinger.*

heritage *see* inheritance

hesitancy *see* hesitation

hesitation/hesitancy Both words can refer to the state of hesitating, but only *hesitation* can be used for an instance of hesitating: 'Why the hesitation?' 'There was a note of hesitancy in his voice,' 'The award winner's hesitation spoiled the effect of her speech.'

higgledy-piggledy *see* helter-skelter

high *see* tall

Hindi/Hindustani/Hindu *Hindi* and *Hindustani* are languages, and *Hindu* the people: 'Hindi is spoken mainly in north central India,' 'Hindustani is a dialect of Hindi spoken in Delhi and serving as a lingua franca throughout India,' 'A Hindu is not just someone who lives in northern India but a person whose religion is Hinduism.'

Hindu *see* Hindi

Hindustani *see* Hindi

hire/rent To *hire* something is to pay for the use of it for a fairly brief time: 'We're late, so we'd better hire a taxi,' 'The club hired a hall for their monthly meeting.' To *rent* is to do the same, but usually for a fairly long period: 'Do you rent your TV or did you buy it?' 'Laura rented an apartment while she was in college.' The verbs are also the action of the person who lets out these things: 'The owner of the van was prepared to hire it out to us for the day,' 'The farmer rented out the field every summer to campers.' *See also* let.

historic/historical A *historic* event is an important one, or one that may come to be regarded as important: 'The two heads of state signed a historic agreement.' A *historical* event is one that belongs to history, so that it actually took place: 'King Arthur is generally believed to be a historical figure, though some regard him as legendary.'

historical *see* historic

histrionics *see* hysterics

hoard/horde A *hoard* is a store or accumulation of things: 'An important hoard of Roman coins was found in a field in Suffolk.' A *horde* is a large group of people: 'There were hordes of bargain hunters at the sales.'

Holland/Netherlands/Low Countries *Holland* is a popular name for the *Netherlands,* the country north of Belgium. This second name means literally 'lower lands,' but the *Low Countries* are more extensive in area, and comprise Belgium, Luxembourg and the Netherlands: 'Benelux, the customs union of the Low Countries, is named from the first syllables of *Be*lgium, the *Ne*therlands and *Lux*embourg.'

home *see* house

homely *see* homy

homy/homely *Homy* (or *homey*) refers to something cosy and informal, like a home: 'What a lovely little homy house this is!' *Homely* relates to something simple and unpretentious, as one often finds in a home: 'Berry always had a nice homely cup of tea in the morning,' *'Home is home, though it be never so homely'* (John Clarke).

honorable/honorary *Honorable* means having honor: 'After the scandal he did the honorable thing and resigned.' *Honorary* means given as an honor (as distinct from something gained by a person's own effort): 'The writer was awarded an honorary degree.' It is the first of these that gave the courtesy title: 'The Hon. Jonathon Porritt inherited the title of baronet on the death of his father.'

honorary *see* honorable

hoodoo/voodoo A *hoodoo* is a person or thing that brings bad luck, otherwise a 'jinx': 'There seems to be a hoodoo on my watch: it's always stopping.' *Voodoo* (which gave the word) is a religious cult involving witchcraft, or a person who practices it: 'The photo showed a young Haitian girl possessed by a *loa* or voodoo god.'

horde *see* hoard

horrible/horrid In the popular sense, both words are used for something unpleasant. *Horrible* is slightly stronger, however, while *horrid* is more emotionally charged, and so perhaps more frequently applied to people: 'Horrible weather, isn't it?' 'I've made a horrible mistake,' 'That was a horrid thing to do,' 'Why did they paint the fence such a horrid color?'

horrid *see* horrible

house/home A *house* is a building for living in: 'Our house is one of the oldest on the street,' A *home* is the place where one lives, whether a *house* or not: 'She has made her apartment into a proper home.' The two therefore may or may not be synonymous: 'The children are eating us out of house and home.'

hove *see* heaved

hub/nub The *hub* of something (properly something round such as a wheel) is its center or focal point: 'At one time Carnaby Street was the hub of the fashion world.' The *nub* of something (properly a lump or chunk of something solid) is its point or gist: 'The nub of the story is this: she turned out to be his mother.'

human/humane *Human* relates to people: 'As members of the human race we ought to act more responsibly.' *Humane* relates to being kind and sympathetic, as *human* beings should ideally be: 'The dog was old and blind, and it was our sad but humane duty to have him put down.'

humane *see* human

humanist/humanitarian A *humanist* is a supporter of humanism, the philosophy that values human needs and rational (not religious) ways of solving human problems: 'Sir Philip Sidney was a famous humanist of the Renaissance period.' A *humanitarian* is concerned with improving human lives by means of social reform: 'Humanitarians of the 19th century were described as believing in the "Religion of Humanity".'

humanitarian *see* humanist

humbled/humiliated Both words refer to a state in which someone has been 'put down a peg.' *Humbled* implies a lessening of self-importance, however, while *humiliated* implies a lessening of self-esteem or self-respect: 'I was really humbled by the experience' (it made me realize I was no one special), 'I was really humiliated by the experience' (I felt really ashamed of myself).

humiliated *see* humbled

hurdle/hurtle To *hurdle* is to run jumping over hurdles or obstacles, as in a race: 'He hurdled over the cases on the platform in a dash to catch the train.' To *hurtle* is to move rapidly and violently (and often noisily): 'The train hurtled out of the tunnel.'

hurry-scurry *see* helter-skelter

hurtle *see* hurdle

hustle *see* bustle

hypercritical *see* hypocritical

hyperthermia *see* hypothermia

hypocritical/hypercritical To be *hypocritical* is to be insincere or two-faced; to be *hypercritical* is to be over-critical, especially of trivial faults: 'It would be hypocritical of me to say I enjoyed the meal, because I didn't,' 'She was hypercritical of the way he drove, even of the way he held the wheel.'

hypothermia/hyperthermia *Hypothermia* is the condition of having a very low body temperature: 'Hypothermia can occur among the elderly when they are in a room that is not properly heated.' *Hyperthermia* is a rarer condition and is the opposite: that of having a very high body temperature: 'Hyperthermia can be artificially induced in a patient for therapeutic purposes.' The difference in meaning is due to the Greek prefixes: *hypo-* means 'under' and *hyper-* means 'over.'

hysterics/histrionics *Hysterics* is an attack of hysteria, or something resembling it, such as a fit of uncontrollable laughter: 'When I told Gwen the story she went into hysterics.' *Histrionics* is a melodramatic display of emotion, like that of a 'hammy' actor: 'There's no need for such histrionics: you've made your point already.'

I

ideal/idyllic If something is *ideal,* it is perfect or exactly right: 'The field was an ideal site for the house.' If it is *idyllic,* it is also *ideal* but in an aesthetic or even poetic sense: 'The meadow was an idyllic spot, and we wondered if we could camp there.'

idle/indolent An *idle* person is lazy, or is simply not doing anything, or at any rate doing very little: 'Some of the students were very idle.' If someone is *indolent,* the implication is that he or she dislikes the necessary work: *'As writers become more numerous, it is natural for readers to become more indolent'* (Goldsmith).

idyllic *see* ideal

i.e. *see* e.g.

ignorance/innocence Both words have to do with a 'state of unknowing,' with *ignorance* a lack of knowledge and *innocence* an unawareness of it: 'In my ignorance, I arrived early' (I didn't know this was wrong), 'In my innocence, I arrived early' (it never occurred to me that it was wrong).

ill/sick *Ill* can refer to a state of being or feeling unwell for a short or a long time, whether slightly or seriously: 'He felt quite ill when he saw the bloodstain,' 'She is seriously ill and has been laid up for three months now.' *Sick,* apart from its reference to vomiting, is used only for a long-term or permanent illness: 'The missionaries did what they could to minister to the sick.' Additionally, *ill* is used in the media for people who have been hurt or injured: 'The driver is seriously ill in the hospital' (yet he has no illness). *Sick,* too, is used for a person away from work for health reasons: 'I was out sick last week.'

illegal/illicit Something *illegal* is forbidden by law: 'It is illegal for a motorcyclist not to wear a crash helmet.' If a thing is *illicit,* it is done by someone who knows that it is disallowed by law but that under different circumstances it could be legal: 'The crew was involved in an illicit import of drugs' (it is basically legal to import drugs, but not the way they did it).

illegible/unreadable Both words can be used for something that is difficult or impossible to read, but *unreadable* commonly applies to something that is too dull or difficult to be worth reading: 'His signature was quite illegible,' 'This novel is absolutely unreadable: how can people write such stuff?'

illicit *see* illegal

illness/disease An *illness* may be slight or severe, short or long, and usually relates to some unspecified or general disorder: 'She has made a good recovery after her recent illness.' A *disease* is usually a lengthy or serious thing, and often implies a disorder in a particular part of the body or bodily system: 'Impetigo is a contagious skin disease.'

illusion *see* delusion

imaginary/imaginative As applied to people, the difference is obvious: an *imaginary* child is one that doesn't exist, but an *imaginative* child is one with a vivid imagination. As applied to things, the difference is more subtle: 'He planned an imaginary route for the journey' (not a real one), 'He planned an imaginative route for the journey' (one that made good use of his imagination).

imaginative *see* imaginary

imbrue *see* imbue

imbue/imbrue To *imbue* is to instill or inspire a person with something or (literally) to steep or soak an object with something: 'My visit to Rome imbued me with a real sense of history,' 'Her handkerchief was imbued with a spicy perfume.' To *imbrue,* as a rare word, means to stain or permeate, often tellingly: 'The murderer's hands were imbrued with blood.'

immeasurable *see* immense

immense/immeasurable *Immense* means very great or huge: 'Oliver had an immense amount of work to get through.' *Immeasurable* relates to something that is literally so great that it cannot be measured: 'I owe you immeasurable thanks for all your care and kindness.'

immersed *see* submerged

immigrant/emigrant/émigré/migrant An *immigrant* is someone who comes into a country: 'Many Mexican immigrants to the U.S. made their home in Los Angeles.' An *emigrant* is a person who leaves a country to live elsewhere (as an *immigrant*): 'The number of British emigrants to Australia has declined in recent years.' An *émigré* is a political or religious refugee, such as French refugees at the time of the French Revolution (hence the word's French form): 'The Russian émigrés were placed with families wherever possible.' A *migrant* is a person who moves from one country to another: 'The migrant workers arrived regularly every summer.'

imminent *see* eminent

immoral/amoral An *immoral* person or thing has low or corrupt moral standards: 'She lived on her immoral earnings as a prostitute,' 'Some might find this book immoral.' An *amoral* person or thing has no moral standards: 'Some tribes were known to be quite amoral, with no sense of right or wrong.'

immovable/irremovable Something *immovable* cannot be moved; something *irremovable* cannot be removed: 'Not only is the sideboard heavy and immovable, but the wine stain on it is irremovable.'

immunity/impunity *Immunity* is freedom from something, often something disagreeable or harmful: 'An annual flu shot is supposed to offer immunity from the disease.' *Impunity* is freedom from punishment or retribution, or more generally from the unpleasant consequences of an action: 'The thieves knew the alarm was not working and so broke into the building with impunity.'

impel *see* compel

imperial/imperious *Imperial* literally refers to an emperor, and so relates to someone or something that is like an emperor, in other words, is grand or commanding: 'Some officers treated their servants with imperial condescension.' *Imperious* relates to a person or thing that is domineering or arrogant: '"Enough!" he commanded, in an imperious voice.'

imperious *see* imperial

impersonate/personate To *impersonate* someone is to pretend to be that person or to imitate him or her, often for entertainment or satirical purposes: 'Jason was a genius at impersonating the science teacher.' To *personate* someone is to act the part of that person, whether in a play or for criminal purposes: 'Nora was able to obtain the payments by personating the old lady.'

impertinent *see* insolent

impetuous *see* compulsive

impinge *see* infringe

implement *see* instrument

implicit *see* explicit

imply/infer Strictly speaking, to *imply* something is to mean it indirectly, and to *infer* it is to deduce it: 'Are you implying that he is innocent?' 'From what you say I infer that you are not too keen on the idea.' The two words are often used interchangeably, however.

impracticable *see* impractical

impractical/impracticable If a thing is *impractical,* it cannot be carried out or put into practice: 'Your idea is impractical: it will never work.' If something is *impracticable,* it either cannot be put into practice for some reason, despite being feasible in general, or it is unsuitable or inappropriate: 'It would be impracticable to set off that early: it will still be dark.'

impromptu *see* extempore

impudent *see* insolently

impugn/impute To *impugn* something is to express doubts about it: 'She impugned his actions.' To *impute* something is to put the responsibility for it on someone else, or to attribute it to him or her: 'He imputed his inability to calculate sums of money to poor teaching at school.'

impulsive *see* compulsive

impunity *see* immunity

impute *see* impugn

in/at With regard to towns, *in* is used in the broadest sense, while *at* implies a reference to a particular location in the town concerned: 'She lives in St. Louis' (somewhere there), 'He changed trains at St. Louis' (at the station).

inapt *see* inept

inartistic/unartistic If someone is *inartistic,* he or she is unable to appreciate art or see things from an artistic viewpoint: 'I'm afraid I'm rather inartistic when it comes to knowing a good painting from a bad one.' If someone is *unartistic,* he or she has no ability as an artist: 'I have made a sketch of the house, but it's not very good as I'm quite unartistic.'

inchoate *see* incoherent

incident *see* accident

incidental/accidental If something is *incidental,* it happens or is likely to happen in conjunction with something else: 'This ticket is not only cheaper than the others but has the incidental advantage of insuring a seat.' If a thing is *accidental,* it happens or is likely to happen independently of anything else: 'Kerry lived only a short bus ride from the office: an accidental advantage that she greatly appreciated.'

incite *see* excite

incoherent/inchoate *Incoherent* usually relates to thoughts or words that are 'rambling' or ill-ordered: 'He had been drinking, and muttered some incoherent remark about the time.' *Inchoate,* not a common word, is used for something that has only just begun to form, especially a body or mass of something: 'According to one theory, the Earth was originally an inchoate mass of gas.'

inconsequent/inconsequential Something *inconsequent* has no logical connection with what has gone before: 'When I invited her out, she made some inconsequent remark about her mortgage.' Something *inconsequential* is of no consequence, that is, it is unimportant: 'The play's many inconsequential episodes detracted from the main plot.'

inconsequential *see* inconsequent

incredible/incredulous *Incredible* is used for something unbelievable or difficult to believe; *incredulous* is used for someone who is disbelieving: 'When he described his incredible escape, she listened with an increasingly incredulous expression.' *Compare* credible.

incredulous *see* incredible

indifferent/diffident *Indifferent* means not caring or impartial: 'She was quite indifferent to my problems.' *Diffident* means lacking confidence or shy: 'Many people are diffident when it comes to performing in public.'

indignation *see* anger

indolent *see* idle

indubitably *see* doubtless

in effect *see* in fact

inept/inapt An *inept* remark is an absurd or clumsy one: 'He said a few inept words by way of an introduction' (they were not well chosen). An *inapt* remark is an inappropriate one: 'He mumbled a few inapt words by way of an apology' (they were quite wrong for the occasion).

inequity/iniquity *Inequity* is unfairness or injustice: 'Some members grumbled about the inequity of the voting system.' *Iniquity* is wickedness or immorality: 'The newspaper columnist wrote a powerful piece condemning the iniquity of the government.' 'The disco was said by some to be a den of iniquity, with alcohol and drugs freely available.' *See also* equable.

inestimable *see* estimable

in fact/in effect *In fact* is used to indicate a true or amended statement of something that is untrue or uncertain, or to expand on something just mentioned: 'In fact, she never wrote the letter,' 'I really like John, in fact I like him more than anyone.' *In effect* is used to clarify or summarize something: 'We now come to what is, in effect, the key part of the story,' 'You will start work tomorrow, but in effect your pay will be for the whole week.'

infamous *see* famous

infantile/infantine Both words relate to something typical of a young child. They have a subtle difference, however, similar to that between *childish* and *childlike:* 'I've never seen such infantile behavior' (like that of a spoiled child), 'Her imagination was both innocent and infantine,' *'Genius has somewhat of the infantile:/But of the childish not a touch or taint'* (Robert Browning).

infantine *see* infantile

infectious/contagious In medical terms, an *infectious* disease is one spread by germs: 'Typhoid and typhus are both highly infectious diseases.' In figurative terms, the word is used for something irresistibly 'catching': 'Her infectious laughter brightened the meal.' Medically, *contagious* is used for a disease spread by bodily contact: 'Scarlet fever is a contagious disease formerly known as scarlatina.' Figuratively, the word is used for something that spreads rapidly: 'His enthusiasm for the project was contagious, and we soon joined in.'

infer *see* imply

infinite/infinitesimal The two words are opposites, since *infinite* is used for something endless *(see* infinity), while *infinitesimal* is used for something so small that it is virtually negligible: 'Jonathan took infinite trouble over the work,' 'There was an infinitesimal decrease in the number of people out of work last month.'

infinitesimal *see* infinite

infinity/eternity *Infinity* is an endless or boundless space, time or quantity: 'There are an infinity of reasons why it is wrong to go.' *Eternity* is endless time only: 'We waited an eternity for the bus.'

inflammable/flammable The two words both have the same meaning, and indicate something that can easily catch fire: 'Paint is often highly inflammable,' 'Most tank vehicles have a symbol showing that they carry flammable liquid.' The form *flammable* arose because the prefix *in-* of *inflammable* was often understood to mean 'not' (as in *infertile)* whereas it actually means 'into.'

inflicted/afflicted To be *inflicted* with something (almost always something unwelcome) is to have it imposed on oneself: 'We were inflicted with a visit from the in-laws over Christmas.' To be *afflicted* with something is to be stricken by it and suffer under it: 'Poor Joan was often afflicted with toothaches when younger.'

informant/informer An *informant* is somebody who gives information (in general); an *informer* is someone who gives specific information to the police about a criminal: 'The journalist was reluctant to identify his informant,' 'The man was found guilty on the evidence of an informer.'

informer *see* informant

infringe/impinge To *infringe* something is to violate or break it: 'The umpire watched carefully to insure that none of the players infringed the new rule.' To *impinge* on a person or thing is to encroach on him or her or it, and so spoil or hamper something: 'May I impinge on your precious time a little?'

ingenious/ingenuous *Ingenious* is used for something done with ingenuity, that is, cleverly or enterprisingly: 'Sally had an ingenious method of keeping the bread fresh.' *Ingenuous* applies to something done innocently or artlessly: 'Timmy's an ingenuous child: he asked if the eggs were the same color as the chicken that laid them.'

ingenuous *see* ingenious

inhabitable *see* habitable

inherent/innate The two words are close, but if something is *inherent* it is part of one's nature and one can do little about it, while if it is *innate* it is also part of one's nature but is inborn and can perhaps be modified or even radically altered: 'He has an inherent dislike of cats' (it is part of his nature), 'He has an innate dislike of cats' (he has always had it).

inheritance/heritage An *inheritance* is something such as property or money that has passed to an heir, or passed down by natural means, such as a gift for languages: 'The title passed to the eldest son by inheritance.' The word can also be used in a wider sense: 'Printed books have long been an inheritance of the human race.' A *heritage* is a grander word used frequently to apply to something valuable or beneficial that has remained from the past for modern human use, whether it is natural or manufactured: 'English Heritage was set up in 1984 to care for historic buildings and ancient monuments in England.'

inhuman/inhumane Somebody or something *inhuman* lacks normal human qualities such as kindness and pity; an *inhumane* person or thing is cruel, and insensitive to the suffering of others: 'It was inhuman to take the take the child away from her parents like that,' 'Many people are concerned about the inhumane treatment of animals.'

inhumane *see* inhuman

iniquity *see* inequity

innate *see* inherent

innocence *see* ignorance

innuendo *see* insinuation

innumerable *see* numerous

inquiry *see* query

insanitary/unsanitary *Insanitary* means unhealthy; *unsanitary* means lacking sanitation: 'In the rural district, many of the inhabitants were living in insanitary conditions, with only primitive sanitation,' 'Some of the prisons were completely unsanitary, with no water and no toilet facilities.'

insert/inset In its best-known sense, an *insert* is a printed or written sheet enclosed in a publication, envelope or the like: 'The paper had an insert advertising a new cleaning service.' An *inset* is a small picture, map or the like set within the borders of a larger one: 'The prices were shown in an inset in the top left-hand corner of the advertisement.'

inset *see* insert

insidious/invidious Something *insidious* is gradually and stealthily harmful or destructive: 'Cancer is often an insidious disease,' 'His constant criticism had an insidious effect on morale and goodwill.' Something *invidious* causes resentment or unpopularity, especially if it is seen to be unfair: 'Teachers are often faced with invidious duties,' 'You have put me in an invidious position, and I am tempted to refuse.'

insignia/regalia *Insignia* are distinguishing badges or emblems of some kind: 'The airline's insignia appeared on the plane's fuselage and tail fin.' *Regalia* are ceremonial emblems or robes of royalty or some high office: 'The queen's regalia was on public display at the museum.'

insinuation/innuendo/insinuendo An *insinuation* is an artful suggestion or hint, usually about something unpleasant: 'The insinuation was that he had acted dishonestly.' An *innuendo* is similar, but in its commonest form is an added remark that is more obviously derogatory and usually more direct: '"We all know about *him*," she said, by way of innuendo.' An *insinuendo* is a blend of the two: 'I can't stand his constant insinuendos: they make me sick.'

insinuendo *see* insinuation

insipid *see* tepid

insolent/impudent/impertinent/pert The words are roughly in order of strength, so that *insolent* refers to a remark or the like that is offensively rude or insulting: 'How dare you make such an insolent comment?' *Impudent* is used for something shameless, although not necessarily insulting: 'Tim made the impudent suggestion that he should get more allowance.' An *impertinent* remark is one that is out of place, but if made by anyone else could have been reasonable: 'Asking how much she earned was rather an impertinent thing to do.' A *pert* remark is a saucy or 'cheeky' one, but one that may even be rather clever: 'When asked if he would be late, the boy's pert reply was: "I don't know: I can't tell the future, can I?"'

insouciant *see* nonchalant

instant/instantaneous If something is *instant,* it happens immediately, at once: 'Any employee who broke this rule was faced with instant dismissal.' Something *instantaneous* also happens immediately, but often as a consequence of something else, that is, at the instant of its occurrence: 'Death was instantaneous' (at the moment of the accident, heart attack, etc. that caused it).

instantaneous *see* instant

instinctively/intuitively Something done *instinctively* is done automatically, without any conscious thought or deliberation: 'I instinctively moved to the back of the crowd so as not to be seen.' Something done *intuitively* is done because the doer has the innate ability or knowledge to do it, either from experience or simply as a 'gut feeling': 'She intuitively chose the longer route' (she knew it was the right one but could not immediately explain why).

instrument/implement An *instrument* is usually more precise or complex than an *implement:* 'The human eye is a delicate optical instrument.' An *implement* is a tool or device for performing a particular function: 'This is a handy little implement: it opens both cans and bottles.'

insulate/isolate To *insulate* somebody or something is to protect him or her or it from something; to *isolate* a person or thing is to keep him or her or it apart for some reason (possibly also for protection): 'To what extent should children be insulated from sex and violence on TV?' 'The sexual offender was isolated in the prison for his own protection.'

insure *see* assure

intense/intensive If something is *intense*, it is great or powerful: 'The heat was intense,' 'I was filled with intense curiosity.' If it is *intensive,* it is concentrated: 'The city was subjected to intensive bombardment,' 'The course was an intensive one, with little free time and frequent tests,' 'After her accident Jill spent three weeks in intensive care.'

intensive *see* intensely

interior/internal If something is *interior*, it is inside rather than outside: 'I painted the interior wall of the house' (the inside part of the outer wall). If a thing is *internal*, it is wholly inside, but may have some connection with what is outside: 'I painted the internal walls of the house' (the ones right inside it, not the inside part of the outer wall), 'She had been suffering from severe internal pain for some days.' *Compare* exterior.

interment/internment *Interment* is the burial of a corpse: 'The interment will take place immediately after the service.' *Internment* is the imprisonment or confinement, without trial, of an enemy or terrorist: 'The internment of suspected terrorists was in force in Northern Ireland in the early 1970s.'

internal *see* interior

internment *see* interment

intrusive/obtrusive An *intrusive* person or thing is one that takes liberties by interposing or interrupting without permission: 'He must learn to control his intrusive manner: he's always butting into other people's conversations.' If a person or thing is *obtrusive*, she or he or it is blatant, so that one is forced to take notice: 'Couldn't you choose a less obtrusive color?'

intuitively *see* instinctively

invective/inveighing *Invective* is an abusive or sarcastic verbal attack: 'A member of the audience heckled the speaker with a tirade of invective, accusing him of deliberate procrastination.' *Inveighing*, the noun of *inveigh*, is a vigorous verbal attack, but not necessarily an abusive one: 'The parishioners were used to the minister's constant inveighing against the decline of morals.'

inveighing *see* invective

invidious *see* insidious

invigorate *see* enervate

invoice *see* account

Iran/Iraq *Iran*, formerly familiar as Persia, is a country in southwest Asia bordered to the west by *Iraq*: 'The Iran-Iraq War, or Gulf War, lasted from 1980 to 1988.'

Iraq *see* Iran

irregardless *see* regardless

irremovable *see* immovable

irrupt *see* erupt

isolate *see* insulate

iterate *see* repeat

its *see* it's

it's/its *It's* means 'it is' or 'it has': 'It's a long way yet, and it's started to rain.' *Its* means 'belonging to it' (whatever 'it' is): 'Oh, the poor little chick: it's lost its mother.'

J

jabber *see* gibber

jaded/jaundiced Someone or something that is *jaded* is tired and lacks freshness, especially after too much of something: 'He looked jaded after the party,' 'Many people have rather a jaded appetite after Christmas.' *Jaundiced* relates to jealousy and spite, and to being bitter about things: 'He takes a jaundiced view of just about everything on television, saying that most of the programs are not worth watching.'

jargon *see* slang

jaundiced *see* jaded

jazzy/snazzy *Jazzy* relates to bright colors: 'She was wearing a jazzy scarf.' *Snazzy* is used for something flashily stylish: 'He was wearing his snazzy new sweat suit, with a bold black logo.'

jealousy *see* envy

jejune *see* juvenile

jetsam *see* flotsam

jewel/gem A *jewel* is a precious or semiprecious stone, or an artificial stone that resembles one, especially when worn as an ornament: 'The ring contained a single jewel,' 'The Crown Jewels are a popular tourist attraction in the Tower of London.' A *gem* is also such a stone, but is one (a gemstone) regarded as specifically cut, polished and set in jewelry: 'The diamond is not only a precious and valuable gem but hard to cut.' Both *jewel* and *gem* are used figuratively for someone or something precious, with *jewel* suggesting a decorativeness and *gem* a usefulness, like the stones themselves: '*Yet three fill'd Zodiacs had he been/ The stage's jewel*' (Ben Jonson), 'The babysitter is a real gem.'

jibe *see* gibe

jinn/genie/genius A *jinn* (or *djinn*) is a spirit in Muslim mythology who could assume human or animal form: 'When Aladdin rubbed the lamp, a powerful jinn appeared.' A *genie* is another form of the same word, from the French (as if deriving from the Latin *genius*, 'spirit'): *'I just rub my jolly old lamp and out pops the genie bringing fame and fortune'* (Salman Rushdie). A *genius* is a highly talented person, or the talent itself, as well as the spirit (Latin, *genius)* of something: *'I have nothing to declare except my genius'* (Oscar Wilde), *'The genius of our constitution is opposed to the assumption of power'* (J.C. Calhoun).

jocose *see* jocular

jocular/jocose/jocund/jovial *Jocular* relates to jokes and joking in general: 'He is a jocular fellow.' *Jocose* is used for playful people or words: 'He met us with a jocose remark about the weather being "lovely for ducks but lousy for drakes."' *Jocund* is used for a playful or cheery mood or temperament: *'A poet could not but be gay,/In such a jocund company'* (Wordsworth). *Jovial* applies to someone or something that is hearty and good-humored (but not necessarily amusing): 'Santa Claus gave a jovial laugh, "Ho-ho-ho!"'

jocund *see* jocular

join/joint Both words denote a place where two things join up. A *join,* however, refers more to the visual appearance of the things joined, whereas a *joint* usually relates to the site of a physical joining up: 'If you look where the flooring was extended you can hardly see the join,' 'The pipe developed a leak in one of its joints.' *See also* junction.

joint *see* join

jovial *see* jocular

judicial/judicious *Judicial* pertains to a judge or judgment, as in a court of law, as well as applying more generally to a person or thing that is fair or just: "A special judicial body was set up to determine a fair rent.' *Judicious* is used for good judgment: 'The announcer made a judicious pause at this point.'

judicious *see* judicial

junction/juncture A *junction* is a place where things join: 'Clapham Junction in London claims to be the busiest railroad station in the world.' A *juncture* is a critical stage in a period of time: 'It is hard to say at this juncture what the outcome will be.' *See also* join.

juncture *see* junction

juvenile/jejune *Juvenile* is used for young people or their actions or views: 'William played some juvenile practical joke on us.' *Jejune* is used for a person or thing that is puerile or naive: 'It would be very jejune to suppose that the city council will actually decide anything.' (The word literally means 'hungry,' and took on this meaning by false association with *juvenile,* or the French *jeune,* 'young').

K

keck *see* retch

keel over *see* heel over

killer *see* assassin

kinky/quirky/kooky *Kinky* is used for someone or something deviant, especially sexually, although it can also apply to something that is bizarrely attractive: 'There was a kinky ad scrawled on the wall of the ladies' room,' 'The telephone was designed like a snake, very kinky.' *Quirky* is used for something eccentric or mildly unusual: 'He has a quirky habit of watching TV standing up instead of sitting down.' *Kooky* (from *cuckoo)* means crazy or cranky, but usually in an enjoyable way: 'The comedienne won many devotees with her kooky jokes and songs.'

kipper/bloater Both these fish are a form of salted and smoked herring. A *kipper* is one that has been split, however, while a *bloater* has not: 'Kippers make a tasty meal at any time,' 'Bloaters are so called because they are bloated.'

kooky *see* kinky

L

labor/belabor To *labor* something is to do it persistently: 'There's no need to labor the point.' To *belabor* someone or something is to whip or attack him or her or it: 'The horse's rider was belaboring it to go even faster,' 'The manager started belaboring us with insults.'

la-di-da/lardy-dardy *La-di-da* is used for (and imitates) exaggeratedly refined speech or manners: '"Oh yes, absolutely fabulous," she said in her la-di-da way.' *Lardy-dardy* is used more for manners, especially a languid dandyism or foppishness: 'He's not too keen on opera, saying it's too stuck up and lardy-dardy for his liking.'

lady/woman Aside from any class differences, *lady* is generally accepted as the courteous term for a *woman,* especially when elderly: 'I think this lady was here before me,' 'What a nice old lady she is,' 'Who's that woman over there?' 'I asked the woman if she would keep my place.' *Compare* gentleman.

lag/laggard/sluggard A *lag* is a convict or seasoned criminal, or someone who suggests one: 'He's a wily old lag.' A *laggard* is someone who dawdles or lags behind: 'Eventually the laggards arrived, many of them having walked rather than run.' A *sluggard* (related to *slug)* is someone who is perpetually lazy or idle: *'Go to the ant, thou sluggard; consider her ways, and be wise'* (Bible: Proverbs 6:6)

laggard *see* lag

languid *see* limpid

lapse *see* elapse

lardy-dardy *see* la-di-da

lascivious *see* licentious

latitude/longitude *Latitude* is used for the distance of a place north (N) or south (S) of the Equator, expressed in degrees (°) and minutes ('). *Longitude* is its equivalent, measured east (E) or west (W) from the Greenwich meridian. The coordinates of a place are given with *latitude* first and *longitude* second: 'The South Atlantic island of Ascension lies at a latitude of 7°57′S and a longitude of 14°22′W.'

Latvia/Lithuania *Latvia* borders *Lithuania* on the Baltic Sea: 'The three republics of Estonia, Latvia and Lithuania run north to south in alphabetical order.'

laudable/laudatory A *laudable* person or thing is praiseworthy: 'The inhabitants made a laudable effort to save the building, but it was too late.' *Laudatory* is used for a person or thing that expresses praise: 'Many tombstones have laudatory inscriptions relating to those buried there.'

laudatory *see* laudable

lawful *see* legal

lawyer *see* attorney

lay *see* lie

leaflet *see* brochure

lease *see* let

lecherous *see* licentious

legal/lawful If a thing is *legal,* it is authorized or permitted by law: 'It is perfectly legal to park here.' If it is *lawful* (the word usually precedes a noun) it is done according to the law: 'The crowd was asked to disperse in a lawful manner,' 'The elder son was the lawful heir to the estate.'

legionary/legionnaire Both are members of a legion, with a *legionary* being in the Roman army and a *legionnaire* belonging to the French Foreign Legion or some other modern legion: '"Legionnaire's disease" is a form of bacterial pneumonia that broke out among members of the American Legion at a conference in Philadelphia in 1976.'

legionnaire *see* legionary

lend/loan To *lend* something is to let a person use it temporarily: 'Can you lend me $10?' 'She lent me a pen.' To *loan* something is basically the same, although the word implies that the period of borrowing is longer or the thing lent is more valuable: 'The paintings were loaned by gracious permission of Her Majesty the Queen.' *Loan* also serves as the noun of *lend:* 'Thanks for the loan of your bike.'

lengthy *see* long

leniency/lenity *Leniency* (or *lenience*) is a state or condition of being lenient or tolerant: 'The teacher showed unexpected leniency, and let the boys off with a warning.' *Lenity,* a rarer word, is the more positive quality of being sparing or merciful: 'The judge displayed lenity whenever he felt it was genuinely justified.'

lenity *see* leniency

let/lease To *let* is to rent out something, usually on a long-term basis: 'Louise found it profitable to let the top two rooms to lodgers.' To *lease* is to obtain the use of something, also normally long-term, in return for payment: 'The school leases a bus for its sports teams when they are playing away.' *See also* hire.

liable/likely Both words refer to a probability. *Liable* means that something will probably happen because it has happened in the past: 'The road is liable to flooding.' *Likely* means that something will probably happen even though it may not have happened before: 'If you stroke the cat's fur up the wrong way, she is likely to bite you.'

libel/slander In law, *libel* is defamation (the publishing of what is false or derogatory) in permanent form, such as in writing, printing and radio and TV broadcasts, while *slander* is not in permanent form, so that it is in spoken words or in gestures: 'The actor issued a writ of libel,' 'Slander is not legally a crime unless it can be proved that special damage was done to the person or persons concerned.'

Liberia/Libya *Liberia* is in West Africa and *Libya* in North Africa: 'Liberia is a modern country, named for the liberated slaves who settled here in the 19th century; Libya is an ancient country, existing from biblical times.'

Libya *see* Liberia

licentious/lascivious/lecherous A *licentious* person is one who is sexually unrestrained or promiscuous: 'Many regarded the official's behavior as unbecomingly licentious.' A *lascivious* person is lustful: 'She took great exception to his lascivious remarks.' A *lecherous* person has an unbridled sexual appetite, and actively seeks unrestrained or promiscuous sex: 'We were warned of his possible lecherous advances.'

lie/lay To *lie* is to be in a horizontal position: 'The book lies on the desk.' To *lay*, often popularly used instead of *lie*, is to put or set in a lying position: 'I laid the book on the desk.' One cannot thus *lie* something, and one must always *lay* something, that is, *lie* takes no direct object, while *lay* always does.

lifelong/livelong *Lifelong* relates to something that lasts a lifetime: 'She had a lifelong ambition to visit China.' *Livelong* relates to something that lasts as long as the time mentioned, often implying that the time spent was tedious: 'For the whole livelong day nothing happened.'

lightening *see* lightning

lightning/lightening *Lightning* is the flash that accompanies (or precedes) thunder; *lightening* is the act of becoming lighter: 'After the storm, with its thunder and lightning, we sensed a marked lightening of the oppressive atmosphere.'

likely *see* liable

limerick/clerihew Both terms denote forms of comic verse, and both are usually about people. The *limerick* is often about an imaginary person, and is typically as follows: '*There was a young lady called Claudia/Whose dresses grew gaudier and gaudier,/She thought it was cool/ To wear them to school/Till her teacher said, "Not any more, dear"*' (anonymous). The *clerihew* is always about a famous person, and has a freer form: '*Prime Minister John Major/Was hardly an old stager,/He cut little ice/By simply being nice*' (anonymous).

limpid/languid *Limpid* (nothing to do with *limp*) means clear or lucid: 'We could see the stones under the cool and limpid water,' 'Her eyes were a soft and limpid blue.' *Languid* (nothing to do with *liquid*) means lazy because lacking energy: 'He gave me a languid wave from his chair,' '*Art thou weary, art thou languid,/Art thou sore distressed?*' (J.M. Neale).

linage/lineage *Linage* relates to the number of lines in something written or printed: 'Payment for the article was based on linage.' The word can also be spelled *lineage,* but this spelling usually has another sense, that of a person's line of descent: 'We can trace our lineage back to the 15th century,' '*He was of the house and lineage of David*' (Bible: Luke 2:4).

lineage *see* linage

liqueur *see* liquor

liquor/liqueur As a drink, *liquor* usually means spirits, such as whiskey or gin: *'Candy is dandy, but liquor is quicker'* (Ogden Nash). A *liqueur* is a special type of sweetened and flavored spirits, such as Benedictine or Cointreau: 'We rounded off the meal with a small liqueur each.'

lissom *see* lithe

listen *see* hear

litany *see* liturgy

lithe/lissom The two words are up to a point synonymous, although *lithe* refers to a body that is supple and bends easily, while *lissom* (a contraction of *lithesome)* emphasizes the agile and graceful aspect of its movements: 'The spectators were quick to applaud the lithe young gymnast,' 'The lissom dancer entranced us all with her perfect poise and timing.'

Lithuania *see* Latvia

liturgy/litany A *liturgy* (from the Greek *leitorgia*, 'ministry') is the form of public services practiced by a particular church: 'We were moved by the beauty and solemnity of the Orthodox liturgy.' A *litany* (from the Late Greek *litaneia*, 'prayer') is a form of prayer consisting of a series of requests and responses, as well as generally a lengthy list or recital of something: *'Here followeth the Litany, or General Supplication'* (Book of Common Prayer), 'The applicant was faced with a litany of queries about her work experience.'

livelong *see* lifelong

livid/lurid *Livid* is used for a grayish color, or popularly for a rage or fury: 'The player had a livid bruise on his arm,' 'A livid sky threatened snow,' 'He was simply livid when I told him.' *Lurid* is used for anything sensational or horrific, or for something bright and glowing: 'The local paper gave all the lurid details,' 'The lurid glow of the sunset promised unsettled weather.' Sometimes, however, *lurid* is used to mean pale and ghastly, making it close to *livid:* 'The snow and ice were made more lurid by the leaden sky above.'

Lloyds/Lloyd's *Lloyds* (occasionally, especially formerly, *Lloyd's)* is a British bank; *Lloyd's,* always with the apostrophe, is the London international insurance market, properly *Lloyd's Register of Shipping:* 'There is a branch of Lloyds not far from Lloyd's in the City of London.'

Lloyd's *see* Lloyds

loan *see* lend

loath/loth/loathe Both *loath* and *loth* are used to express reluctance: 'Freddie seemed loath to depart,' 'Nothing loath, we set off for the next stage of our journey,' 'He was loth to do anything that would upset her.' The verb of disliking is *loathe:* 'I loathe these boring meetings.'

loathe *see* loath

locale *see* location

locality *see* location

location/locality/locale A *location* is the place where something is situated: 'The new condominiums were built in a pleasant riverside location.' A *locality* is similar, but unless qualified ('exact locality') has a wider sense: 'Our hotel was in an attractive locality not far from the sea.' A *locale* is a place linked to a particular event or series of events: 'The director found an ideal locale for his new film.'

loch/lough A *loch* is a lake or arm of the sea of Scotland: *'On the bonnie, bonnie banks o' Loch Lomond'* (anonymous). A *lough* is the same in Ireland: 'Lough Neagh, in Northern Ireland, is the largest lake in the British Isles, and is five times larger than the second largest, Loch Lomond.'

lonely/lonesome A *lonely* person is one without friends or companions, and a *lonely* place is a remote one: 'He lived alone, but said he was never lonely,' *'O bold majestic downs, smooth, fair and lonely'* (Robert Bridges). *Lonesome* means the same, but stresses the sense of loneliness or isolation: *'Are you lonesome tonight?'* (ballad), *'Like one, that on a lonesome road/Doth walk in fear and dread'* (Coleridge).

lonesome *see* lonely

long/lengthy Something *lengthy* is very *long,* often tiresomely so, when applied to time: 'The chairman made a long speech' (it took a long time), 'The chairman made a lengthy speech' (it was too long). However, *lengthy* can have a positive sense when it implies thoroughness: 'After a lengthy examination, the doctor pronounced the patient fit to resume work' (he went to great lengths to produce his professional opinion).

longitude *see* latitude

loose *see* lose

loosen *see* lose

loot/booty *Loot* implies valuable goods or properties that have been stolen: 'The thief made off with his bag of loot.' *Booty* is also something stolen, but with the implication that the thieves have some sort of right to their plunder (as a 'prize'), and that it is shared among them: 'The islanders were amazed at the rich booty yielded by the wreck.'

lose/loose/loosen To *lose* someone or something is to have him or her or it taken away, or to be unable to find him or her or it: 'Bob lost his best friend in the accident,' 'I don't want to lose the only copy that I've got.' To *loose* something is to let it go or release it: '*Who is worthy to open the book, and to loose the seals thereof?*' (Bible: Revelation 5:2). To *loosen* something is to make it less tight: 'Larry loosened his tie, as it was hot.'

loth *see* loath

lough *see* loch

lour *see* glower

Low Countries *see* Holland

lower *see* glower

lumber *see* encumber

lunch/dinner/supper Time-wise, *lunch* is a midday meal, *dinner* is an evening meal, and *supper* is another word for an evening meal. A *dinner* is usually more substantial than a *supper,* and is generally 'classier': 'Do you go out to dinner much?' Household pets invariably have a *dinner,* whenever it is: 'I'll give these bits to Tiddler for her dinner.'

lure/allure The *lure* of a person or thing is his or her or its attraction, or the property that he or she or it has to entice, often to something harmful or dangerous: 'The mouse could not resist the lure of the bait.' The *allure* of someone or something is his or her or its innate (and often not deliberate) power to attract in an agreeable way: 'We couldn't resist the allure of a swim in the sea.'

lurid *see* livid

lustful *see* lusty

lusty/lustful *Lusty* is used for a thing or person that is vigorous or hearty: 'Tommy tucked into the steak with a lusty appetite.' *Lustful* involves lust and sexual desire: 'Pauline was plagued with lustful thoughts.'

luxuriant *see* luxurious

luxurious/luxuriant *Luxurious* is used for something that has or gives luxury: 'The house was expensively furnished, with luxurious carpeting throughout.' *Luxuriant* is used for something rich and abundant: 'Joanna slowly brushed her long, luxuriant hair,' 'We were awed by the luxuriant ornamentation of the Buddhist temples.'

M

macrocosm *see* microcosm

madam/Madame *Madam* is used as a polite form of address to a woman, especially one whose name is not known: 'Can I help you, madam?' *Madame* is a title adopted by some professional women, or given to a woman who is not British or American: 'Madame Vestris was a popular actress and singer on the London stage,' 'Have you been to Madame Tussaud's?'

Madame *see* madam

Magdalen College/Magdalene College *Magdalen College* is in Oxford, and *Magdalene College* is in Cambridge: 'Both Magdalen College and Magdalene College have chapels dedicated to St. Mary Magdalene.' Both college names are pronounced like maudlin. (A mnemonic: Magdalen and Oxford are shorter names than Magdalene and Cambridge.)

Magdalene College *see* Magdalen College

magic/magical *Magic* relates to magic: 'Dreams are like magic spells: we are held captive and have no power to escape.' *Magical* relates to something that *seems* like magic: 'It was a magical moment: the whole coast was suddenly bathed in the rays of the setting sun.'

magical *see* magic

magisterial/magistral In the strictest sense, *magisterial* relates to a magistrate and *magistral* to a master. However, *magisterial* also refers in a more general sense to someone or something that has or displays authority: 'The head waiter came to our table, and with a magisterial gesture placed a menu before us.'

magistral *see* magisterial

magnificent/munificent *Magnificent* means grand or fine: 'The water-falls were a magnificent sight,' 'She left the charity more than ten thousand dollars: a magnificent gesture.' *Munificent* means generous and liberal: 'Lord Nuffield was a munificent benefactor, endowing both the Oxford college and the foundation now named after him.'

magniloquence/grandiloquence Both words are used for pompous-sounding speech, but *grandiloquence* also implies that the speaker (or writer) uses long words that most people do not understand: 'Some of Shakespeare's characters have speeches that are deliberate displays of magniloquence,' 'According to his biographer Boswell, the famous lexicographer Dr. Jonson was often guilty of affected grandiloquence.'

Malawi *see* Mali

Malaya/Malaysia *Malaya* forms the southern part of the Malay Peninsula (apart from Singapore at its tip), and with Sarawak and Sabah, on the island of Borneo, comprises the country of *Malaysia:* 'Malaya is West Malaysia, while Sarawak and Sabah are East Malaysia.'

Malaysia *see* Malaya

male/masculine *Male* relates to the sex of living things in general, and when applied to humans, emphasizes the physical aspects of being a boy or man: 'The males in the herd protected the females,' 'The male voice is deeper than the female.' *Masculine* relates to the general characteristics of a boy or man, even when applied to a girl or woman: 'She had a deep, masculine voice.' *Compare* female.

malevolent/malicious Someone or something *malevolent* wishes ill or harm to others: 'He gave me a malevolent look when I got the job and he didn't' (although he didn't actually do anything harmful). A *malicious* person or thing causes harm to others, often for reasons of spite or jealousy: 'She found the malicious gossip very hurtful.'

malfunction/dysfunction A *malfunction* is the failure of a machine to work properly: 'There seemed to be a major malfunction in the computer.' A *dysfunction* is a failure of the human body to work properly: 'The specialist diagnosed a dysfunction of the thyroid gland.'

Mali/Malawi *Mali* is a country in northwest Africa; *Malawi* is a country in southeast Africa: 'Mali has French as its official language, while Malawi has English.'

malicious *see* malevolent

malign/malignant *Malign* is used for something bad or harmful: 'Did Rasputin really have such a malign influence on the Russian royal family?' *Malignant* is used for something *designed* to hurt or harm: 'He gave me a malignant look,' 'Her letter was a malignant attack on the owner, whom she accused of deception.' *Compare* benign.

malignant *see* malign

man *see* gentleman

maniacal *see* manic

manic/maniacal *Manic* relates to mania (in the proper medical sense): 'He was suffering from manic depression.' However, it is also loosely used to denote something frenzied or lively: 'Film goers have long enjoyed the manic humor of the Marx Brothers.' *Maniacal* relates to a maniac, or to something behaving like one: 'He gave a shriek of maniacal laughter.'

manifold/manyfold *Manifold* is generally used to mean little more than 'many and varied': 'Her manifold interests keep her busy in local society.' *Manyfold* means 'many times': 'If every country could provide its own energy, water and other necessities, the usefulness of the Earth's resources would be increased manyfold.'

manikin *see* mannequin

mannequin/manikin Both words are now rather old-fashioned, but as applied to people, a *mannequin* is a (female) fashion model, and a *manikin* is a (male) dwarf: 'Mannequin parades were a regular feature of the fashion world in the 1930s,' 'The children loved the story about the giant and the manikin.'

mantel *see* mantle

mantle/mantel The words have the same origin but different meanings. A *mantle* is a cloak, or something that covers like a cloak: *'At last he rose, and twitch'd his mantle blue;/To-morrow to fresh woods and pastures new'* (Milton), *'But, look, the morn, in russet mantle clad,/Walks o'er the top of yon high eastern hill'* (Shakespeare). A *mantel* is a shelf over a fireplace, now better known as a *mantelpiece:* 'An elegant ormolu clock stood upon the mantel.'

manyfold *see* manifold

marginal/minimal In their general sense, *marginal* means 'small' and *minimal* 'very small': 'There has been a marginal increase in the cost of living,' 'As I stayed with friends, not at a hotel, my expenses were minimal.'

marital/matrimonial Both words refer to marriage. *Marital* is more personal, relating to the husband or the wife (or to both husband and wife): 'The couple began to experience marital problems' (differences between husband and wife), 'They looked forward to a long life of marital happiness.' *Matrimonial* is more impersonal, relating to marriage as a state: 'They began to experience matrimonial problems' (something went wrong with the marriage).

market/mart A *market* is a place, indoors or out, where goods are bought and sold: 'There is a market every Friday.' A *mart* is the same, but although an old-fashioned word, is still used for certain special types of *markets:* 'The used-car mart buys and sells secondhand cars.'

marquess *see* marquis

marquis/marquess The title is normally spelled *marquis* for a foreign nobleman (next in rank above a count), and *marquess* for a British nobleman (next in rank above an earl, but below a duke): 'The Marquis de Sade, who gave his name to sadism, was not really a marquis at all, but a French count,' 'The Marquess of Bath opened Britain's first safari park at Longleat in 1967.'

marshal *see* martial

mart *see* market

martial/marshal The words have similar associations, but are not related. *Martial* relates to war: 'Martial law was imposed on the country by the rebel forces.' A *marshal* is an officer's rank, and also a person who either organizes crowds, or who helps the competitors at a public event: 'Field-Marshal Montgomery was popularly known as Monty,' 'Marshals along the route told the cyclists which way to go.'

masculine *see* male

masochism *see* sadism

masterful *see* masterly

masterly/masterful Something *masterly* is clever or skillful, as befits a master: 'The ball player hit a masterly line drive that insured his team's victory.' A person or thing that is *masterful* is imperious or commanding, befitting one who is master: 'She is a proud and master-ful woman, and intimidating on first acquaintance.'

material/materiel *Material* is what is used for making things: 'There is plenty of material here for the job.' *Materiel* (or *matériel)* is all the equipment used by a military force or other organization, such as a business: 'For an army to function efficiently, its materiel must be as effective as its personnel.'

materiel *see* material

matrimonial *see* marital

maudlin/mawkish *Maudlin* means tearfully sentimental: 'After a few drinks, he would sing some weepy old song in a maudlin voice.' *Mawkish* means sentimental in a false or sickly manner: 'Some people are put off the novels of Dickens by the mawkish streak that runs through many of them.'

maunder/meander To *maunder* is to move aimlessly or idly: 'He was just maundering about, reluctant to start work.' To *meander* is to wander aimlessly, or without any definite direction: 'The tourists meandered about the streets of the town.'

Mauretania *see* Mauritania

Mauritania/Mauretania/Mauritius *Mauritania,* in northwest Africa, arose out of the ancient region of *Mauretania. Mauritius* is a small island republic east of Madagascar and the African continent: 'Mauritania and Mauretania are named after the Moors who inhabited this part of Africa, while Mauritius, formerly a Dutch possession, is named after Maurice of Nassau, Prince of Orange.'

Mauritius *see* Mauritania

mawkish *see* maudlin

maxim/axiom/aphorism A *maxim* is a short or pithy saying or proverb expressing, usually for purposes of edification, what is held to be a general truth: 'Her favorite maxim was: "More haste, less speed."' An *axiom* is not really a saying, but the expression of a clear or obvious principle: 'For most children it is an axiom that school means work.' An *aphorism* is a *maxim* that is particularly common or well known, and that is not necessarily quoted for purposes of edification: 'It's an old aphorism that it is better to be a good servant than a bad master.'

meadow *see* field

meander *see* maunder

meantime *see* meanwhile

meanwhile/meantime The words are interchangeable in meaning to refer to the time between two events, or to something that happens at the same time as something else. However, *meanwhile* is more common as an adverb, and *meantime* as a noun: 'Meanwhile, back at the ranch,' 'I'll be writing a letter in the meantime.'

mediate *see* arbitrate

melodic/melodious Although there is some overlap between the two meanings, *melodic* is more a technical term, relating to a melody or line of music, while *melodious* is used for music or a sound that is tuneful or pleasant to listen to: 'It is easy to detect the melodic structure of many instrumental compositions,' *'By shallow rivers, to whose falls/ Melodious birds sing madrigals'* (Marlowe).

melodious *see* melodic

melody *see* tune

mendacity/mendicity *Mendacity* (or *mendaciousness)* is lying or deceit: 'We were tired of the government's mendacity, saying one thing and doing another.' *Mendicity* (or *mendicancy)* is the state of being a beggar: 'Mendicity is rife in many parts of India,' *'There is a certain class of clergyman whose mendicity is only equaled by their mendacity'* (Archbishop Temple).

mendicity *see* mendacity

mentholated/methylated The words relate respectively to *menthol* (obtained from oil of pepper*mint)*, and the poisonous liquid *methyl* alcohol: 'I'll buy some mentholated cough drops,' 'The alcohol in methylated spirits is unfit to drink, but even so, some alcoholics drink it with fatal results.'

meretricious/meritorious *Meretricious* is used for something apparently attractive, but actually of little value: 'Beware of meretricious advertisements, tempting you to buy goods that are not worth the money.' *Meritorious* is used for something or someone that deserves praise or reward: 'In the past, schools awarded prizes "For Meritorious Conduct."'

meritorious *see* meretricious

metal/mettle *Metal* always has a literal sense: 'Iron and steel are metals regularly used in construction.' *Mettle* is abstract, and refers to 'spirit' or courage: 'Sharon showed her mettle and won the race easily,' 'I was on my mettle, ready for all comers.' *(Mettle* arose as a form of *metal,* the association coming from the toughness of iron, for example, and the toughness of a courageous person.)

metaphor *see* simile

meter/metre There are two meanings for the same word: a *meter* is a measure (just more than three feet), and also a measuring device: 'The gas meter is about a meter from the back door,' 'The speedometer showed how fast we were traveling in kilometers per hour.' The British spelling for the word in both usages is *metre.*

methylated *see* mentholated

metre *see* meter

metric/metrical *Metric* has to do with the meter (see above) that is the unit of length, while *metrical* relates to the meter that is found in verse: 'Britain converted its currency to the metric system in 1971,' 'A hexameter is a line of verse with six metrical feet.'

metrical *see* metric

mettle *see* metal

Mexico/New Mexico *Mexico* is a country in southern North America; *New Mexico* borders it as a southern state of the United States: 'The capital of Mexico is Mexico City,' 'New Mexico's largest city is Albuquerque.'

microcosm/macrocosm A *microcosm* is something that represents the universe, or humanity, in miniature: 'A single human being is a microcosm of the whole of humanity,' 'Their village was a microcosm of our world.' A *macrocosm* is essentially the converse, and is a term either for the universe, or for any complete structure that contains smaller structures: 'Society is the macrocosm of each of its individual members.'

middle *see* center

Middle Ages *see* Dark Ages

Middle East/Near East/Far East The *Middle East* is a general term for all the countries between Sudan, in Africa, and Iran, in Asia. The *Near East* is an alternative name for this region, but was formerly more narrowly applied to its western countries, i.e., those bordering the Mediterranean. The *Far East* is a general name for the countries of eastern Asia, notably China and Japan: 'The Middle East originally lay midway between the Near East and the Far East.' *See also* oriental.

migrant *see* emigrant

mildew *see* mold

militate *see* mitigate

million/billion The usual meaning of *a million* is a thousand thousands (1,000,000): 'The population of Africa is estimated to be more than five hundred million.' The traditional meaning of *a billion* is a million millions (1,000,000,000,000), but the value of a thousand millions (1,000,000,000), standard in the United States, is now increasingly common: 'The prefix *giga-* is used by scientists to indicate a multiple of one billion, so that a gigavolt is 1,000,000,000v.'

minced meat *see* mincemeat

mincemeat/minced meat *Mincemeat* is normally understood as a mixture of dried fruit, spices and the like, although the word is sometimes used to apply to *minced meat,* or *mince,* which is meat that has been minced or chopped up small. This usage is more common in Britain than in the United States: 'Shepherds' pie is made with minced meat, while mince pies are made with mincemeat.'

minimal *see* marginal

minuscule *see* minute

minute/minuscule Both words relate to something very small. *Minute,* however, is used more generally, while *minuscule* can additionally imply that what is small is also unimportant: 'The water contained minute traces of lead,' 'The poll showed a minuscule lead for the Republicans over the Democrats.' *(Minuscule* is frequently misspelled *miniscule* by association with words starting with *mini-.)*

misanthropist/misogynist/misogamist A *misanthropist* (or *misanthrope)* is someone who hates or dislikes other people, whether men or women: 'He was something of a misanthropist, preferring his own company to that of others.' A *misogynist* is a man who hates or dislikes women: 'The Greek dramatist Euripides was a misogynist, and all the women in his plays are bad women.' A *misogamist,* as a rare word, is someone who hates marriage: 'St. Jerome was a noted misogamist, preaching in support of the monastic life, and extolling the virtues of virginity.'

misogamist *see* misanthropist

misogynist *see* misanthropist

mistrust *see* distrust

misuse *see* abuse

mitigate/militate To *mitigate* something is to moderate it or make it less severe: 'The offense was mitigated by the fact that the offender had not seen the warning notice.' To *militate* against something is to affect or influence it adversely: 'The bad weather militated against the planned outing.'

moan/groan Both words are used for the inarticulate sound made by someone in pain or distress, but a *moan* is generally more a soft, long, and possibly even high-pitched sound, while a *groan* is usually a deep, relatively loud, and mostly brief sound: 'The moans of the wounded were heard in the hospital,' 'The boxer sank to the canvas with a groan.'

mobile/movable Something *mobile* is intended to be moved quickly and easily: 'The villages have a weekly visit from the mobile library.' Something *movable* is physically able to be moved: 'The TV stand is designed to be movable.'

mode *see* 1) fashion, 2) mood

moderate *see* modest

modern/modernistic *Modern* relates to anything contemporary, or in the present; *modernistic* is a rather derogatory term referring to something conceived to be *modern,* especially in art and religion: 'The modern shopping center is spoiled by its modernistic architecture.'

modernistic *see* modern

modest/moderate As applied to size, amount and the like, both words refer to something average, not particularly large and not particularly small. However, *modest* suggests (almost approvingly) that what is mentioned could well have been larger: 'They grow vegetables on a modest scale' (they could grow more, but they are content with what they have), 'They grow vegetables on a moderate scale' (neither small nor large).

modus operandi/modus vivendi A *modus operandi* (Latin, 'way of working') is either the way a person deals with a particular task, or else the way in which a thing works: 'Their modus operandi for the annual spring cleaning was to put all the furniture in the garden.' A *modus vivendi* ('way of living') is a temporary arrangement by which two people who are opposed to each other or in dispute can live or work together until their disagreement is settled: 'The business partners managed to achieve a sort of modus vivendi.'

modus vivendi *see* modus operandi

Mogul/Mongol In their original senses, a *Mogul* was a member of the Muslim dynasty of Indian emperors set up in 1526, while a *Mongol* is a person who lives in Mongolia: 'The Moguls took their name from the Mongols, as they were descendants of Timer (Tamerlane) the Great, the famous 14th-century Mongol conqueror.'

Mohammedan *see* Muslim

moist *see* damp

mold/mildew *Mold* is the fine, furry growth of fungi that appears on old or stale food: 'The rolls had lain uneaten for several days, and many were covered in mold.' *Mildew* is the thin, white or blue coating of fungi that appears on plants and on materials such as paper and leather when exposed to moisture: 'The room was very damp, with a patch of mildew in one corner of the ceiling.'

momentary/momentous *Momentary* relates to something short-lived, or lasting only a few moments: 'There was a momentary interruption of the power supply,' 'It needs only a momentary lapse of attention and you could ruin the whole thing.' *Momentous* is used for something seriously important, or of great moment: 'I made the momentous decision to resign,' 'The finale was a momentous occasion, with all the players giving of their best.'

momentous *see* momentary

Mongol *see* Mogul

monogram/monograph Although both words have the same literal sense ('one writing,' from the Greek), a *monogram* is a design of two or more letters combined as a single figure, while a *monograph* is a scholarly study of a single subject: 'His handkerchiefs had his initials in the corner as a monogram,' 'Monica has just completed her monograph on early medieval hagiography.'

monographs *see* monograms

monologue/soliloquy Both are terms for a speech by one person alone. In a *monologue,* however, the speaker is talking to (or at) others, while in a *soliloquy* he is talking to himself: 'Shakespeare's *Hamlet* has a number of monologues, and a famous soliloquy by Hamlet himself in his "To be or not to be" speech.'

Monterey/Monterrey *Monterey* is a city in western California; *Monterrey* is a city in northeast Mexico: 'Both Monterey and Monterrey are named for the Count of Monterey, the Spanish viceroy of Mexico.'

Monterrey *see* Monterey

mooch *see* moon

mood/mode A *mood* is a prevailing state of mind or attitude: 'The boss was in a confrontational mood' (he felt like confronting people). A *mode* is (among other things) the way or state in which a person or machine operates: 'The boss was in a confrontational mode' (as if he had been 'programmed' to act in a manner familiar to those who worked with him).

moody/broody A *moody* person is generally gloomy or sullen: 'Why are you so moody today?' A *broody* person is both *moody* and depressed, as if wanting something that is unobtainable: 'Gillian became increasingly broody as the evening progressed.'

moon/mooch/mope To *moon* about is to be idle or aimless, as if moonstruck: 'She spent the whole morning just mooning about the house.' To *mooch* is to hang around, or wander about aimlessly, or even suspiciously: 'He was seen mooching about at the back of the store.' To *mope* is also to go around aimlessly, but in a gloomy or apathetic manner, as when lovelorn: 'After the separation, he spent several days moping about the town.'

moor *see* heath

moot *see* move

mope *see* moon

morale *see* morals

morals/morale *Morals* are a person's standards of behavior, or principles of right and wrong, while his *morale* is his state of confidence and optimism: 'His morals were impeccable, and his morale consistently high.'

morgue *see* mortuary

mortgagee/mortgagor Since many people have mortgages, it is important to know which is which. The *mortgagee* is the person or organization to whom the property is mortgaged, and the *mortgagor* is its buyer, who is taking out a mortgage: 'The mortgagee is usually a bank or loan company, and the mortgagor one of its regular customers.'

mortgagor *see* mortgagee

mortuary/morgue A *mortuary* is a room or building in which dead bodies are kept before being buried or cremated: 'Most hospitals have a mortuary.' A *morgue* is usually a building only. The word is also used figuratively, which *mortuary* is not: 'It's like a morgue in here: shall we turn the fire on?'

Moslem *see* Muslim

motion *see* resolution

motivation *see* motive

motive/motivation A *motive* is what prompts a person to do something, or to act in a particular way; *motivation* is the prompting itself: 'I wish I knew what her motives were,' 'Many of the students were lazy, and lacked motivation to work.'

mot juste *see* bon mot

motor *see* engine

moue *see* pout

mourn/grieve To *mourn* is to express one's grief or sorrow, especially when someone has died: 'The old man never ceased to mourn the death of his wife, and visited her grave regularly.' To *grieve* is to experience such an emotion, but not necessarily to express it openly: 'No one could tell that she was grieving for the loss of her father.'

movable *see* mobile

move/moot To *move* a point or matter is to make a formal request or application for it to be discussed or acted on: 'Mr. Black then moved that the meeting be closed.' To *moot* a point is to raise it: 'Mr. White mooted the possibility of appointing a new secretary.'

mucous/mucus *Mucous* is the adjective of *mucus,* which is the stuff in your nose: 'Mucus is produced by the mucous membrane.' *Compare* callous and its noun.

mucus *see* mucous

munificent *see* magnificent

murderer *see* assassin

Muslim/Moslem/Mohammedan/Mussulman A *Muslim* is a follower of the religion of Islam: 'The Muslim population is estimated to be about one million.' *Moslem* is an alternative form of the name: 'The chief Moslem place of worship is the mosque.' A *Mohammedan* is a formerly common name for a Muslim, but one never used by the Muslims themselves: 'The Mohammedan is so called from his worship of Mohammed.' A *Mussulman,* in archaic English, is also a Muslim, with the name influenced by *man: 'Prayer, fasting, and alms are the religious duties of a Musulman* [sic]' (Gibbon). *Muslim* and *Islam* (and *salaam)* are directly related words, from an Arabic source meaning 'surrender,' i.e., to God. The name of Mohammed, founder of Islam, at one time popular in the form *Mahomet,* is now often spelled in its more correct form of *Muhammad.*

Mussulman *see* Muslim

mutual *see* reciprocal

mysterious/mystic/mystical *Mysterious* relates to something difficult to explain, and possibly also awesome in an 'otherworldly' sense: 'There was a mysterious silence in the woods,' 'Several people reported seeing mysterious lights in the sky.' *Mystic* is somewhat similar, but emphasizes the supernatural or spiritual factor: 'We heard of mystic rites and ceremonies,' 'Miranda had a mystic beauty that long haunted me.'

Mystical is the same as *mystic,* but relates solely to what is spiritual: 'Trees had a mystical power for the Druids.'

mystic *see* mysterious

mystical see mysterious

mythical/mythological In its general sense, *mythical* relates to anything imaginary, while both *mythical* and *mythological* refer to mythology, and especially to the myths of classical times: 'What happened to that mythical fortune of his?' 'Her favorite mythological character in Greek legend was Ganymede.'

mythological *see* mythical

N

nadir/zenith Because of the exotic form of the words (they are both Arabic in origin), they are sometimes wrongly applied to the extreme point that each denotes. The *nadir* of something is its lowest point, and the *zenith* is its highest: 'Her spirits soared from the nadir of despair to the zenith of happiness.'

naked/nude *Naked* is the general term for an unclothed state; *nude* relates mainly to art and pornography, or to nudism: 'In the summer he liked to sleep naked,' 'Picasso painted several nude portraits,' 'Naked children were playing on the beach, although nude bathing was officially not allowed there.' *See also* naturists.

narration/narrative Both words can be used for a story, but properly a *narration* is the act of telling the story (of narrating it), while a *narrative* is the story itself (what is narrated), especially the parts that are not conversation: *'This narrative is not meant for narration/But a mere airy and fantastic basis'* (Byron).

narrative *see* narration

nationalize/naturalize To *nationalize* an industry is to put it under government ownership: 'Most of the companies nationalized by the British Labour Party were privatized by the Conservatives.' To *naturalize* a person is to give an immigrant the nationality of the adopted country: 'He married a naturalized Polish girl who had come to the United States with her parents.'

naturalize *see* nationalize

naturalist/naturist A *naturalist* is a person who is interested in botany or zoology: 'Sheila is an enthusiastic naturalist, and has a particular interest in woodland life.' A *naturist* is a nudist: 'A section of the sea front at South Beach is reserved for naturists.' *See also* naked.

naturist *see* naturalist

naught/nought *Naught* means 'nothing' in certain idiomatic expressions: 'All his plans came to naught when the firm went bankrupt.' *Nought* is the figure '0' (zero): 'How many noughts are there in a million?'

nauseating/nauseous *Nauseating* applies to something or someone that makes a person feel nausea: 'There was a nauseating smell in the kitchen,' 'I think he's a nauseating person.' *Nauseous* can also mean this, but is frequently used figuratively for something disgusting, or literally for a person who feels nausea: 'A colleague pestered her with his nauseous attentions,' 'Many of the passengers felt nauseous during the sea crossing.' *See also* obnoxious.

nauseous *see* nauseating

nautical/naval *Nautical* relates to ships, sailors and life at sea generally: 'The speed of one nautical mile an hour is called a knot.' *Naval* has to do with the navy: 'He looked smart in his naval uniform,' 'The United States is regarded as the greatest naval power in the world.'

naval/navel The words are unrelated in origin and meaning. *Naval* has to do with the navy (*see* nautical); the *navel* is the umbilicus ('belly button'): 'He was dressed as a naval officer,' 'A navel orange has a small pit like a navel in the top.'

naval *see* nautical

navel *see* naval

Near East *see* Middle East

necessaries/necessities *Necessaries* are things that are regarded as necessary but which are in fact not actually essential: 'Have we got all the necessaries for the picnic?' *Necessities* are things that really are necessary: 'Food, clothing and a roof over your head are the necessities of life.'

necessities *see* necessaries

nefarious/felonious *Nefarious* is used for someone or something evil or wicked: 'There is no doubt he bought the tools for some nefarious purpose.' *Felonious* is a more precise word in that it usually relates to a serious or violent crime, even murder: 'The new employee was believed to have had something of a felonious past.'

neglectful/negligent A *neglectful* person is someone who has neglected something, on one or more occasions: 'When it came to the garden, she was rather neglectful.' A *negligent* person is regularly or constantly *neglectful,* or is so by nature: 'The nurse was accused of being negligent in her duties.'

negligent *see* neglectful

neophyte *see* novice

net/gross A *net* (or *nett)* amount is one after deductions have been made: 'The net weight of the parcel, without its packing and wrapping, was 4 pounds.' A *gross* amount is one that includes all regular additions: 'His gross salary was $5,000 a month, but 25% was deducted for taxes and social security.'

Netherlands *see* Holland

New Mexico *see* Mexico

niceness/nicety *Niceness* is the quality of being nice; a *nicety* is a subtle distinction or detail: 'Because of the niceness of the weather we were able to have drinks in the garden,' 'It is not always easy to appreciate the niceties of meaning in similar words.'

nicety *see* niceness

niche *see* nook

Niger/Nigeria *Niger* is a country to the north of *Nigeria* in West Africa: 'Niger and Nigeria are named for the Niger, which flows south through both countries to the Gulf of Guinea.'

Nigeria *see* Niger

noisome *see* obnoxious

nonchalant/insouciant *Nonchalant* means indifferent or coolly unconcerned: 'He kept a nonchalant eye on the game.' *Insouciant* means blithely carefree: 'He whistled an insouciant tune as he walked down the street.'

nook/niche A *nook* is a cosy corner, a place that is secluded or remote: 'The cottage nestled in a nook of the hills.' A *niche* is a recess or other location that is ideal for containing something: 'We used the niche in the garden wall to plant an apricot tree,' 'Mary settled into the job quickly and soon found her niche.'

notable/noticeable If something is *notable,* it is considerable and worth noting: 'There has been a notable decrease in the number of automobile accidents this year.' If a thing is *noticeable,* it has been noticed and is significant, even though it may be quite small in itself: 'Catherine has made noticeable progress in her studies this term.' (If she had made 'notable' progress, it would have been to a remarkable degree, and could imply that she was making poor progress before.)

note/tone In the nonmusical sense, a *note* is a characteristic element or atmosphere: 'The speech took on a positive note' (the speaker had something positive to say). A *tone* is a general quality or style: 'The speech took on a positive tone' (the speaker's voice and manner sounded positive).

noticeable *see* notable

nought *see* naught

nourish *see* nurse

novice/neophyte A *novice* is a beginner, or someone new to something: 'Veronica tried her hand as a novice reporter for the local paper.' A *neophyte* is also this, but the word (literally meaning 'new plant') implies that the person is being introduced to a new routine or skill, and that he or she is committed to it: 'Some of the regular staff regarded the neophytes with suspicion.'

noxious *see* obnoxious

nub *see* hub

nude *see* naked

numerable *see* numerous

numerous/numerable/innumerable *Numerous* means great in number: 'He called on numerous occasions' (several times). *Numerable* is used for something that can be numbered or counted: 'There were so many islands that they were scarcely numerable.' *Innumerable* means countless, and is stronger in sense than *numerous:* 'He called on innumerable occasions' (very many times).

nurse/nurture/nourish/cherish To *nurse* someone or something is to tend or foster her or him or it: 'She patiently nursed him back to health,' 'He still nurses a grudge against his boss.' To *nurture* is to raise, train or bring up: 'The children were well nurtured in both speech and manners.' To *nourish* is to provide food or nutriment, that is, what is necessary for life and growth: 'The gardener took care to see that the greenhouse plants were adequately nourished.' To *cherish* a person or thing is to hold her or him or it dear: 'We have known each other since childhood, and it is a friendship I cherish.' There is a degree or overlap in the words, however, so that children and plants (for example) can be both nurtured and nourished *and* cherished while they are growing.

nurture *see* nurse

nutritional *see* nutritious

nutritious/nutritional *Nutritious* relates to something that is nourishing; *nutritional* relates to the process of nourishing, i.e., to nutrition itself: 'Two nutritious meals a day should meet the nutritional requirements of most people.'

nymph/sylph A *nymph* is a minor goddess of Greek mythology in the form of a young and beautiful maiden who personifies a natural object such as a tree, river, mountain or the like: '*Nymphs and shepherds, come away*' (Thomas Shadwell). A *sylph* is an imaginary being said to inhabit the air: 'The Swiss alchemist Paracelsus is thought to have invented the word "sylph" from the Latin *sylvestris,* "of the wood," and *nympha,* "nymph."' Both words are used for a beautiful young woman, with *sylph* implying that she is noticeably graceful or 'airy': 'His sister was small but not petite: perhaps more of a nymph than a sylph.'

O

O/oh *O,* usually written with a capital letter, is used when addressing someone or something, especially in poetry or classical literature: *'O Captain! my captain!'* (Walt Whitman), *'O Lord, in thee have I trusted'* (Book of Common Prayer). *Oh* is much more common, is not a capital unless it begins a sentence, and is used to introduce a call or exclamation: 'Oh, George, can you take this?' 'Oh no, I've done it again!'

obdurate *see* obstinate

object/subject The *object* of one's attention or interest is its focus or target: 'For many years she was an object of his affection,' 'The object of the exercise is to cut costs.' The *subject* of one's attention is what has been selected for examination, treatment, or the like: 'She saw him as an original subject for a portrait,' 'What is the subject of your present research?'

obligated s*ee* obliged

obliged/obligated If you are *obliged* to do something, you have to do it: 'You are not obliged to answer.' If you are *obligated* to do something, you are legally or morally compelled to do it: 'She felt obligated to help.' Further, *obliged,* not *obligated,* is used for a physical obligation: 'Passengers were obliged to remain in their seats.'

obnoxious/noxious/noisome If a person or thing is *obnoxious,* he or she or it is objectionable or highly undesirable: 'He is an obnoxious little boy: why can't his mother teach him some manners?' Something *noxious* is poisonous or harmful: 'The town was evacuated when noxious gases escaped from the broken pipe.' *Noisome* also has this sense, but is mostly used (as a rather 'affected' word) for a smell that is unpleasant or disgusting, rather than actively harmful: 'A noisome stench emanated from the dung heap.'

obscure/abstruse/obtuse/obtruse Something *obscure* is unclear or uncertain: 'He appeared to be speaking some obscure dialect that we couldn't understand,' 'The family is an ancient one but of obscure origins.' If a thing is *abstruse,* it is difficult to understand or recondite: 'The abstruse language of the writer alienated many who wished to study the subject.' An *obtuse* thing or person is indistinct or dull: 'The patient was suffering from an obtuse pain in the stomach' (i.e., not an acute one), 'Can't you understand what I'm saying? You're very obtuse!' *Obtruse* is sometimes used as a colloquial (but nonstandard) blend of *abstruse* and *obscure*: 'The rules of this game are very obtruse.'

observance *see* observation

observation/observance *Observation* relates to observing in the literal sense: 'The hospital kept her overnight for observation.' *Observance* relates to observing in the sense of marking or keeping: 'Wearing black at memorial services is now a custom more honored in the breach than the observance.'

obsolescent *see* obsolete

obsolete/obsolescent If something is *obsolete,* it is out of date or no longer used: 'When the automobile was invented, horse-drawn vehicles became obsolete.' *Obsolescent* is used for something that is in the process of becoming *obsolete:* Most telephones now have keypads, and phones with dials are obsolescent.'

obstacle/obstruction An *obstacle* is something that hinders literal or figurative progress, and that therefore needs to be overcome or removed: 'The children enjoyed the obstacle race,' 'The immigrant's lack of English proved no obstacle to his practical ability.' An *obstruction* is something, often of an unknown nature, that prevents movement or progress or makes it very difficult: 'The water could not escape because of an obstruction in the pipe.'

obstinate/obdurate An obstinate person is one who will not give way or yield, usually unreasonably: 'She's such an obstinate child, always wanting her own way.' An *obdurate* person is one who is determined not to be swayed from a particular course or decision, especially for moral reasons: 'Neil was obdurate that he would play no part in the deception.'

obstruction *see* obstacle

obtruse s*ee* obscure

obtrusive *see* intrusive

obtuse *see* obscure

occidental *see* oriental

occupied/preoccupied To be *occupied* with something is to be busy doing it: 'Roger was occupied with the decorating' (he was busy doing it, so I did not disturb him). To be *preoccupied* with something is to be engrossed in it: 'Roger was preoccupied with the decorating' (he was so absorbed in it that I could not attract his attention).

oculist/optician An *oculist* is now a dated word (except in American English) for a person who is licensed to perform eye tests and to prescribe glasses but who does not have a medical degree: 'She was referred to an oculist.' An *optician* is a qualified medical person who prescribes and sells glasses and contact lenses: 'The optician recommended an eye test every two years.' (Most opticians are now officially known as ophthalmologists.)

odious/odorous If a thing is *odious,* it is disgusting or hateful; if it is *odorous,* it has a smell, usually a pleasant one: 'What an odious person!' 'The odorous ingredients of the ointment leave an agreeable aroma on the skin.'

odium/odor/opprobrium *Odium* is dislike or hatred of someone or something: 'The college president was exposed to the odium of the students when he introduced the new rules.' To be in a bad *odor* with someone is to be the object of his or her disapproval: 'I'm in a bad odor with the garage at the moment because I still owe it for the service.' *Opprobrium* is reproach or censure: 'The congressman's dubious conduct made him an object of opprobrium among many of his constituents.'

odor *see* odium

offer/proffer Both verbs refer to presenting something for consideration or acceptance, but whereas *offer* can be used in almost any context, *proffer* is much more formal, and often relates to something abstract: 'May I offer you a cup of tea?' 'May we proffer our sincere congratulations?'

official/officious *Official* relates to someone or something formal or authoritative: 'Here is an official announcement,' 'Arthur Smith was there in his official capacity as chairman.' *Officious* is used for a person who is unnecessarily keen to offer advice or services, often intrusively or embarrassingly so: 'Guests were greeted by an officious little man who made it his business to take their coats.'

officious *see* official

oh *see* O

older *see* elder

omnipotent *see* omniscient

omniscient/omnipotent *Omniscient* means knowing everything; *omnipotent* means having great or unlimited power (literally 'all powerful'): 'I agree he knows a lot, but he's not quite as omniscient as he thinks,' 'In the former Soviet Union the KGB were virtually omnipotent.'

operative *see* operator

operator/operative An *operator* is a person who operates a machine or piece of equipment, while an *operative* is often simply a term for someone who does a menial job, albeit a specific one: 'As a crane operator, he found his work much less interesting than when he had been a rodent operative or ratcatcher (as some people called it).'

oppression/repression Both nouns refer to a form of subjugation or restraint. As used for a political or generally strict regime, however, *oppression* indicates direct subjugation, while *repression* implies a restriction on normal rights and liberties: 'Many people emigrated in the early years of oppression,' 'The harsh rules of the religion led to the repression of many trivial pleasures.' *Repression* is thus the term relating to the psychological state (*see* depression).

opprobrium *see* odium

optician s*ee* oculist

oral *see* aural

oration/orison An *oration* is a formal or grand speech: 'There then followed a long but rather moving funeral oration.' An *orison* (which formerly also meant this) is a literary word for a public or private prayer, and is almost always used in the plural: *'The fair Ophelia! Nymph, in thy orisons/Be all my sins remember'd'* (Shakespeare).

orchestrate/organize Both words can be used in the sense of arranging something effectively. In the media, however, *orchestrate* often has an unfavorable sense, applying to something carefully 'staged': 'Union leaders orchestrated a demonstration against the company.' *Organize,* however, mostly has a favorable or simply neutral sense: 'The meeting was well organized, and there were no incidents.'

ordinance/ordnance An *ordinance* is an authoritative rule or law:

'Residents are bound by the ordinances of the city council.' *Ordnance* is military supplies and ammunition: 'The Ordnance Survey, famous for its maps, arose from the Board of Ordnance, the government department responsible for the army's military supplies.'

ordnance *see* ordinance

organize *see* orchestrate

orient/orientate Both words relate to finding one's direction or bearing, although *orient* is frequently applied in a figurative sense, and *orientate* in a literal one: 'Students need to orient themselves when first entering college,' 'Orienteering is the sport of running across country, orientating your position and course as you go with a map and compass.' As adjectives, however, both words can be used figuratively: 'I settled for a science-oriented course,' 'The trade unionist's approach was bound to be politically orientated.'

oriental/occidental *Oriental* is eastern, pertaining to the orient, while *occidental* (a much less common word) is western, pertaining to the occident (equally rare): 'The oriental countries are usually regarded as those lying east of Europe, while the occidental are to the west of Asia.'

orientate *see* orient

orison *see* oration

ornamental *see* ornate

ornate/ornamental If something is *ornate,* it is richly decorated: 'The tourists admired the ornate stonework of the church.' If a thing is *ornamental,* it serves as an ornament: 'The mantelpiece was full of ornamental trinkets.' Something *ornate* thus may have a practical use, but something *ornamental* is not intended for use.

orotund *see* rotund

orthopedic/pediatric Confusion between the terms exists because *orthopedic* (literally 'straight child') formerly related to the medical science of correcting bone deformities in children. It now relates to bone deformities and diseases in general, so that *pediatric* (literally 'child medicine') relates solely to the medical treatment of children: 'The patient needed orthopedic treatment for his spine,' 'A children's hospital ward is officially known as a pediatric ward.'

ostensibly *see* ostentatiously

ostentatiously/ostensibly To do something *ostentatiously* is to do it openly or pointedly, so that those present see it being done: 'Janet disliked cigarette smoke, and ostentatiously opened the window when he lit up.' To do something *ostensibly* is to do it for an apparently obvious or stated reason but actually for quite a different one: 'He asked if I could lend him $200, ostensibly to settle a debt' (but actually to back a winner in the horse race).

outrageous/outré If a thing is *outrageous,* it is very bad or offensive: 'That's an outrageous lie, and you know it!' If something is *outré,* it exceeds the bounds of normal politeness or decency: 'I thought her dress rather outré for such a formal occasion.'

outré *see* outrageous

overtone *see* undertone

P

package *see* packet

packet/package/parcel A *packet* is basically a small *package,* i.e., a 'pack-ette': 'The men waited eagerly for Friday and their weekly wage packet.' A *package* in turn is a small *parcel,* or a collection of things that are packed or boxed, especially one ready for mailing: 'The post office has a special cheap rate for small packages sent abroad.' A *parcel* is anything wrapped and ready to be taken or sent somewhere: 'Matthew decided it would be cheaper to take the parcel himself rather than mail it.'

paean/paeon A *paean* (or *pean*) is a song of praise or triumph: 'The artist saw his work as a paean to nature.' A *paeon* is a special metrical unit of four syllables in Greek verse: 'Gerard Manley Hopkins is one of the few English poets to use paeons in his writings.'

paeon *see* paean

pagan *see* heathen

palate/palette The *palate* is literally the roof of the mouth, and so the means of testing the taste of something, or the pleasure of taste itself: 'Too much junk food can ruin your palate,' 'The white wine appealed to her palate.' A *palette* is properly the board on which an artist mixes paints to make different colors. It is thus also the colors themselves, or anything that is noteworthy because of its mixed colors: 'We rose early to admire the blue, yellow and red palette of the dawn.'

palette *see* palate

palpate/palpitate Both words relate to medical vocabulary. To *palpate* someone is to feel his or her body with the hands by way of examination: 'The doctor palpated the child's abdomen and asked if it hurt where he pressed.' To *palpitate,* of the heart, is to beat rapidly: 'His heart palpitated after even the slightest exertion.'

palpitate *see* palpate

pamper *see* pander

pamphlet *see* brochure

panacea/placebo A *panacea* is a remedy, or supposed remedy, for all ills: 'Some people regard herbal tea as a virtual panacea,' 'Modern technology cannot yet provide a panacea for all problems in the home.' A *placebo* is an inactive or 'sham' drug given to calm a patient or to serve as a control when compared with the effects of the real drug. It is thus also anything given as a sop, to humor someone: 'The shop did not reimburse me, but offered me a discount on my next purchase as a placebo.'

pander/pamper To *pander* to someone is to give in to everything he or she asks, however unreasonable: 'He pandered to her every wish and whim.' To *pamper* someone is to spoil him or her by overindulgence: 'She liked to pamper herself with a cup of Turkish coffee after supper.'

panoply *see* canopy

Paraguay/Uruguay *Paraguay* is a country in central South America, and *Uruguay* is a country to the south of it: 'Paraguay is a landlocked state, but Uruguay is on the coast.'

paralyzed/petrified To be *paralyzed* is to be unable to move or function for some reason: 'Colin was almost paralyzed with cold and hunger,' 'The strike paralyzed many parts of the city.' To be *petrified* is to be rooted to the spot (literally 'turned to stone') with fear or dread: 'When I saw the snake I was absolutely petrified.'

parameter/perimeter Apart from the mathematical use of the word to denote a quantity that does not vary in one case but does in others, a *parameter* is now used generally as a limit of some kind: 'We have to work within the parameters of our budget (i.e., not overspend). This leaves *perimeter* as either a mathematical term for the outer edge of a geometric shape or as the boundary of an area: 'Guards patrolled the perimeter fence.'

parcel see packet

parlous/perilous *Parlous* is used for something in an uncertain or dangerous situation, or in one that is generally very bad: 'Many industrialists expressed concern about the parlous state of the economy.' *Perilous* applies to something that is more obviously dangerous or fraught with difficulty: 'The overland expedition to the North Pole was a perilous undertaking.'

parochial *see* provincial

parody/pastiche A *parody* is a satirical or witty imitation of something: 'Stella Gibbons's novel *Cold Comfort Farm* is a parody on the "brooding" rural fiction of her day.' A *pastiche* is essentially the same, but is more an imitation of style than of content: 'His performance was a pastiche of the way the part should really be acted.'

parricide/patricide *Parricide* is the killing of one or both of one's parents, or the person who does this; *patricide* is the killing of one's father, or the person who does this: 'In killing his mother, Agrippina, the emperor Nero was a parricide, not a patricide.'

part/piece/portion A *part* of something is an incomplete bit of it: 'Part of the road was under water.' A *piece* of something is a *part* of it that is usually complete on its own: 'Would you like a piece of cake?' A *portion* of something is a *part* of it that has been allotted or measured out: 'Two portions of french fries, please.'

partially *see* partly

particular/peculiar The *particular* features of something are those that are special to it: 'A particular advantage of this job is that we work flexible hours.' The *peculiar* features of something are unique to it, or are unexpected or surprising: 'This style of architecture was peculiar to the 1930s,' 'Robert showed a peculiar lack of interest in the program.'

partly/partially *Partly* is the opposite of *wholly*, and so means 'in part': 'I was only partly dressed when the bell rang,' 'Pam said she was only partly responsible for the mess.' *Partially* is the opposite of *completely*, and so means 'not fully,' 'not entirely': 'The road was partially blocked by the fallen tree (but we got through), 'The house was partially hidden by the trees (but we could see it).

passed *see* past

past/passed *Past* is never a verb: 'The time for pleasure is past' (adjective). 'We ate there several times in the past' (noun), 'It's half past seven already' (preposition), 'Sandra hurried past' (adverb). *Passed* is always a verb: 'Sandra passed in a hurry,' 'Many of the students had already passed the exam.'

pastiche *see* parody

pastry/pasty/patty/pâté A *pastry* is a small, fancy cake, made wholly or partly with pastry: 'We were served a choice of pastries with our tea.' A *pasty* is a pastry pie filled with something savory or (much less often) sweet, such as meat, mixed meat and vegetables, or fruit: 'Chris often had a Cornish pasty for his lunch.' A *patty* was formerly a small pie, but is now a flat, round cake of uncooked meat: 'I'll get some hamburger patties for the children's lunch.' *Pâté* (once made with *pastry,* but no longer) is a paste or spread of finely ground liver, meat or fish, usually served as an hors d'oeuvre: 'A popular form of pâté is *pâté de foie gras,* made from goose liver.'

pasty *see* pastry

pâté *see* pastry

pathos/bathos *Pathos* is the quality of something, such as speech or music, that evokes a feeling of pity or sorrow: 'The mother told her tale with such pathos that tears came to the eyes of many present.' *Bathos* is either insincere *pathos* or a descent 'from the sublime to the ridiculous': 'The play was rather moving in places, but the episode where the two take a shower together was pure bathos.'

patricide *see* parricide

patty *see* pastry

peaceable *see* peaceful

peaceful/peaceable *Peaceful* has to do with a state of peace or calm: 'The park was a peaceful scene, with children playing and adults strolling.' *Peaceable* has to do with wanting or seeking peace: 'The deer is a peaceable animal,' 'We reached a peaceable settlement.'

peal/chime A *peal* is usually a series of changes rung on a set of bells, while a *chime* is a melodious ringing of bells, whether a *peal* or an actual tune: '*Oh, peal upon our wedding,/And we will hear the chime,/ And come to church on time*' (A.E. Housman).

peculiar *see* particular

pedagogue *see* pedant

pedal/peddle To *pedal* is to move by pedaling, as on a bicycle; to *peddle* is to sell things from door to door: 'The young craftsman pedaled the streets, peddling his wares wherever he could.' The words are not related.

pedant/pedagogue A *pedant* is a person who is stuffily precise about matters of detail: 'He's a real pedant, and insists on having his checks printed with his full name.' A *pedagogue* is similar, but is a person who is either a teacher or who behaves like one: 'My stylist is such a tiresome pedagogue: she doesn't have to tell me how to look after my hair!' Both terms have a derogatory flavor.

peddle *see* pedal

pediatric *see* orthopedic

pendant/pendent A *pendant* is an ornament hanging from a chain worn around the neck: 'He bought his girlfriend a silver chain and pendant.' *Pendent* is a formal or poetic adjective used for something hanging: 'The boat brushed aside the pendent boughs of the weeping willows.'

pendent *see* pendant

peninsula/peninsular *Peninsula* is the noun for a land mass that projects into the sea, and *peninsular* is its adjective: 'The Iberian peninsula, or Spain and Portugal, was the scene of the Peninsular War.'

peninsular *see* peninsula

perceptive/percipient/perspicacious/perspicuous A *perceptive* person understands something readily or intuitively: 'So you realized I had lost? That was very perceptive of you.' A *percipient* person is similar, but notices whatever it is quickly: 'The youngest members of the class were often the most percipient.' A *perspicacious* person is one who discerns or who understands something without needing an explanation: 'He was a perspicacious student of human nature and knew how we would react.' A *perspicuous* person is easy to understand: 'We then heard Anna's account, which although long was wonderfully clear and perspicuous.'

percipient *see* perceptive

percolate *see* pervade

peremptory *see* perfunctory

perennial *see* annual

perfume/scent/fragrance A *perfume,* as well as being the familiar cosmetic, is the pleasant smell or odor of something, especially that of a substance used commercially to produce it: 'The heady perfumes of the orient are too strong for many western visitors.' A *scent* is either a manufactured *perfume* or the natural and distinctive smell of something, typically flowers: 'The strong scent of the roses filled the room.' A *fragrance* is either a commercial term for a *perfume* or any pleasant *scent,* especially a sweet or delicate one: 'The scent of the silk suggested the fragrance of a freshly opened packet of tea.'

perfunctory/peremptory If a thing is *perfunctory,* it is done carelessly or quickly, or in a routine way: 'He took a perfunctory shower before coming down to breakfast.' If something is *peremptory,* it is usually sharp and authoritative: 'Our conversation was interrupted by a peremptory knock at the door.'

perilous *see* parlous

perimeter *see* parameter

perk *see* privilege

permeate *see* pervade

pernickety *see* finicky

perpetrate/perpetuate To perpetrate something (usually something bad) is to do it or carry it out: 'This is the latest crime he has perpetrated.' To *perpetuate* something is to make it continue or last: 'The students have perpetuated the tradition.'

perpetuate *see* perpetrate

perquisite *see* requirement

persecute/prosecute To *persecute* someone is to treat her or him cruelly or to hound her or him; to *prosecute* someone is to bring a charge against that person in a court of law: 'The young men persecuted the shopkeeper so persistently that he prosecuted them.'

persistence/pertinacity/tenacity/tenaciousness *Persistence* is the quality of continuing with something until it is achieved: 'Thanks to his persistence, Max finally got his money back.' *Pertinacity* is a dogged or stubborn *persistence:* 'The wrestlers fought and grappled with almost equal pertinacity.' *Tenacity* is the quality of holding fast, not necessarily with any ultimate aim in mind: 'The bulldog is famous for its tenacity: when it gets hold of something it will not easily let go.' *Tenaciousness* is the same, with the word often used in a nonliteral sense: 'He was respected for the tenaciousness of his opinions.'

persistent *see* consistent

personage/personality As applied to a well-known person, a *personage* is important or distinguished, while a *personality* is famous and popular, especially in the world of entertainment or sports: 'The state funeral was attended by royal and political personages from all over Europe,' 'TV personalities often get invited to open things.'

personal/personnel *Personal* relates to a particular person or particular people: 'This is my personal copy, so please take care of it,' 'The shop prides itself on its personal service,' 'Geraldine is his personal assistant.' *Personnel* has to do with the staff or employees of a company or organization, including the armed forces: 'A personnel carrier is a ship that transports troops,' 'The personnel manager is responsible for the terms of employment and welfare of the workforce.'

personality *see* personage

personate *see* impersonate

personnel *see* personal

perspective/prospect In their literal senses, a *perspective* is a view that stretches into the distance, while a *prospect* is a wide view generally: 'From the hill we had a fine perspective of the whole valley,' 'From the hill a magnificent prospect opened before us.' In their figurative senses, which are more common, a *perspective* is a viewpoint, or way of looking at something, while a *prospect* is an outlook or an expectation of something: 'If you look at things from a proper perspective, you'll see that the prospect is pretty good.'

perspicacious *see* perceptive

perspicuous *see* perceptive

pert *see* insolent

pertinacity *see* persistence

perturbed *see* disturbed

pervade/permeate/percolate To *pervade* is to make the presence of something constantly felt: 'The scent of the flowers pervaded the house,' 'My father's influence pervaded my early years.' To *permeate* something is to pass through it gradually or subtly so as to fill it: 'News of the President's arrival began to permeate the waiting crowd.' To *percolate* is to do the same, although the suggestion is of something filtering or flowing, such as a liquid: 'The dawn light percolated through the closed curtains,' 'Oriental influences have percolated into some western styles of art.'

perverse/perverted A *perverse* person is obstinate or 'difficult,' and *perverse* feelings are unreasonable or excessive: 'He has a perverse dislike of standing on line for anything,' 'She took a perverse pleasure in making him wait.' A *perverted* person is one whose behavior is abnormal or corrupt, especially sexually: 'The gang took a perverted pleasure in recording their victim's cries.'

perverted *see* perverse

pestilence/plague Both words are (or were) used to denote a deadly epidemic that kills many people. A *plague* is perhaps generally regarded as more sudden and destructive than a *pestilence,* although the words are very close in meaning: 'The most infamous of all pestilences was the bubonic plague.'

petrified *see* paralyzed

Pharisee *see* Philistine

phase *see* phrase

Philistine/Pharisee In its figurative sense, a *Philistine* is a boor or uncultured person: 'He was something of a Philistine, not caring for art or music.' A *Pharisee* is a self-righteous or hypocritical person: 'The old Pharisee told us he was collecting for charity, but he was simply after our money.'

phrase/phase A *phrase* is a group of things, such as words or musical notes, that can join with other, similar groups to produce an overall effect: 'The repeated phrases of the song produced a curious sense of peace and happiness.' A *phase* is a stage in the evolution or development of something: 'The country now moved into a new phase in its troubled history.'

phrenetic *see* frantic

picaresque *see* picturesque

pick/choose To *pick* something or someone is to *choose* the thing or person carefully from among a group, especially when members of that group seem very similar to one another: 'Here are the pens: pick the one you want,' 'He was picked to play in the game.' To *choose* something is to select it because it is the best or most suitable: 'He chose a special present for Susan.'

picturesque/picaresque *Picturesque* relates to something pretty or attractive, especially in a quaint or charming way: 'The film makers chose the village because of its picturesque setting.' *Picaresque* relates to a story that deals with the adventures of a likable rogue: 'The novels *Kim* and *Huckleberry Finn* are not only similar in plan but are both picaresque, with a likable rogue of a boy as a traveler.'

pidgin/pigeon The unrelated words have quite different meanings: *pidgin* (from *business)* is a mixed language combining a local language with English and others: 'Pidgin English originated in China.' *Pigeon (see below)* is the familiar bird.

pie *see* tart

piebald/skewbald A *piebald* horse is properly one covered with irregularly-shaped patches of two colors, usually black and white, while a *skewbald* horse has patches that combine white and a color that is not black: *'As quaint a four-in-hand/As you shall see—three pyebalds* [sic] *and a roan'* (Tennyson), 'A skewbald's coat is a combination of white and a color such as brown, chestnut or roan.'

piece *see* part

pigeon/dove Both *pigeons* and *doves* belong to the same family, although *doves* are generally smaller. Where the meanings coincide, *pigeon* is the ordinary 'down-to-earth' word for the bird, while *dove* is more elevated and poetic: 'The pigeons in Washington Square Park in New York are popular with tourists but a plague to the authorities,' 'The dove sent out of the Ark by Noah returned bearing an olive branch, and so became a symbol of peace and freedom from anxiety.'

pigeon *see* pidgin

pile/pyre A *pile* is a heap of something: 'There was a big pile of garbage in the yard.' A *pyre* is a heap of wood or other combustible materials used for burning a corpse: *'For nine long nights through all the dusky air/The pyres thick-flaming shot a dismal glare'* (Pope). However, since a *pyre* is a *pile* of wood, a funeral *pyre* can also be a pile: *'Full bowls of wine, of honey, milk, and blood/Were poured upon the pile of burning wood'* (Dryden).

pilfer *see* purloin

pill/tablet In medicine, a *pill* is usually round or oval and often in the form of a capsule containing a drug or drugs: 'The pills were rattling in the box.' A *tablet* is usually flat and round and made of the drug itself in compressed form, with no outer casing: 'These white tablets are aspirins.'

pillar/column A *pillar* is a tall shaft of some kind used for support or ornamentation (or both). A *column* is an individual *pillar,* especially one that is architecturally important or interesting: 'We stood by a pillar on the portico of the National Gallery in London and admired the view across Trafalgar Square to Nelson's Column.'

pimp *see* ponce

pincers *see* pliers

pine *see* fir

piquant *see* pungent

piteous *see* pitiful

pitiable *see* pitiful

pitiful/pitiable/piteous *Pitiful* relates to someone or something that excites pity or is contemptible: 'The aftermath of the fire was a pitiful sight, with many houses completely destroyed,' 'Jessica's knowledge of geography is pitiful: she thought Athens was in Egypt.' *Pitiable* relates to a person or thing that is lamentable or wretched: 'The old woman was in a pitiable plight, with no one to care for her.' *Piteous* is used for evidence of suffering and misery, evoking pity: 'The crowds of undernourished and starving children were a piteous sight.'

placebo *see* panacea

plague *see* pestilence

plain *see* plane

plane/plain Both words can apply to a flat or level area. A *plane* is a more or less technical term for a flat surface: 'The sides of a pyramid rise on an inclined plane to meet at its apex, 'Joe tried to raise the level of conversation to a more elevated plane.' A *plain* is a level tract of country: '*A gentle knight was pricking on the plain*' (Spenser).

plangent *see* pungent

playwright *see* dramatist

pleasantness/pleasantry *Pleasantness* is the quality of being pleasant: 'Spain is popular with tourists for the general pleasantness of the weather.' A *pleasantry* is a humorous remark or joke, or an attempt at one: 'Jean smiled politely at her visitor's pleasantries.'

pleasantry *see* pleasantness

pliers/pincers *Pliers* have parallel jaws and were originally designed for *plying*, i.e., bending, although they are now used also for gripping, cutting and pulling things such as wire or nails: 'I extracted the broken light bulb with a pair of pliers.' *Pincers* are similar but are often larger and have rounded jaws designed for *pinching*: 'Try using these pincers for getting the nails out of the floorboards.'

plumb/plummet To *plumb* something is to descend to its lowest point, usually figuratively: 'After the death of her husband, she plumbed the depths of despair.' To *plummet* is to fall or plunge straight down, literally or figuratively: 'The binoculars fell overboard and plummeted to the bottom of the lake,' 'House prices plummeted last year.'

plummet *see* plumb

poetic/poetical Although there is some overlap between the two words, *poetic* usually relates to something that is like poetry, while *poetical* relates to something that *is* poetry: 'The audience admired the poetic grace of the dancer's movements,' 'I bought a secondhand copy of *Tennyson's Poetical Works.*'

poetical *see* poetic

poignant *see* pungent

policy/polity *Policy* is the plan of action or statement of ideals of a government, political party, or the like: 'The government has revised its policy on unemployment benefits.' *Polity* is either the form or process of government or else a country's people organized as a state: 'British political and legal ideas have had an influence on American polity,' 'The polity of a united Europe is based on both trade and trust.' *See also* politic.

politic/political A *politic* action is a prudent one: 'When they started quarreling I thought it politic to leave.' *Political* has to do with politics: 'I see there's another paid political broadcast on this evening.' *See also* policy.

political *see* politic

polity *see* policy

ponce/pimp A *ponce* is a man of effeminate nature, manner or dress: 'His extravagant manner of dressing made him look like something of a ponce.' The same word can also be used for a *pimp,* who is a man (not necessarily effeminate) who finds clients for prostitutes or a brothel and lives off most of their earnings: 'The hotel guests seemed to include a number of prostitutes and their pimps.'

poorness/poverty *Poverty* is the more literal word of the two, while *poorness* tends to be more figurative: 'The couple lived in a state of abject poverty,' 'It was difficult to grow crops because of the poverty of the soil,' 'After paying all that money, we were very disappointed with the poorness of the performance.'

poppet/moppet Both a *poppet* and a *moppet* are affectionate terms for a small child, especially a little girl. *Poppet* is used in the sense of 'darling' to address such a child, however, while *moppet* is mostly not. A *moppet,* too, is a young girl seen as prettily or even precociously dressed, whereas a *poppet* is simply a 'lovable' one: 'Isn't she a poppet?' 'Mothers and their moppets filed into the theater for the auditions.'

pore *see* pour

port/harbor A *port* is a place where naval and merchant ships dock, or a town with such a place. A *harbor* is a place where ships and boats such as fishing or recreational vessels can take shelter. At the same time, a *port* may well serve as a *harbor* for ships wishing to shelter there. Passengers have more to do with *ports* than *harbors:* 'We stayed overnight in a fishing port, and in the evening went down to the harbor.'

portion *see* part

pose/propose/propound To *pose* a question is to ask it or put it forward, often with the implication that it may be difficult to answer: 'I would like to pose a further question.' To *propose* a matter is to suggest it or put it forward: 'The next speaker proposed that the matter be discussed when more facts were known.' To *propound* a matter is to do the same, although the word is a formal one and suggests a serious proposition or a forceful argument: 'The scheme for constitutional reform was the most extensive yet propounded.'

possible/probable If something is *possible,* it could happen but may not; if it is *probable,* it is likely: It is possible the weather will improve tomorrow, and if it does, it is probable we will play the game after all.'

postdate *see* antedate

pour/pore To *pour* is to fall as liquid: 'The rain poured down.' To *pore* is to study something intently: 'We pored over the map, looking for the best route.' Despite the apparent common concept of downward direction, the two words are not related.

pout/moue A *pout* is a sulky look, or one of annoyance: '"I never have any fun," said the child, with a pout.' A *moue* is a disdainful or derisive pout (the French word is the equivalent of the English *mow,* as in 'mops and mows'): I told her that *I* would be the judge or that, whereupon she gave a moue and flounced out.'

poverty *see* poorness

practicable *see* practical

practical/practicable If something is *practical,* it is useful and likely to be successful; if it is *practicable,* it can be carried out, or put into practice: 'You have made a practical suggestion, but I wonder if in this case it will be practicable?' *Compare* impractical.

prate/prattle To *prate* is to talk or chatter too much about something: 'There he goes, prating on about his new car again.' To *prattle* is also to talk at length, but more about unimportant things: 'She was prattling on about the mailman and how he never came at the same time and how he always came with packages while she was out, and so on.'

prattle *see* prate

pray/prey To *pray* is to 'talk' to God; to *prey* on someone or something is to hunt, catch or exploit that person or thing: 'I pray that it won't rain today,' 'It's been preying on my mind for some time now,' 'The praying mantis is so called not because it preys on living insects for its food but because when at rest it folds its front legs as if praying.'

precede *see* proceed

precedence *see* precedent

precedent/precedence A *precedent* is an event or decision that serves as a model for subsequent similar events or decisions: 'There is no precedent for such an action,' 'I was keen not to set a precedent.' *Precedence* is priority: 'Many believe that the needs of others should take precedence over one's own needs,' 'The elder son in a family usually has precedence over the younger.'

precipitately/precipitously To do something *precipitately* is to do it hurriedly and without regard for the consequences: 'She took offense at his words and precipitately left the room.' To do a thing *precipitously* is to do it rashly and often vigorously or violently: 'On hearing the explosion, he dashed precipitously into the street.'

precipitously *see* precipitately

preclude *see* exclude

precondition *see* condition

predicate *see* predict

predict/predicate To *predict* something is to foretell or forecast it: 'He predicated that many would leave the party the worse for wear.' To *predicate* something is to state that you think it is true: 'The weather report predicated that the flooding had been caused by a combination of high winds and heavy rain.' To *predicate* one thing on another, however, is to state that you believe the first thing you mention to be true only if the second one is: 'The treatment of patients should be not predicated upon their ability to pay.'

predilection/proclivity A *predilection* for something is a special preference for it: 'He has a predilection for chocolates.' A *proclivity* is a natural inclination toward something, especially something bad or undesirable: 'She has a proclivity for chocolates' (but they make her put on weight). *See also* propensity.

predominate/preponderate To *predominate* is to be more numerous or powerful than others in a group: 'Oak trees predominate in this forest.' To *preponderate* has the same sense, although the word suggests a weightiness that implies a significant superiority in numbers or authority: 'In the next town we came to, it was the Muslim population that preponderated' (the Christians were outnumbered and had little influence).

pre-empt *see* prevent

preface *see* foreword

prefatory *see* preparatory

preliminary *see* preparatory

premise/premiss *Premise* is the standard spelling for the word relating to a building or to a reasoned idea: 'The office's premises are vacant,' 'I am basing my premise on what you told me.' However, *premiss* is an alternative spelling for the second sense, especially in its use as a term in logic: 'The two first parts of an argument in logic are known as the major premiss and the minor premiss.'

premiss *see* premise

premonition *see* presentiment

preoccupied *see* occupied

preparatory/prefatory/preliminary A *preparatory* remark prepares listeners for what is to come: 'The speaker made a few preparatory remarks about the facilities available for delegates.' A *prefatory* remark is an introductory one: 'The guest of honor said he would like to make a brief prefatory statement before the toast.' A *preliminary* remark is one made beforehand, for whatever reason: 'The announcer said a few preliminary words before the recital began.'

preponderate *see* predominate

prerequisite *see* requirement

prerogative *see* privilege

prescience *see* presentiment

prescribe/proscribe The two verbs are virtual opposites. To *prescribe* something is to recommend or authorize it: 'The doctor prescribed a course of antibiotics,' 'The laws prescribe a strict penalty for this offense.' To *proscribe* something is to ban it: 'The import of pornographic material was proscribed by law,' 'The new nationalist party was proscribed.'

presentiment/premonition/prescience A *presentiment* (not a *presentment,* which is a presentation) is a feeling that something undesirable or unpleasant is going to happen: 'Edward had a vague presentiment that he would find no one at home.' A *premonition* is similar, but implies that the feeling is by way of warning, and that the person concerned can perhaps prevent or avoid what lies ahead: 'Penny had a premonition that he had already left' (so she phoned to see if her fears were realized). *Prescience* is knowing or seeing something beforehand, in other words, foreknowledge or foresight: 'With remarkable prescience, James parked the car clear of the trees so that it remained unscathed when the lightning struck.'

preserve *see* 1) conserve, 2) reservation

pressure/pressurize To *pressure* someone is to persuade him or her to do something: 'They were pressured into accepting.' To *pressurize* someone is to do the same, although the word stresses the 'pressing' aspect of the action: 'They were pressurized into accepting' (we put the pressure on until they did).

pressurize *see* pressure

prestigious/prodigious Something *prestigious* is famous; something *prodigious* is great: 'The gallery has a prestigious collection of paintings' (famous ones), 'The gallery has a prodigious collection of paintings' (a very large one). The fact that something famous is often also great means that the words are liable to confusion.

presume/assume To *presume* something is to believe it to be true, although with some uncertainty remaining: 'You'll come, I presume?' (I would be surprised if you didn't, although I would accept your decision). To *assume* something is to take it for granted: 'You'll come, I assume?' (I expect you to, and would like to know why if you don't). *See also* presumptuous.

presumptive *see* presumptuous

presumptuous/presumptive *Presumptuous* relates to taking liberties: 'It was presumptuous of you to place the order without consulting me,' 'I hope it won't seem presumptuous if I serve myself first.' *Presumptive,* a less common word, is used to describe something based on a presumption, that is, something that is probably true but might possibly not be: 'All the presumptive evidence points in his favor,' 'Prince Albert Victor, Duke of Clarence, was the heir presumptive to the throne' (he was next in line after the heir apparent, his father, Albert Edward, Prince of Wales, the future king Edward VII).

pretense/pretext A *pretense* is a false show of something: 'Bob went to bed early under the pretense of being tired' (he wasn't really, but he pretended to be because he wanted to escape from the boring company). A *pretext* is a reason given for something when it was not the true reason: 'Ann went to Boston under the pretext of visiting her brother' (she said she was, but she wasn't really: she was seeing her boyfriend).

preternatural *see* supernatural

pretext *see* pretense

prevaricate/procrastinate To *prevaricate* is to avoid saying what should be said: 'The doctor prevaricated, fearful of telling the patient the truth.' To *procrastinate* is to put off doing something: 'Let's not procrastinate any longer: we have wasted enough time as it is.'

prevent/pre-empt To *prevent* someone or something is to stop him or her or or it: 'I managed to prevent the sale of the house' (I stopped it from being sold). To *pre-empt* a person or thing is also to stop him or her or it but by taking action in advance: 'I managed to pre-empt the sale of the house' (I acted so as to stop the sale from getting under way in the first place).

preventative *see* preventive

preventive/preventative The words are often used interchangeably to denote whatever prevents something else from happening or occurring, especially when it is undesirable. However, *preventative* is often applied to an actual object, especially in noun form, while *preventive* is mostly reserved for an abstract concept, and remains an adjective: 'Preventive medicine regards vitamin C as an effective preventative against colds.'

previous/prior Both words relate to something coming before something else in time. *Prior* implies, however, that it is also more important: 'I'm afraid I can't come, as I have a previous engagement' (I am already booked that day), 'I'm afraid I can't come, as I have a prior engagement' (not only am I already booked, but my engagement is more important than the one you are offering me).

prey *see* pray

prim/prissy/sissy A *prim* person is affectedly precise or proper, with the implication that he or she is also prudish: 'My aunt was a prim and unsmiling woman who believed every word of the Bible to be true.' A *prissy* person is fussily *prim,* especially in an exaggerated way: 'The older girl gave me a prissy look as if to say that *she* would never do anything like that.' A *sissy* is effeminate, weak or cowardly, or a combination of these: 'He's rather a sissy, and seems scared of mixing with the others,' 'Tom said wearing gloves was sissy.'

prima facie *see* a priori

primary *see* prime

prime/primary *Prime* has the sense of being first in importance or quality: 'The president made his TV speech in prime time, when his audience would be greatest.' *Primary* relates mainly to being first in time, order or importance (but not quality): 'A good primary education can influence a child's performance at the secondary level,' 'A primary reason for advertising is to make people aware of new or improved products.'

primeval/primordial *Primeval* relates to the earliest stages of life in the world: 'Our primeval ancestors would be hard put to live the way we live now.' *Primordial* relates to the *very* earliest times, when life was only just forming or beginning: 'Science fiction writers sometimes take their readers back to the primordial moment when everything began,' 'Although he's a modern composer, his music has a wild and primordial quality.'

primordial *see* primeval

primp *see* prink

principal *see* principle

principle/principal A *principle* is a firm belief or conviction that one has about something, or a rule or law about the way something works: 'It would be against my principles to do such a thing,' 'A thermometer works on the principle that mercury expands when warm and contracts when cool.' A *principal* is the head of a school: 'She became principal in 1991.' *Principle* is always a noun, but *principal* can also be an adjective meaning 'main,' 'chief': 'My principal objection is the cost.'

prink/primp To *prink* oneself up is to dress carefully and finely, and admire oneself while doing so: 'Hugh spent ages prinking himself up before the mirror.' To *primp* is to dress similarly, but in an ultra-correct or proper manner (the word is related to *prim*): '*In tropical heat/ Nobody who's sweet, survives/We powder and primp/And try to be sympathetic*' (Noël Coward).

prior *see* previous

prissy *see* prim

privilege/prerogative/perk A *privilege* is a special benefit or advantage that someone enjoys: 'A well-behaved prisoner can earn certain privileges.' A *prerogative* is an exclusive right to something, as typically held by a person of rank, wealth or authority: 'Senior civil servants enjoy first class air travel as one of their prerogatives.' A *perk* (short for a *perquisite*) is a benefit that an employee enjoys in addition to a salary: 'Free phone calls at work was one of the boss's perks that the rest of us envied.' *See also* requirement.

probable *see* possible

procedure/proceedings A *procedure* is the way of doing or arranging something: 'There is a special procedure for reserving seats at these events.' The *proceedings* are the courses of events as they happen: 'At this point in the proceedings I decided I'd had enough.'

proceed/precede To *proceed* is to go forward, especially after stopping or turning: 'The parade then proceeded up Main Street.' To *precede* is to go in front: 'The parade was preceded by two majorettes, tossing and twirling their batons.'

proceedings *see* procedure

proclaim *see* announce

proclivity *see* 1) predilection, 2) propensity

procrastinate *see* prevaricate

procure *see* secure

prodigious *see* prestigious

prodigy *see* progeny

produce/products *Produce,* as a noun, chiefly refers to things that have been produced by being grown, such as food: 'Denmark is famous for its farm produce.' *Products* are things that have been produced either by a natural process or by being manufactured: 'France is well known for its agricultural products,' 'The company was keen to promote its new product.'

products *see* produce

proffer *see* offer

profligate *see* prolific

progeny/prodigy/protégé *Progeny* is a collective word for offspring or children: 'The whole family was there: mother, father and their sizeable progeny.' A *prodigy* is an unusually talented child: 'Mozart gained early fame as a prodigy, giving public performances of his own compositions at the age of six.' A *protégé* is a (usually young) person who is guided or helped by someone else, by implication usually older and wiser: 'He came to regard Justin as his protégé, encouraging and advising him in his studies whenever he could.'

prognosis *see* diagnosis

prohibit *see* forbid

prolific/prolix/profligate *Prolific* means producing abundantly: 'She was a prolific writer, turning out as many as ten novels a year for much of her life.' *Prolix* is used for something excessively lengthy or long-winded, typically a speech or piece of writing: 'He aspired to be a poet, but his poems were prolix and inelegant.' *Profligate* means extravagant and wasteful: 'The company was criticized for its profligate spending on advertising.'

prolix s*ee* prolific

prone *see* prostrate

pronounce *see* announce

propensity/proclivity A *propensity* for something is a natural tendency toward it or disposition for it: 'Andrew has a propensity for fast cars.' A *proclivity* is similar, but implies a predisposition for something undesirable or unhealthy: 'John suffered from a proclivity to colds, so he steered clear of crowded places.' *See also* predilection.

prophecy *see* prophesy

prophesy/prophecy *Prophesy* is the verb, and *prophecy* the noun: 'I prophesy that you'll hear from him by the end of the week,' 'Unfortunately, her prophecy proved to be wrong.'

propitious s*ee* auspicious

proportional/proportionate *Proportional* is used for something that corresponds in size or amount to something else, so that it is in proportion to it, with the proportion usually changing: 'The workers' pay was proportional to the amount of work they actually did,' 'Several politicians favor proportional representation, whereby each party has a number of seats in proportion to the number of votes its candidates get.' *Proportionate* means the same, but often relates to a fixed proportion: 'The punishment was proportionate to the crime.'

proportionate *see* proportional

proposal/proposition A *proposal* is a plan put forward for acceptance or rejection: 'My proposal is that we should start work tomorrow.' A *proposition* is almost always an advantageous offer: 'I have considered your proposition, and it seems very fair to me.'

propose *see* pose

proposition *see* proposal

propound *see* pose

proscribe *see* prescribe

prosecute *see* persecute

prospect *see* perspective

prostrate/prone/supine *Prostrate* means lying face downwards, often as the result of some accident or illness: 'He was knocked over and lay prostrate for some minutes before getting up.' *Prone* means the same. It usually lacks the suggestion of being suddenly struck down, however, although it can apply to patients in bed: 'The medical students were advised not to move patients from the prone position unless it was absolutely necessary,' 'The fitness club instructor demonstrated the prone position.' *Supine* is the opposite, and means lying on one's back, face up: 'The beach was full of sun worshipers, supine on the sand.'

protagonist *see* antagonist

protégé *see* progeny

protest/protestation A *protest* is an objection to something: 'The demonstrators made their protest known,' 'I wish to register a strong protest.' A *protestation* is simply a formal declaration of something, especially in cases of doubt: 'The accused redoubled his protestations of innocence,' 'Despite my protestations, they insisted on helping.'

protestation *see* protest

provided *see* providing

providing/provided *Providing* implies the positive fulfillment of a condition, so that if one thing happens, another will: 'Providing we drive carefully, we should be home by seven' (if we do, we will be). *Provided* means the same, but is more negative, implying that the second thing will not happen unless the first does: 'Provided we drive carefully, we should be home by seven' (if we don't, we won't be). The two words are often used interchangeably, however.

provincial/parochial As used for attitudes or opinions, *provincial* can have a 'rustic' overtone, characteristic of one who lives out of town: 'Further north, people tend to have a more provincial outlook.' *Parochial,* in the same kind of way, means narrow or even bigoted: 'For such a cultured person, Wendy's interests are really very parochial.'

prudent/prudential A *prudent* decision (for example) is a wise and cautious one, and to be commended, but a *prudential* decision, which is one dictated by prudence, may turn out not to be such a good idea after all: 'I took the prudent step of not paying for the goods until they had arrived,' 'Prudential solutions to problems are not necessarily the best solutions.'

prudential see prudent

psychiatrist *see* psychologist

psychologist/psychiatrist A *psychologist* is a person whose special study is human or animal behavior: 'A psychologist is interested in not only what people are thinking but what they do.' A *psychiatrist,* a medical specialist, is concerned exclusively with the working of the mind, and in particular with mental disorders: 'Norman's doctor referred him to a psychiatrist.'

puke *see* retch

punctilious *see* punctual

punctual/punctilious Someone who is *punctual* is on time, or does something at the agreed time: 'He was always punctual in renewing his subscription' (he always did it on time). Someone who is *punctilious* is careful to carry out duties correctly: 'He was always punctilious in renewing his subscription' (he always did exactly as required, including being on time).

pungent/poignant/piquant/plangent *Pungent* is used for something sharp to the taste or smell, or in a figurative sense for something powerful: 'There was a pungent reek of onions in the kitchen,' 'John made a pungent speech attacking the spending cuts.' *Poignant* is used for something distressing or painful to the senses: 'The autobiography opened with a poignant description of the writer's unhappy childhood.' *Piquant* is used for something agreeably *pungent:* 'The sauce had a piquant flavor that improved the taste of the dish.' *Plangent* is used for a resonant and mournful sound: 'The distant bell of the chapel began to toll its plangent note.'

puny/pusillanimous: *Puny* is used for a person or thing that is small or weak (or both): 'He was a puny little fellow only five feet tall,' 'The boy's puny efforts to climb the fence met with jeers from the others.' *Pusillanimous* applies to someone who is cowardly or faint-hearted: 'The government was accused of adopting a pusillanimous line on the issue.'

pupil/student In general, the words refer to the age of the learner: a *pupil* is in elementary school, and a *student* in high school or college.

purloin/pilfer Both words involve stealing, but to *purloin* something is more to take something for one's own use, while to *pilfer* is to take something relatively small: 'I managed to purloin some food from my host's fridge,' 'She was caught pilfering the small change from the cash register.'

purposefully *see* purposely

purposely/purposefully To do something *purposely* is to do it deliberately or on purpose: 'Please don't move those books: I put them there purposely.' To do something *purposefully* is to do it with determination: '"Carrots, here I come," he said, and strode purposefully into the garden.'

pusillanimous *see* puny

pyre *see* pile

Q

quality *see* quantity

qualmish *see* queasy

quantity/quality The two characteristics, although in some ways similar, should be distinguished: *quantity* relates to measure (size, weight, number, etc.), while *quality* relates to degree ('measure') of excellence: 'The quality of a manufacturer's output does not necessarily depend on its quantity.'

quarrelsome/querulous A *quarrelsome* person is quick-tempered and likely to pick a quarrel; a *querulous* person or temperament is irritable or fretful: 'As soon as he has anything to drink he is bad-tempered and quarrelsome,' 'The old fellow has such a querulous and jaundiced view of everything: why can't he just enjoy life for once?'

queasy/qualmish/squeamish To feel *queasy* is to feel sick: 'I had eaten rather a lot, and was beginning to feel queasy.' *Qualmish* relates to qualms, that is, to a sudden feeling of sickness or unease, whether physical or mental: 'I was feeling rather qualmish after the trip,' 'Clare felt more than a little qualmish at the thought of her plan.' *Squeamish* applies to someone who is easily nauseated or sickened: 'There's no need to be so squeamish: it's only a squashed spider.'

querulous *see* quarrelsome

query/inquiry/enquiry A *query* is a single question, often asked when something is doubtful or needs clarification: 'Are there any queries?' 'I have a query about my phone bill.' An *inquiry* is a request for information: 'I'll make some inquiries about that.' It is also an official investigation: 'Shareholders demanded a public inquiry.' *Enquiry* has the same sense as *inquiry,* and is the preferred form in Great Britain.

quiescent *see* quiet

quiet/quiescent If a person or thing is *quiet,* he or she or it is making little or no noise: 'The children are unusually quiet this evening.' If something is *quiescent,* it is both *quiet* and inactive: 'The terrorist organization was quiescent for a while.'

quirky *see* kinky

quiver *see* shiver

quorum *see* quota

quota/quorum A *quota* is the fixed or due amount of something: 'That's your quota of drinks for this evening.' A *quorum* is the number of people required to be present for business to be transacted: 'It looks as if we have a quorum now, so shall we put it to a vote?'

quote/cite To *quote* something is to repeat somebody's words by way of illustration or as an authority: 'You can quote the Bible to support many unexpected arguments, if you choose carefully.' To *cite* is also to do this, but implies that the quoted words or passage are authoritative: 'May I cite Jackson on this?'

R

rabbit *see* babble

rabid *see* avid

racialist/racist The words are often used interchangeably, but a distinction can be made. A *racialist* is someone who believes in the superiority of one race (usually white) over another (usually black or colored), and who voices his or her views when surrounded (and outnumbered) by representatives of the 'other' race: 'Many white racialists in South Africa were bitterly opposed to the release of the ANC leader Nelson Mandela.' A *racist* is more of a theorist, believing that race is what determines a person's characteristics, so that some races are superior to others: 'Critics remain divided regarding the extent to which Rudyard Kipling was or was not a racist.'

racist *see* racialist

rack/wrack *Rack* is used for something painful or harmful: 'She lay still, racked with pain,' 'He racked his brains but could not think of an answer,' 'This country is going to rack and ruin.' *Wrack* is simply an alternative form of *rack,* but in the three examples quoted, it is rare (some would say wrong) in the first two senses, and common in the third ('wrack and ruin').

rage *see* anger

raise/rear To *raise* children (especially in American usage) is to bring them up: 'I was raised on a farm.' To *raise* animals is to breed them, and to *raise* crops or plants is to make them grow: 'Some fish farms now raise oysters as well,' 'He raised the finest strawberries in the country.' To *rear* children (especially in British usage) is to bring them up and educate them: 'It is not always easy for a single parent to rear a family.' To *rear* animals is to breed and keep them, and to *rear* crops is to grow and produce them: 'They went in for sheep-rearing,' 'Some crops are harder to rear than others.' *Rear* thus generally has a more comprehensive sense than *raise.*

raise *see* rise

rancid *see* rank

randy/raunchy/rangy *Randy* is used for someone or something lustful or lecherous: 'We grew rather tired of his randy behavior.' *Raunchy* has a similar sense, but implies crudeness and 'earthiness': 'A drunk at the table next to ours began to sing a raunchy song.' *Rangy* is used for a thin, long-legged and often rather ungainly person or animal, and implies the freedom to roam or wander at will: 'We were welcomed with a smile and a handshake by a tall, rangy Australian.'

rangy *see* randy

rank/rancid A *rank* smell or taste is an offensively strong one: 'My clothes stank for days from the rank cigar smoke.' A *rancid* smell or taste is similar, but is used for something that has gone bad or is 'off,' such as stale cheese: 'There was nothing in the cupboard but a dish of rancid butter.'

rapacious/voracious *Rapacious* is used for someone greedy and grasping, especially with regard to money: 'The landlord plagued us with his rapacious demands for rent.' *Voracious* is used for someone who has a large appetite for something; 'Mary is a voracious reader, getting through three novels a week.'

rapscallion *see* rascal

rapt *see* wrapped

rascal/rapscallion/rogue The words more or less coincide in their casual use for a 'naughty' person. They can be distinguished, however. A *rascal* is a dishonest person who is also cunning or sly: 'The two rascals were sent to prison for their swindles.' A *rapscallion* is similar, but the term implies that the person is not only dishonest but disreputable: 'The tourists were accosted by an evil-looking rapscallion pretending to be a genuine beggar.' A *rogue* is essentially a cheat or fraud: 'Some of the vendors at the fair were undoubtedly rogues.'

raunchy *see* randy

ravage/ravish To *ravage* is to destroy or lay waste: 'The storms ravaged the wood, uprooting many trees.' To *ravish* is to seize and carry off by force, and hence to rape (which originally meant carrying off a woman with the aim of forcing her to have sex): 'The dog was living wild, and farmers feared it could ravish their flocks.' From this bad 'carrying off' sense came the good one of 'transporting' with delight: 'The visitors were ravished by the beauty of the landscape before them.'

ravening *see* ravishing

ravenous *see* ravishing

ravish *see* ravage

ravishing/ravenous/famished/ravening *Ravishing* is used for someone or something delightful or very beautiful: 'He was stunned when a ravishing blonde walked in.' *Ravenous* means very greedy because hungry: 'The farmhands had a ravenous appetite.' *Famished* means the same, but implies a shortage or absence of food: 'The escaped prisoner was famished after two days without food.' *Ravening* means the same as *ravenous,* but is mostly used for animals: 'The children clamored around the ice cream truck like ravening wolves.'

reach *see* retch

realism *see* reality

reality/realism *Reality* is the state of being real, or the state of things as they actually are: 'Some psychiatrists hold that dreaming is a necessary escape from reality.' *Realism* is the appearance of *reality,* otherwise an acceptance of facts rather than fantasies: 'Many problems can be solved if we approach them with realism.'

reap/wreak To *reap,* in its figurative sense, is to get or gain something as a consequence of an earlier action: 'After all that hard work it is only right that you should reap your reward,' *'They have sown the wind, and they shall reap the whirlwind'* (Bible: Hosea 8:7). To *wreak* is to cause something damaging: 'The neighbors plotted to wreak their revenge,' 'The flood wrought havoc in the town.'

rear *see* 1) back, 2) raise

rebate *see* refund

rebuff *see* rebut

rebuke *see* reproach

rebut/rebuff To *rebut* something is to prove it false by means of evidence or argument: 'The physicist rebutted the standard theories regarding the creation of the universe.' To *rebuff* a person or thing is to check her or him or it by snubbing or rejecting: 'I rebuffed his offer of help as I didn't trust him.' *See also* refute.

recall/recollect To *recall* something is to remember it, to bring it back to mind: 'He recalled the happy days of his youth.' To *recollect* means the same, but implies that what is remembered is specific or detailed, and can be recalled only with an effort, by collecting one's thoughts: 'I quite clearly recollect paying the bill.'

recant *see* retract

receipt/recipe A *receipt* is the written or printed acknowledgment of a payment: 'It is a good idea to keep receipts in case of a claim or a query.' In the past, a *receipt* was the word for *recipe,* which is now a set of instructions for preparing a food dish: 'Do you know a good recipe for chocolate cake?'

recipe *see* receipt

reciprocal/mutual *Reciprocal* relates to something done by one person or side in return for something (usually similar) done by another, whereas *mutual* relates to something done simultaneously by both sides: 'The two nationals had a reciprocal agreement on trade' (if one traded in an agreed way, the other would), 'The two nations had a mutual agreement on trade' (they traded simultaneously on the same conditions).

reckless/feckless To be *reckless* is to be careless of the consequences of one's action: 'She was accused of reckless driving.' To be *feckless* is to be weak or ineffectual (literally without *feck,* a Scottish form of *effect):* 'He was a feckless father, out drinking much of the time.'

recollect *see* recall

reconcile/conciliate To *reconcile* people or things is to bring them together so that they are compatible: 'I did my best to reconcile the two, although there was little love lost between them,' 'In accounting, it is essential to reconcile the credits with the debits.' To *conciliate* someone is to win him or her over when he or she is hostile or unfriendly, usually by doing or saying something that will please that person: 'Although I was promoted to regional manager instead of Fred, I conciliated him by saying that at least he wouldn't have the hassle of moving.'

recoup *see* recover

recourse *see* resource

recover/recoup To *recover* something is to get it back generally: 'We managed to recover our losses' (we made good). To *recoup* something is to regain or replace it exactly, especially where money is concerned: 'We managed to recoup our losses' (we got our money back).

recur *see* reoccur

red/ruddy *Red* is the standard word for the color; *ruddy* often implies a glowing *red:* 'The red sky augured well for the following day,' 'His red cheeks suggested a fondness for the bottle,' 'The ruddy sky suggested a storm was brewing,' 'With her ruddy cheeks and bright eyes she looked a picture of health.'

redolent *see* reminiscent

redouble/reduplicate To *redouble* something is to increase it (literally by twice as much): 'We redoubled our efforts to complete the work on time.' To *reduplicate* something is to repeat it (strictly speaking just once, so that it is doubled): 'When children begin to talk they often reduplicate words, such a "bobo" and "bick-bick."'

redound *see* resound

reduplicate *see* redouble

refer *see* allude

refund/rebate A *refund* is a return of money paid for something: 'If you are dissatisfied with the product in any way, you are entitled to a full refund.' A *rebate* is a partial *refund* of an amount paid or payable, if certain conditions are observed: 'The firm offers a rebate to customers who pay their bills before the end of the month.'

refurbished *see* refurnished

refurnished/refurbished Premises that have been *refurnished* have been supplied with new furniture: 'We rented an apartment that had only just been refurnished.' If a place had been *refurbished,* it has been modernized, redecorated or re-equipped, or all three, so that it is neat and clean: 'The dingy old museum had been completely refurbished.'

refute/repudiate To *refute* something is to prove it wrong or deny it: 'I refuted his claim to be the senior person there' (I knew that I was, and I could prove it), 'I wish to refute this accusation' (I deny it). To *repudiate* something is to refuse to accept it: 'I repudiated his claim to be the senior person there' (there must surely have been someone senior to him). *See also* rebut.

regal *see* royal

regalia *see* insignia

regardless/irregardless The two words look as if they should be opposites, but they have the same sense, with *irregardless,* actually a non-word, originating as a humorous blend of *irrespective* and *regardless:* 'We went by air, regardless of the cost,' 'He continued his meal, irregardless of the fact that others were waiting.'

regime/regimen A *regime* is a generally prevailing method or system of doing something: 'The staff found life much easier under the new regime.' A *regimen* is a course of beneficial treatment, sometimes one that a person follows independently: 'We had to follow a strict regimen, and were told what we could and could not eat.'

regimen *see* regime

regretfully/regrettably *Regretfully* means 'with regret': 'When I asked if he sold beer, he shook his head regretfully,' 'Regretfully, I must decline your kind offer.' *Regrettably* means 'in a way that should be regretted': 'We had a regrettably poor response to our appeal,' 'Regrettably, you are no longer eligible for the grant.'

regrettably *see* regretfully

reign/rein To *reign* is to rule, while to *rein* is to check. Hence the expression 'give free *rein*' (not *reign),* meaning to allow freedom to someone or something that might otherwise have been held in check (like a horse by its reins): 'She gave the gardener free rein to work as he thought best,' 'Judy gave free rein to her imagination about what she would do if she won the lottery.'

rein *see* reign

reiterate *see* repeat

relation/relationship The *relation* between two things is the specific thing that they have in common: 'Most doctors are convinced of the relation between smoking and lung cancer.' The *relationship* between two things is often more general, or although specific is doubtful: 'Some people think there is little relationship between cholesterol and heart attacks.'

relation/relative As used for a member of the family, there is little difference between the words. However, a *relation* tends to be someone with a regular connection, such as an aunt or grandson, while a *relative* may be someone more remote: 'He held a big party for all his friends and relations,' 'She is a distant relative of mine.'

relationship *see* relation

relative s*ee* relation

relegate *see* delegate

reliable/reliant *Reliable* is used for someone or something that can be relied on: 'Don't worry, she's very reliable.' *Reliant* means dependent: 'They're entirely reliant on government welfare payments for their income.'

reliant *see* reliable

relic/relict A *relic* is something that has survived or been kept from the past, especially something interesting or valuable: 'The museum had an interesting display of relics from shipwrecks,' *'Fair Greece! sad relic of departed worth!'* (Byron). *Relict* is also sometimes used in the same sense, especially in the plural: 'The walls of the director's office were decorated with relicts of the company's early years.' Its chief use, however, is as a scientific term for a remnant of some earlier species or natural formation: 'Some rare plants are often relicts that have survived in a favorable ecological environment.'

relict *see* relic

reluctant/reticent If you are *reluctant* to do something, you don't want to do it: 'I was reluctant to invite her.' If you are *reticent* about something, you don't want to say anything about it: 'She was reticent about the invitation.'

remediable *see* remedial

remedial/remediable Something *remedial* is intended as a remedy; something *remediable* is able to be remedied: 'He has remedial treatment once a week for his backache,' 'All is not lost, and the situation is perfectly remediable.'

reminiscent/redolent If a thing is *reminiscent* of something, it reminds you of it: 'The resort was reminiscent of the one we had stayed in earlier.' If a thing is *redolent* of something, it strongly evokes it: *'On every side Oxford is redolent of age and authority'* (Emerson). *(Redolent* literally means 'having the odor of.')

remission/remittance *Remission* is the condition of being freed from something: 'The prisoner got six months' remission for good behavior,' 'The disease may well have periods of remission, when it will not progress.' A *remittance* is money given as payment for something: 'I enclose my remittance for the goods.'

remittance *see* remission

remonstrate *see* demonstrate

rent *see* hire

reoccur/recur To *reoccur* is to occur or happen again: 'All right, I'll let you off this time, but don't let it reoccur.' To *recur* is either to *reoccur* or to occur repeatedly: 'Her hay fever recurred every summer.'

repairable *see* reparable

reparable/repairable *Reparable* is used only for abstract things: 'The accountant advised that the loss was probably reparable' (the money could be recovered or made up). *Repairable* is used only for concrete things: 'Do you think these shoes are repairable?'

repeat/reiterate/iterate To *repeat* something is to do it again: 'Would you mind repeating that?' To *reiterate* is also to *repeat,* but usually with the aim of emphasizing what has already been said or done: 'I reiterate: we should oppose this ban.' To *iterate* is a formal alternative for *repeat* in the sense 'say again': 'The ambassador iterated his request for a meeting.'

repel/repulse To *repel* someone or something is to drive her or him or it back: 'The troops successfully repelled the attack.' To *repulse* is to do the same, but with greater force: 'After a long struggle, the front-line detachment successfully repulsed the advancing enemy.' In a figurative sense, to *repel* is to produce a feeling of disgust in someone: 'His ingratiating manner repels me.' To *repulse* is to reject coldly or discourteously: 'She repulsed his well-meaning offer.'

repellent *see* repulsive

repertoire/repertory A *repertoire* is properly the range of acts, songs, dances and the like that a particular company or actor can perform, and hence anyone's 'stock' of similar things: 'Uncle Jeff has a good repertoire of corny jokes.' A *repertory* can be the same, but the word usually refers more precisely to the plays that a company performs at one theater over a period of time: 'Many famous performers started their career in repertory companies.'

repertory *see* repertoire

repetitive/repetitious Both words relate to something that repeats, but whereas *repetitive* is usually neutral in tone, *repetitious* implies that the repeating is unnecessary or tedious: 'I could heart the loud repetitive beat of the disco music,' 'The chairman's speech was lengthy and repetitious, and I longed for it to end.'

replenishment/repletion *Replenishment* is the act of filling something up, or the thing that is used to fill something up: 'The assistant manager regularly monitored the replenishment of stocks in the store.' *Repletion* is the state of being filled up: 'The shelves were filled to repletion with every kind of food.'

repletion *see* replenishment

replicate *see* reproduce

reportedly *see* reputedly

repository *see* depository

repression *see* 1) depression, 2) oppression

reproach/reprove/rebuke To *reproach* someone is to blame him or her for something: 'I reproached her for her forgetfulness.' To *reprove* someone is to blame and scold him or her simultaneously: 'The teacher frequently had to reprove the boy for his outbursts of temper.' To *rebuke* someone is to scold him or her for what he or she is doing or has done: 'The speaker rebuked anyone who interrupted him.'

reproduce/replicate Generally, to *reproduce* something is to produce a copy of it, while to *replicate* something is to produce a precise or detailed copy of it: 'Our new copier can reproduce color photos,' 'The artist specialized in replicating paintings by Constable.'

reprove *see* reproach

repudiate *see* refute

repugnant *see* repulsive

repulse *see* repel

repulsive/repugnant/repellent Something *repulsive* is disgusting or 'sick-making': 'There was a repulsive mess where the dog had been.' Something *repugnant* is unpleasant or 'off-putting': 'I find your suggestion rather repugnant.' Something *repellent* (or *repellant*) is *repulsive,* but the word implies that the thing actively turns you away or puts you off: 'When Susie became a vegetarian, the very sight of meat was repellent to her.' There is considerable overlap in all three words, however.

reputedly/reportedly *Reputedly* is used for something that is alleged to be true: 'The beach was reputedly one of the finest' (people said that it was, and it probably was). *Reportedly* is used for something that is rumored: 'The beach was reportedly one of the finest' (people said that it was, but it might not have been).

requirement/requisite/perquisite/prerequisite A *requirement* is generally what is necessary for something: 'It is a requirement that you live here for at least six months.' A *requisite* is something that is essential or indispensable: 'The firm provided all requisites for the work.' A *perquisite,* or *perk,* is an additional benefit of some kind (*see* privilege). A *prerequisite* is something required as a prior condition: 'Good eyesight is a prerequisite for a driving test.'

requisite *see* requirement

reservation/reserve/preserve As applied to tracts of land set apart for a particular purpose, a *reservation* is the usual term for a territory in the United States or Canada that is occupied by Native Americans: 'The Apaches were sent to Florida after they refused to remain on a reservation in Arizona.' A *reserve* is usually associated with animals, especially wildlife, and with trees and plants: 'There are around 500 national and local nature reserves in Great Britain.' A *preserve* is similar, but is a place where game or fish are protected, usually for sport: 'The castle moat had been turned into a preserve for carp and pike.'

reserve *see* reservation

resin/rosin *Resin* is the sticky stuff that oozes from certain trees, or a similar synthetic substance used for making plastics: 'Resin exudes naturally from the fir and pine.' *Rosin* is the product made from the natural substance and used for the bows of stringed instruments, the shoes of boxers and ballet dancers, and the hands of gymnasts, among other things: 'The cellist rubbed her bow carefully with rosin.'

resolution/motion If a *resolution* is passed at a meeting, it means that a proposed action is agreed; if a *motion* is passed, the proposed action will actually take place: 'The meeting passed a resolution to ban smoking at all future meetings' (they were all agreed it was a good idea), 'The meeting passed a motion to ban smoking at all future meetings' (they agreed to ban smoking, and they did ban it).

resort *see* resource

resound/redound In a figurative sense, to *resound* (literally 're-echo') is to be famed or celebrated: 'The name of Shakespeare resounds down the ages.' To *redound* is to have favorable or unfavorable effect on somebody or something: 'Her bravery redounds to her credit.' (The word may have been influenced by *renown).*

resource/resort/recourse A *resource* is something that one can turn to when needed: 'The pilot knew that his only resource was to eject and parachute to safety.' A *resort* is something one *actually* turns to for help, especially when all else has failed: 'As a last resort, I contacted the police.' The word is also a verb: 'Whenever she had a headache, she would resort to lying on the bed with her eyes closed.' *Recourse* is the act of *resorting* to someone or something: 'When roused, he would frequently have recourse to bad language.'

respectable/respectful *Respectable* is used for a person or thing that is worthy of respect or that is decent and proper: 'They are a respectable middle-aged couple,' 'Although he had just had a shower, he was perfectly respectable wrapped in a bath towel.' *Respectful* means showing respect: 'We kept a respectful distance from the car in front.'

respectably/respectively *Respectably* relates to someone or something that is respectable: 'The children were respectably dressed in their blue and grey uniforms' (they looked neat and tidy in them). *Respectively* relates to each person or thing separately: 'The children were respectively dressed in their blue and grey uniforms' (one was wearing a blue uniform and the other a grey). *See also* respectable.

respectful *see* respectable

respectively *see* respectably

restive *see* restless

restless/restive *Restless* is used for a person or thing that has or gives little rest: 'She spent a restless night worrying about the bills,' *'Never more, Sailor,/Shalt thou be/Tossed on the wind-ridden/Restless sea'* (Walter de la Mare). *Restive* is used for a person or thing that is uneasy, or impatient of authority: 'Horses can be restive creatures, anxious to be moving when they should be standing still.'

restraint *see* constraint

retch/reach/keck/puke To *retch* is to vomit suddenly, or attempt to do so: 'The very thought of the meal made him retch.' To *reach* is a colloquial form of the same word, probably associated with the idea of reaching out or over: 'We had a really rough crossing, and I reached several times.' To *keck* is to make the sound of someone about to vomit: 'She tried to swallow the pills, but they kept making her keck.' To *puke* actually is to vomit, but the word is often used figuratively for someone or something that disgusts or nauseates: 'He really makes me puke.'

reticent *see* reluctant

retire/retreat In military terms, to *retire* is to withdraw for tactical or strategic reasons: 'After launching the attack, the platoon retired to their new base.' To *retreat* is to make an obligatory withdrawal when faced with a superior force: 'The enemy retreated behind the lines.' These two senses are carried over into general use: 'I then retired for the night,' *'But see, the shepherds shun the noonday heat,/The lowing herds to murm'ring brooks retreat'* (Pope).

retort/riposte To *retort* is to reply angrily or defiantly: '"Speak for yourself," she retorted.' To *riposte* is to respond quickly and sharply to a particular statement or situation: 'When Hitler invaded Poland, Britain riposted by declaring war on Germany.'

retract/recant To *retract* a statement or opinion is to withdraw it, often voluntarily: 'The accused later retracted his confession.' To *recant* is to *retract* or deny what one has said, usually under pressure: 'During her trial, Joan of Arc refused to recant her declaration that she had heard voices from God.'

retreat *see* retire

retroactive *see* retrospective

retrospective/retroactive If something is *retrospective*, it applies to the past as well as to the present and the future: 'The legislation was made retrospective.' If something is *retroactive*, it is made effective from a past date: 'The law was made retroactive to January 1st' (as if it had been introduced then).

revenge *see* avenge

reverend *see* reverent

reverent/reverential/reverend *Reverent* relates to a feeling or expression of reverence: 'The mourners stood in reverent silence by the grave.' *Reverential* is similar, but often relates more to a show of respect rather than of genuine reverence: 'The usher gave a reverential bow to the judge.' *Reverend* in its broadest sense is used for someone or something treated with reverence, especially when old or holy: *'How reverend is the face of this tall pile,'/Whose ancient pillars rear their marble heads'* (Congreve). From this is gained its use as a clergy title: 'The sermon was preached by the Reverend Charles Potter.'

reverential *see* reverent

reversal/reversion A *reversal* is the turning of something to the opposite of what it was: 'His good fortune suffered a cruel reversal' (i.e., his luck changed for the worse). A *reversion* is a return to an earlier condition or state: 'For some time after the introduction of the new currency, many people demanded a reversion to the old money.'

reverse *see* converse

reversion *see* reversal

review/revue A *review* is a re-examination, survey or report: 'This schedule is subject to review,' 'Most company reports include a financial review of the year,' 'I quite agreed with the review of the TV program.' A *revue* (the French equivalent) is a theatrical entertainment, either of song and dance, and purely for pleasure, or satirical in some way: 'After the war many traditional spectacular revues turned into night club or strip-tease shows,' 'One of the great TV satirical revues is *Saturday Night Live.'*

revolt/revolution A *revolt* is a rebellion or uprising against authority, usually by a particular or local group of people: 'In the Peasants' Revolt of 1381, the English peasants demanded an end to serfdom.' A *revolution* is a much bigger affair, and is the overthrow of a political system or government: 'The Russian Revolution of 1917 overthrew the Romanov dynasty and set up a Communist state,' 'Louis XVI of France: "C'est une révolte?" Duc de la Rochefoucauld-Liancourt: "Non, Sire, c'est une révolution".'

revolution *see* revolt

revolve/rotate The two words are largely synonymous. However, to *revolve* is used for one thing going around another, whereas to *rotate* is used only for something turning around its own center: 'The Moon revolves around the Earth, and the Earth rotates on its own axis.'

revue *see* review

reward/award A *reward* is a recompense for something deserved, often a single, specific action: 'The owner offers a reward to anyone finding the missing dog,' 'Virtue is its own reward.' An *award* is an official recognition of prowess or excellence in a particular field, often over a period of time: 'The actress has won three Tony awards.'

rheumatism/arthritis *Rheumatism* is a disease of the joints or muscles; *arthritis* of the joints only: 'The old lady asked the doctor for something for her rheumatism, but he said she actually had a touch of arthritis.'

right/ripe The time is *right* to do something when a particular moment is reached: 'The time was right to propose a second plan.' The time is *ripe* for something when it has been 'brewing' for some time, and the right moment has arrived or will arrive: 'The time will soon be ripe to try something more complicated,' 'When time is ripe—which will be suddenly,—/I'll steal to Glendower and Lord Mortimer' (Shakespeare).

rigorous *see* vigorous

rim/brim The *rim* of something is its edge or border: 'It looked as if the rim of the cup was cracked.' The *brim* of something is the inside top part, by or at the *rim*, when it is full: 'The glass had been filled to the brim.'

ring/wring To *ring* is to make a resonant sound or mark with a circle: 'Did the phone ring?' 'Someone is ringing at the door,' 'I had to ring the misprints in the article.' To *wring* is to squeeze, whether literally or figuratively: 'Did you wring out your washcloth?' 'It wrings my heart to see the way they treat their children.'

ripe *see* right

riposte *see* retort

rise/arise/raise To *rise* is to move upwards: 'The sun began to rise,' 'That morning I rose early.' To *arise* is to *rise* in a poetic or archaic sense, but otherwise is to come into notice or 'turn up': '*I will arise and go to my father*' (Bible: Luke 15:18), 'A fresh doubt then arose in my mind.' To *raise* is to lift something or move it upwards: 'I raise this toast in memory of absent friends.'

risky *see* risqué

risqué/risky Something *risqué* is slightly indecent or 'near the knuckle': 'He told a rather risqué joke.' Something *risky* is hazardous or may well go wrong: 'Investing in stocks and bonds is a risky business.'

rite/ritual A *rite* is a special ceremony, often a religious or socially significant one: 'The Aborigines undergo rites of initiation at puberty.' A *ritual* is the prescribed formula or established procedure for carrying something out, usually formally: 'The ritual of the Orthodox Church in many ways resembles that of the Catholic Church,' 'A stroll in the park after lunch was part of her daily ritual.'

ritual *see* rite

rogue *see* rascal

role/roll A *role* (or *rôle*) is an actor's part in a play or the duties undertaken by somebody: 'Versatile actors can play many different roles,' 'The proud father took on a new role: that of babysitter.' A *roll* is a list of people: 'John checked the electoral roll to see if he was entitled to vote.'

roll *see* role

root out/rout out To *root out* something is to remove it or eliminate it completely: 'The government said it was determined to root out corruption.' To *rout out* somebody is to force him or her out of a place: 'We were routed out of bed to pack our things.'

rosin *see* resin

roster *see* rota

rota/roster Both words relate to a list of people, setting out the order in which they carry out their duties. If there is a difference, it is that a *rota*

(Latin for 'wheel') has a regular and repeating 'round' of names and duties, while a *roster* is more concerned with the individuals and their duties: 'There was a rota for doing the dishes' (everyone did them in turn), 'The truck drivers worked according to a roster' (they knew when and where each one had to drive).

rotate *see* revolve

rotund/orotund *Rotund* is used for a plump or fat person: 'I could see his rotund figure waddling up the street.' *Orotund* applies to a tone of voice that is grandiloquent (see **magniloquence**) and even pompous: 'The minister was famous for the orotund delivery of his sermons.'

rouse/arouse Apart from the general sense of 'to wake,' the two words have different shades of meaning. To *rouse* is to create or excite a strong feeling or emotion: 'She was roused to action by pangs of jealousy' (which she did not previously have). To *arouse* is to stimulate a feeling that is already latently present: 'The sight aroused the crew's sense of pride and patriotism' (which they already had).

rout/route A *rout* is an overwhelming defeat, usually one ending in disorder: 'After the tenth home run, the game became a rout.' A *route* is the course taken by someone or something: 'We came home by the shortest route.' As verbs in the past tense the two words look identical: 'The army was routed over the hill' (it was defeated there), 'The army was routed over the hill' (it was sent that way).

route *see* rout

rout out *see* root out

royal/regal As used for a monarch, *royal* has more to do with the monarchy, together with its status and ceremonies, while *regal* has to do with the monarch as a person. 'The guard fired a royal salute' (not a 'regal' one), 'The fashion model had a regal bearing that was the envy of her colleagues' (not a 'royal' one).

ruckus *see* rumpus

ruction *see* rumpus

ruddy *see* red

rude/rudimentary One of the senses of *rude* is 'primitive': 'Our ancestors used rude stone implements for building.' *Rudimentary* also has this sense, but implies that what is described is imperfectly formed or developed: 'The Manx cat has only a rudimentary tail.'

rudimentary *see* rude

ruin/ruination *Ruin* is severe damage or complete financial loss; *ruination* is the act of being ruined, or the thing or person that causes ruin: 'If we don't win more orders we face ruin' (we'll be broke), 'These account sheets spell ruination' (they mean we'll be ruined), 'Do stop— you'll be the ruination of me!'

ruination s*ee* ruin

rumpled *see* crumpled

rumpus/ruction/ruckus A *rumpus* is a noisy disturbance or commotion of some kind: 'Hey, you kids, stop that rumpus at once!' A *ruction* (often plural) is similar, but usually involves a quarrel or argument: 'She knew there would be ructions if she arrived late for any reason.' A *ruckus* is more or less a combination of the two: 'There was usually a ruckus in the locker room after the game.'

rural/rustic *Rural* has to do with the country or countryside, as opposed to the town: 'Rural amenities are inevitably more basic than urban ones,' 'Teresa loved the peaceful rural setting of the place.' *Rustic* has to do with the country as being characteristically simple, quaint or attractive: 'I sat for a while on the rustic seat under the oak,' 'The couple lived in rustic simplicity in a little village.'

rush/dash To *rush* is to hurry, perhaps carelessly or clumsily: 'She rushed to the store before it closed.' To *dash* is to go somewhere at great speed: 'He dashed downstairs to answer the door,' 'The fox dashed into the wood.' Compare also the implications of: 'I must rush!' (or I will be late), 'I must dash!' (it is already late).

rustic s*ee* rural

S

saccharin/saccharine *Saccharin* is the artificial sweetener: 'She always had saccharin in her coffee, not sugar.' *Saccharine* is used to describe something excessively sweet: 'She gave me a saccharine smile.'

saccharine see saccharin

sacred/sacrosanct If something is *sacred* (apart from the literal sense of being holy), it is respected and important: 'His morning hour in the bathroom is sacred' (he has to have it), 'Is nothing sacred?' If a thing is *sacrosanct,* it is so *sacred* in this sense that it cannot be changed or altered: 'His morning hour in the bathroom is sacrosanct' (he and it are categorically unavailable then).

sacrosanct see sacred

sadism/masochism *Sadism* is the desire to inflict pain on others for sexual pleasure; *masochism* is the desire to have pain inflicted on oneself for the same reason: 'Sadism is named after the French soldier and writer, the Marquis de Sade; masochism after the Austrian novelist Leopold von Sacher Masoch.'

salary/wages *Salary* is usually reckoned by the year and paid monthly or weekly; *wages* are usually reckoned, and paid, weekly or daily: 'His salary has been frozen for six months,' 'Most workers get their wages on Friday.'

sally *see* sortie

salon/saloon A *salon* is generally associated with fashion, and a *saloon* with entertainment: 'The hotel had both a beauty salon and a dancing saloon.'

saloon *see* salon

salubrious *see* sanitary

salutary *see* sanitary

Salvador/San Salvador/El Salvador *Salvador* is a large city and port in eastern Brazil. *San Salvador* is the capital of *El Salvador,* a country in Central America formerly known as *Salvador:* 'The name Salvador is both Spanish and Portuguese for "Savior".'

same/similar If two things are the *same,* they are identical; if they are *similar* they are not quite the *same:* 'We have the same tastes in music' (our musical tastes are identical), 'We have similar tastes in music' (our tastes are broadly the same, although we have particular preferences that distinguish us).

sample *see* example

sanitary/salutary/salubrious *Sanitary* relates to health and hygiene generally: 'The hospital maintained the highest sanitary conditions,' 'We had a snack in a not very sanitary café.' *Salutary* relates to something beneficial: 'There's nothing like a salutary swim before breakfast,' 'Let that be a salutary warning to you.' *Salubrious* is used for something favorable to health and well-being: 'The campers planned to move to a more salubrious site.'

San Salvador *see* Salvador

sarcastic/sardonic *Sarcastic* is used for a sneering speech or tone of voice, with the speaker often deliberately saying the opposite of what is expected: '"Of course, that wouldn't occur to you, would it?" he snapped, with a sarcastic leer.' *Sardonic* relates to irony or mockery, often in a grimly humorous way: '"What sort of breakfast do you call this? I'm the breadwinner, not the burnt toast winner," he said with a sardonic sneer.'

sardonic *see* sarcastic

sat *see* sitting

sated/satiated/saturated To be *sated* is to be satisfied to the full: 'After a good lunch, their appetites were entirely sated.' To be *satiated* is to have too much of something, so that in many cases one grows tired of it: 'My interest in pop music is now quite satiated after watching all those videos.' To be *saturated* is to be completely filled with or by something: 'We lay motionless on the sand, saturated in the warm rays of the sun.'

satiated *see* sated

satire/satyr *Satire* is the method of attacking absurd or bad or imperfect things by making fun of them: 'The comedy was a satire on the police force.' A *satyr* is a creature in classical mythology who was half man and half goat: *'And the hoofed heel of a satyr crushes/The chestnut-husk at the chestnut-root'* (Swinburne).

saturated *see* sated

satyr *see* satire

saunter *see* stroll

savor *see* flavor

scamp/skimp/scrimp/stint To *scamp* something is to do it hastily or perfunctorily: 'It's not good for you to scamp breakfast like that.' To *skimp* is virtually the same, but suggests an inadequate or incomplete action: 'Polly usually skimped on the cleaning.' To *scrimp* is to be very sparing or economical: 'She scrimped and saved to buy the new dress.' To *stint* is to be miserly or mean with something: 'There's no need to stint on the milk, there's plenty more in the fridge.'

scant *see* scarce

scanty *see* scarce

scarce/scant/scanty/sparse If something is *scarce,* it is in short supply: 'Cucumbers are scarce this summer.' *Scant* is usually used for something abstract that is smaller in amount than expected: 'The critics paid scant attention to her next novel.' *Scanty* means more or less the same, but mostly applies to a concrete object that is smaller than expected: 'There was only a scanty crop of wheat that year,' 'Her scanty dress drew stares from some, headshakes from others.' *Sparse* is used for something thinly distributed or scattered: 'He carefully combed his sparse grey hair,' 'The population was sparse in the hillier regions.'

scent *see* perfume

schedule *see* scheme

scheme/schedule A *scheme* is a plan of something, or for something: 'He explained his scheme to us.' A *schedule* is a plan or procedure for something, with particular regard to the time needed: 'The new work schedule was an improvement on the old.'

science *see* art

scorn/spurn/shun To *scorn* someone or something is to treat that person or thing with contempt, especially when refusing or rejecting something: 'He scorned all offers of help' (although he may have actually accepted one, albeit reluctantly). To *spurn* actually *is* to reject, but with disdain: 'She spurned all offers of help" (she would not accept any of them). To *shun* a person or thing is to keep away from her or him or it: 'He gradually withdrew into himself and shunned all company.'

Scotch *see* Scottish

Scots *see* Scottish

Scottish/Scotch/Scots *Scottish* is used for things relating to Scotland as a whole: 'The Scottish Highlands are sparsely populated,' 'She was singing an old Scottish song.' *Scotch* is mostly used in fixed phrases relating to objects traditionally (or supposedly) associated with Scotland: 'For supper he had Scotch broth and a couple of Scotch eggs followed by a glass of Scotch whiskey.' *Scots* usually refers to someone native to Scotland: 'He married a Scots girl.'

scowl *see* frown

scream/screech/shriek To *scream* is to give a loud, high-pitched cry, usually through fear, anger, frustration, pain, or other extreme emotion: 'The slave screamed as the whip struck his back,' 'The girls screamed when at last their idol appeared.' To *screech* is to give a disagreeably shrill or harsh cry: '"Leave me alone!" screeched the old woman,' 'An owl screeched in a nearby tree.' To *shriek* is to give a brief, high-pitched cry from any sudden emotion or reaction: 'Sandy shrieked when the window flew open,' 'When I showed Philip the photo, he shrieked with laughter.'

screech *see* scream

scrimmage/scrummage/scrum A *scrimmage* is any general confused tussle or struggle, as also is a *scrum* (although perhaps a more local one): 'There was a real scrimmage outside the store before the sale, and a scrum around the bargain counter as soon as the doors opened.' A *scrummage* (or *scrum)* is a set formation in Rugby football. In American football, a *scrimmage* is the action that takes place between the teams from the moment the ball is put into play until the moment the play is declared dead.

scrimp *see* scamp

scrub *see* bush

scrum *see* scrimmage

scrummage *see* scrimmage

scrumptious/sumptuous *Scrumptious* is a colloquial word used to describe very tasty or appetizing food: 'We had a scrumptious picnic yesterday.' *Sumptuous* can also be used for food, but can apply to anything that is (or looks) expensive and splendid: 'I'm not really used to such sumptuous fare,' 'The portrait was of an aristocratic young lady in a sumptuous dress.'

scupper *see* scuttle

scurry/scuttle To *scurry* is to move rapidly or urgently: 'A mouse scurried across the floor,' 'When the shooting started, we all scurried for cover.' To *scuttle* is to move with short, hasty steps: 'A squirrel scuttled across the road,' 'The old schoolmaster scuttled into his study.'

scuttle/scupper To *scuttle* a ship or boat is to make it sink by cutting holes in the bottom or opening the seacocks (the valves below the waterline) to let water in or pump it out: 'The fleet was scuttled in a matter of days,' 'The crew decided it would be best to scuttle the ship.' To *scupper* is either to *scuttle* one's own ship or to ruin or disable someone or something: 'The city council scuppered his plans to build an extension.'

scuttle *see* scurry

seamy *see* steamy

seasonable *see* seasonal

seasonal/seasonable If something is *seasonal,* it relates to a particular season (often summer): 'He got seasonal work renting deck chairs on the beach.' If a thing is *seasonable,* it is appropriate for the season or occasion: 'The snow was unexpected but seasonable for the time of year,' 'I wanted to give him some seasonable advice.'

seated *see* sitting

section/sector A *section* is a distinctive part of something: 'The paper came in six sections.' 'There was little concern for the underprivileged section of society.' A *sector* is similar, but is more precisely defined and frequently relates to a country's economy: 'An increasing number of companies were joining the private sector,' 'Many self-employed people work in the service sector, in hotels and restaurants.'

sector *see* section

secure/procure To *secure* something is to obtain it for certain: 'I've managed to secure a couple of seats.' To *procure* is to obtain something by care or effort: 'The buyer said it was not always easy to procure the right grade of tea.'

sedulous *see* assiduous

sensibility *see* sensitivity

sensitivity/sensibility/susceptibility *Sensitivity* relates to being sensitive: 'I thought you showed a remarkable lack of sensitivity.' *Sensibility* relates to being sensible, in the sense of having delicate or deep feelings: 'He is a composer of considerable sensibility,' 'His coarse remarks wounded the sensibilities of many of those present.' *Susceptibility* is close in meaning, but relates to being susceptible, that is, easily influenced or impressionable: 'It would be unfair to take advantage of her susceptibility in this matter.' In the plural the word refers to the ease with which a person is hurt or offended: 'At the risk of offending your susceptibilities, I suggest you stop watching such trash.'

sensual/sensuous *Sensual* usually relates to physical and specifically sexual pleasures: 'She delighted in the sensual warmth of the sun,' 'He observed the sensual sway of her hips.' *Sensuous* relates to something that appeals to the senses (sight, smell, hearing, touch, taste), especially when it is luxurious: 'There was a scent of new-mown hay, warm and sensuous,' 'She ran her sensuous fingers down his arm.'

sensuous *see* sensual

sentiment/sentimentality *Sentiment* relates to feelings of tenderness or sadness: 'There's not much room for sentiment when you're a farmer.' *Sentimentality* is exaggerated or affected *sentiment:* 'For many people, Christmas is not so much a season of sentiment as one of self-indulgent sentimentality.'

sentimentality *see* sentiment

seraphic *see* chubby

serial/series A *serial* is a story, program or the like that is told, written or broadcast in stages: 'The new radio serial was very popular' (with the same participants throughout). A *series* is a set of stories or programs on a common theme, with each complete in itself: 'There was an interesting TV series on railroad journeys' (each program had a different person going on a different journey).

series *see* serial

serve/service To *serve* is to perform a service: 'This old coat has served me well over the years,' *'No man can serve two masters'* (Bible: Matthew 6:24). To *service* is to supply a service or services, especially the maintenance of a vehicle or machine: 'I must take the car to be serviced,' 'The industrial complex is serviced by road and rail transport.'

service *see* serve

sewage/sewerage *Sewage* is the waste material that passes through sewers: 'Local residents protested at the amount of untreated sewage being discharged into the sea.' *Sewerage* is the system by which *sewage* is removed and treated, including the sewers themselves: 'The water company's bill included a charge for the sewerage service.'

sewerage *see* sewage

shade s*ee* shadow

shadow/shade A *shadow* is the dark outlines of something seen against a light background, or figuratively a simple image of the real thing: 'The shadow of the tree fell on the house,' *'Life's but a walking shadow'* (Shakespeare). *Shade* is used for a place that is cooler and darker than elsewhere because it is protected from heat or light by an object's *shadow:* 'We sat in the shade of the old oak tree.' *Shade* is normally used for the sun, whereas any light can cast a *shadow.*

shallow/callow A *shallow* person or thing is superficial or lacking in depth: 'Her whole life was simply a shallow existence, trivial and wasteful.' A *callow* person is immature and lacks experience: 'He was the proverbial callow youth, with much to learn about life.'

shindig *see* shindy

shindy/shindig The two words can be used interchangeably, although a *shindy* is often a quarrel or commotion and a *shindig* a noisy party: 'There was a real shindy in the bar yesterday when the bartender refused to serve one group,' 'Shall I see you at the shindig tomorrow?'

ship *see* boat

shiver/quiver To *shiver* is to shake or tremble, especially with cold but also from some strong feeling or emotion, such as fear; 'There was no heat, and we were shivering all morning,' 'She shivered at the thought of what had happened.' To *quiver* is also to tremble in this way, but often less markedly and with part of the body only: 'His fingers quivered nervously as he began to play,' 'The dog snuffled eagerly in the hedge, its tail quivering with excitement.'

shoot/chute In the sense of something steep, a *shoot* is a descent in a stream or river, while a *chute* is a passage or channel down which things can be slid or dropped: 'A single shoot through the rocks carried the canoe down the rapids,' 'Each morning, sheets from the hotel bedrooms were put down the laundry chute.'

shriek *see* scream

shrub *see* bush

shun *see* scorn

sick *see* ill

sieve *see* sift

sift/sieve As used figuratively, to *sift* something is to examine it closely or minutely: 'He sifted through the correspondence on the matter,' 'The detective began to sift the evidence.' To *sieve* someone or something is to submit him or her or it to a selection or weeding-out process: 'We must first sieve out the defaulters.'

signal/single To *signal* something is to communicate or indicate it: 'A new supplier was signaled' (it was indicated). To *single* someone (usually but not always single *out)* is to pick him or her out: 'The boss singled you from the rest,' 'The patients were singled out for special treatment,' *'Bold of your worthiness, we single you/As our best-moving fair solicitor'* (Shakespeare).

silicon/silicone *Silicon* is the non-metallic chemical element used for making microchips: 'The Santa Clara valley, in California, is known as Silicon Valley because many of the country's leading computer firms are located there.' *Silicone* is a compound made from *silicon* that has various domestic and surgical applications: 'Silicone has been widely used as a plastic in breast implants.'

silicone *see* silicon

similar *see* same

simile/metaphor A *simile* is a direct comparison between two things, however unlikely or incompatible: 'His favorite simile for a lazy person was "dozy as a dormouse."' A *metaphor* uses a literal word or phrase in a figurative sense, often (unless hackneyed) evoking a vivid or original mental picture: 'Cheryl was a great lover of metaphor, saying things like "He's out of his tree" and "Look what the cat dragged in."'

simple/simplistic Something *simple* is easy and straightforward: 'The system is a simple one, and works well,' 'He led a simple life, eating frugally and hardly drinking at all.' *Simplistic* is used for something that is oversimplified or at best naively simple: 'The writer gave a rather simplistic analysis of the situation,' 'To say that we need a monarchy because we are insecure without one is simplistic nonsense.'

simplistic *see* simple

single *see* signal

sissy *see* prim

sitting/sat/seated *Sitting* is used for a person who has adopted a seated position: 'She was sitting in the corner.' Some people used *sat* in the same way: 'She was sat in the corner.' However, this is usually regarded as incorrect or at best jarring. *Seated* means the same as *sitting* but emphasizes the type of seat or its location: 'The spectators were seated on benches,' *'Seated one day at the organ,/I was weary and ill at ease'* (Adelaide Ann Proctor).

skeptical *see* cynical

skewbald *see* piebald

skilled *see* skillful

skillful/skilled In their most general senses, *skillful* means showing skill, while *skilled* means having skills: 'The talks were conducted by a skillful negotiator' (who handled matters adroitly), 'The talks were conducted by a skilled negotiator' (an experienced one).

skimp *see* scamp

skulk *see* sneak

slag/slut A *slag* or a *slut* is a woman who looks disreputable and who is regarded as sexually immoral. However, *slag* stresses the sexual side and *slut* the appearance, so that the two are not really incompatible: 'There was real trouble when one carnival queen called the other a slag, a slut and a bitch.' *See also* sloven.

slander *see* libel

slang/jargon Broadly speaking, *slang* is colloquial or nonstandard English, whether generally or as used by a particular group of people, while *jargon* is the regular specialized vocabulary and phraseology used by such a group: 'The children's slang word for days when the school was closed for teacher training was "freebie," while in the jargon of the teachers themselves they were "retread days."'

slattern *see* sloven

slaver/slobber To *slaver* is to let saliva run out of one's mouth, otherwise to drool: 'The dog slavered when it saw its dinner being prepared.' To *slobber* is virtually the same, although the word can apply to food as well as saliva: 'The baby slobbered food onto its bib.'

sledge/sleigh The two words are largely interchangeable, although *sledge* tends to be used more for loads and *sleigh* for people: 'Captain Scott's Antarctic expedition was equipped with motor sledges as well as pony and dog teams,' *'Oh what fun it is to ride in a one-horse open sleigh'* (popular song).

sleek *see* slick

sleigh *see* sledge

slender *see* slim

slick/sleek The two words are close in meaning, although *slick* tends to mean smooth and glossy (or smooth and slippery), while *sleek* means more smooth and shiny. *Slick,* too, is typically used for a road surface, while *sleek* more often applies to hair or an animal's fur: 'The racetrack was slick with rain and grease,' 'We admired the sleek coats of the greyhounds.'

slight *see* 1) slim, 2) slur

slim/slight/slender As used for a person, *slim* means not fat (especially after losing weight), *slight* means *slim* and delicate, and *slender* means *slim* and well-formed. It is of course possible to be more than one of these at the same time: 'A slim young man came into the room,' 'The gymnast's slight and slender figure was the envy of many of the girls watching.'

slink *see* sneak

slit/slot A *slit* is a narrow opening or crack in something: 'We could see what was happening through a slit in the fence.' A *slot* is similar, but is usually intended for the insertion of something: 'I put a coin in the slot, but the machine was apparently empty.'

slobber *see* slaver

slosh *see* splash

slot *see* slit

sloven/slattern A *sloven* is someone who is untidy or dirty in appearance or dress or negligent in his or her work: 'The waiter was a real sloven, wearing a stained jacket and taking ages to bring our orders.' A *slattern* is a woman or girl who is a *sloven:* 'His wife was nothing but a slattern.' *See also* slag.

sludge *see* slush

sluggard *see* lag

slur/slight A *slur* is a remark or accusation, usually a false one, that damages a person's reputation: 'I don't wish to cast a slur on his understandable popularity, but doesn't he have something of a record?' A *slight* is a remark that offends someone: 'All that year, Brenda patiently tolerated the slights of her colleagues.'

slush/sludge *Slush* tends to be more liquid than *sludge,* or *sludge* more solid than *slush:* 'We walked through the slush and wet of the melting snow,' 'We walked through the mud and sludge of the field.'

slut *see* slag

smother/stifle/strangle/suffocate To *smother* someone is to kill him or her by preventing him or her from breathing, the agent often being something choking such as smoke or feathers: 'The Princes in the Tower are believed to have been smothered with pillows as they slept.' To *stifle* a person is to kill him or her or overpower him or her to some extent by covering his or her mouth or nose or by making him or her breathe something other than pure air: 'The atmosphere in here is stifling: please open a window.' To *strangle* someone is to kill him or her by compressing his or her throat (for example with a rope or one's hands) so that he or she cannot breathe: 'Two of the victims had been strangled, and one apparently smothered.' To *suffocate* is to kill or overpower someone by any means that deprives him or her of air: 'I almost suffocated in the heat and smoke of the fire.'

snazzy *see* jazzy

sneak/slink/skulk To *sneak* is to move furtively or stealthily so as not to be heard or seen: 'I found he had sneaked in behind me to watch the TV.' To *slink* is to move both furtively and abjectly: 'The dog slunk away with its tail between its legs.' To *skulk* is to move slyly or lie low, especially when doing something wrong or cowardly: 'The sailors were seen skulking through the back streets,' 'The fox was skulking in the undergrowth.'

snicker s*ee* giggle

snigger *see* giggle

snooze *see* doze

sociable *see* social

social/sociable *Social* relates to society in some way: 'I'm not doing this out of a sense of social duty,' 'The two children were friends, although each came from quite a different social background.' *Sociable* relates to the enjoyment of company: 'She was a sociable old lady, and always liked a good chat,' '*Society is no comfort/To one not sociable*' (Shakespeare).

solecism/solipsism A *solecism* is a mistake in the use of language, or more generally an offense against good manners or etiquette" 'To say "seasonal" when you mean "seasonable" is a solecism,' 'Pouring tea from your cup into the saucer to cool it is a solecism.' *Solipsism* is the theory that there can be no existence apart from one's own: 'Solipsism is an extreme form of subjective idealism.'

solid/stolid/stout As applied to character or temperament, *solid* means reliable or genuine: 'Charlie was a good solid worker, completely dependable,' 'The neighbors were respectable but dull people, typical solid citizens.' *Stolid* is used for someone who is dull and unemotional, or who moves slowly and seriously: 'He gave me his stolid support,'

'The sergeant made his stolid way down the ranks.' *Stout* means brave and strong or firm and strong: 'Despite his wounds, the stout old soldier marched bravely on,' 'He was stout in his support for the plan.'

soliloquy *see* monologue

solipsism *see* solecism

soluble/solvable Both words describe something that can be solved. However, *soluble* is also used for something that is *dis*solved: 'Have you any soluble aspirin?' *Solvable* is thus more often used for problems and puzzles: 'The crossword puzzle was solvable after all.'

solvable *see* soluble

sometime/sometimes *Sometime* (or *some time*) relates to a particular but unspecified time; *sometimes* means occasionally, or from time to time: 'I went there sometime last year' (I can't remember when exactly), 'I went there sometimes last year' (on occasion).

sometimes *see* sometime

sortie/sally A *sortie* is a brief trip to a place, especially an unfamiliar one: 'She enjoyed rare sorties to the shops,' 'We planned our holiday carefully, making sorties to all sorts of new places.' A *sally* is similar, but refers more to the start of a visit or journey: 'For our next sally, I suggest an excursion to Florida.' The word is more common as a verb: 'We sallied forth into the cold, wintry night.'

souse *see* douse

sparse *see* scarce

spasmodically *see* sporadically

spatter *see* splutter

specially/especially *Specially* refers to something done for a particular purpose or in a particular way: 'The rules were specially designed to make the game easy to play,' 'The stores will open specially tomorrow,' 'She was specially interested in the old prints' (she took a particular interest in them). *Especially* relates to the degree to which something is done, and usually means little more that 'very': 'It was not especially late,' 'This is an especially difficult problem,' 'She was especially interested in the old prints' (she was very interested in them).

specimen *see* example

specious/spurious If something is *specious* it seems right or true but is actually wrong or false: 'Your reasoning is specious: you have ignored certain basic facts.' If a thing is *spurious* it is fake or false, and can be seen to be such: 'The woman was known to have made several spurious claims for income support.'

specter s*ee* spook

spire/steeple Strictly speaking, a *spire* is the tall, pointed structure on top of a church tower: 'We climbed to the roof of the tower to see the spire soaring above us.' A *steeple* is either the tower or, more usually, the whole structure, that is, the tower with the *spire* on top: '*The steeple, which has a spire to it, is placed in the middle of the church'* (Laurence Sterne), 'From the hill there was a good view of the town's many steeples.' However, *spire* is now the general word for the whole structure: 'Salisbury Cathedral has the tallest spire in England: 404 feet from the pavement.'

splash/slosh To *splash* a liquid onto something is to wet or drench it in a fairly haphazard way, either accidentally or deliberately: 'The artist splashed paint onto the canvas,' 'When I knocked over my cup, it splashed tea over the table.' To *slosh* a liquid is usually to throw or pour it intentionally, and often noisily or copiously: 'Whenever the plants looked dry, she just sloshed some water over them.'

splutter/sputter/spatter To *splutter* is to make a spitting sound: 'He spluttered angrily, searching for words,' 'The engine spluttered into life.' To *sputter* is similar, but the word emphasizes the actual sound, as a milder spitting or popping: 'The fireworks sputtered, and then went out,' 'The engine sputtered feebly, and then stopped.' To *spatter* is to scatter something wet or liquid: 'Erica tore open the carton, spattering milk everywhere,' 'Tom's pants were spattered with mud.'

spoil/despoil To *spoil* something is to ruin it or make it useless or valueless: 'The new road spoiled the scenery,' 'What a shame you spoiled the table by putting hot dishes on it.' To *despoil* something is to plunder it or rob it of whatever is valuable: 'The construction company despoiled the forest of many fine trees.'

spook/specter Both are ghosts, although the words are unexpectedly unrelated. A *spook* is a relatively 'friendly' ghost: 'Are you afraid of spooks?' A *specter* is a much more serious thing, and the word has gained a figurative sense to denote anything unpleasant or frightening that either 'haunts' from the past or threatens in the future: 'The spec-ter of mass unemployment loomed again.'

sporadically/spasmodically If something happens *sporadically* it hap-pens at intervals, from time to time: 'Many families watch TV only sporadically.' If it happens *spasmodically* it happens intermittently, in 'bursts': 'The couple in front argued spasmodically throughout the journey.'

sprain *see* strain

sprint *see* spurt

spurious *see* specious

spurn *see* scorn

spurt/sprint For a runner, a *spurt* is a sudden increase in pace, while a *sprint* is a stretch of running at high speed: 'Karen put on a spurt, over-took the others, and finished in a spectacular sprint.'

sputter *see* splutter

squeamish *see* queasy

stable/staple *Stable* is used for something firm and steady: 'The country longed for a stable government,' 'It is helpful to maintain a stable diet' (a balanced one). *Staple* is used for something basic or standard: 'Exams were a staple subject of conversation among the students,' 'Many people follow a fairly staple diet' (with the same basic foods).

stairs *see* steps

stalactite/stalagmite A *stalactite* is an icicle-shaped formation of lime that hangs down from a cave roof. A *stalagmite* is the opposite, and extends upwards like a pillar from a cave floor: 'A stalagmite grows higher as the water from a stalactite drips onto it.'

stalagmite *see* stalactite

stalk/stem A *stalk* is the stem, or main central part, of any plant that is not a tree or shrub: 'A vase of long-stalked bluebells stood on the win-dow sill.' However, a tree's trunk can be called its *stem*: 'The stem of a tree conducts water, minerals and food.'

stammer/stutter To *stammer* is to speak with difficulty, hesitating and repeating words: '"I can't - can't - don't know how to thank you," he stammered.' To *stutter* is also to speak with difficulty, but typically involves repeating a single letter rather than a whole word: '"B-b-but you s-s-said you'd t-t-tell me," she stuttered.'

staple *see* stable

starlight/starlit When used adjectivally, *starlight* simply describes a night sky with stars; *starlit* refers more to the visual effect of such a night: 'On starlight nights the comet could be seen quite clearly,' 'The starlit road stretched across the moor.'

starlit *see* starlight

start *see* beginning

statement *see* account

stationary/stationery *Stationary* is used for a person or thing that is not moving: 'The train was stationary in the station.' *Stationery* is written materials, as supplied by a stationer: 'There was plenty of paper in the office stationery store.' (Stationers are so called as at one time they had a regular stall, so were *stationary*, unlike other tradesmen, who traveled with their goods.)

stationery *see* stationary

steamy/seamy *Steamy* usually relates to something exotic, such as a scene in a film or novel: 'She developed a taste for steamy fiction.' *Seamy* is used for something unpleasant or sordid: 'Visitors to the city were mostly unaware of its seamy side.'

steeple *see* spire

stem *see* stalk

stepfather/father-in-law A person's *stepfather* is his or her mother's second or subsequent husband; a person's *father-in-law* is the father of his wife (if a man) or husband (if a woman): 'Janet was not on the best of terms with her stepfather, although her father-in-law was amiable enough.' (The same types of relationships apply to other members of the family, such as stepmother and mother-in-law, stepson and son-in-law.)

steps/stairs *Steps* are usually outside and are either single or restricted in number or else form a flight: 'He almost tripped over the bottom step.' *Stairs* are usually inside and form the main part of a staircase: 'She stood at the top of the stairs.'

stifle *see* smother

stimulant *see* stimulus

stimulus/stimulant A *stimulus* is something that spurs you on or encourages you: 'The thought of seeing her again served as a stimulus to his work that day.' A *stimulant* is either an actual substance that quickens some bodily or mental process, or something less tangible that has such an effect: 'Coffee can keep you awake because of its caffeine, which acts as a stimulant,' *'Public speaking is not only a powerful stimulant but a habit-forming one'* (Dean Acheson).

stint *see* scamp

stolid *see* solid

story *see* floor

stout *see* solid

straight/strait *Straight* is used for something direct, or continuing on an undeviating course: 'The road ran straight for three miles.' *Strait,* a much rarer word, is used for something tight or confining, usually in set phrases or word combinations: 'He said he'd try to keep on the strait and narrow,' 'The mental patient had to be confined in a strait jacket,' 'Aunt Dora was not at all strait-laced.'

strain/sprain To *strain* a part of the body, such as a muscle, is to stretch it too far, usually through overexertion: 'I strained my back trying to lift the motorbike.' To *sprain* something is to twist or wrench it: 'She sprained her ankle when she slipped off the curb.'

strain *see* stress

strait *see* straight

strangle *see* smother

stratagem *see* strategy

strategy/stratagem A *strategy* is a plan or tactic: 'She decided to try a new strategy to make the child eat.' A *stratagem* is basically the same, but the word is more formal and often relates to a military tactic, or implies that the scheme is a cunning one that will put someone at a disadvantage: 'The general discussed the stratagem with his officers,' 'They had s single stratagem: one kept the old lady talking while the other slipped in to look for her money.'

stress/strain From the point of view of mechanics, *stress,* or the force that acts on a thing and tends to pull it out of shape, results in *strain,* the state of being stretched or pulled tightly: 'Civil engineers calculated the stresses and strains of the bridge.'

strict/stringent A *strict* person or thing is severe or precise: 'My father was very strict,' 'Knowledge of word processing is a strict requirement for this job.' Something *stringent* is *strict* in the sense that it must be observed or obeyed: 'The theater imposed a stringent ban on smoking.'

stringent *see* strict

stroll/saunter To *stroll* is to walk in a slow and leisurely way: 'We strolled along the sea front after dinner.' To *saunter* is the same, but the word implies that the pace or manner of walking is deliberately casual: 'The boy sauntered home with his hands in his pockets.'

student *see* pupil

stupor/torpor A *stupor* is the state of being almost unconscious because of disease, drugs or shock: 'He had drunk so much that he lay in a stupor.' A *torpor* is a state of inactivity, lethargy or indifference, often as the result of some physical agent: 'After the late meal and the drink, many of the guests were slumped in torpor,' 'In the spring the earth awakens from its regular torpor.'

stutter *see* stammer

style *see* fashion

subconscious/unconscious *Subconscious* is used for something that influences one's actions but that one is only partly aware of: 'She reacted with subconscious relief' (she instinctively knew things were all right, but she couldn't explain why). *Unconscious* is used for something that influences one's actions although one is unaware of it: 'She reacted with unconscious relief' (she didn't realize she was so reacting).

subject *see* object

submerged/immersed If something is *submerged* it is under the water, often when it would not normally be: 'The canoeist struck a submerged tree-trunk.' If a thing is *immersed* it has been put under the surface of a liquid, often when it is supposed to be: 'Each mug of boiling water held an immersed tea-bag.' In a figurative sense, the two words are virtually identical, although *submerged* suggests a certain concentration: 'He submerged himself in the detailed reports of the case,' 'For the next three months she was immersed in her new duties.'

subsequent *see* consequent

subsidence/subsidy A *subsidence,* however pronounced, is a thing that has subsided or collapsed, or the place where this has happened: 'The road was closed because of the subsidence.' A *subsidy* is a grant of money, typically one made by the government to an industry: 'Farmers were offered an increased subsidy.'

subsidy *see* subsidence

substantial/substantive if a thing is *substantial* it is considerable or sizable: 'We need a substantial improvement in sales' (so that they are greater). If something is *substantive* it is real or actual: 'We need a substantive improvement in sales (not just a cosmetic improvement).

substantive *see* substantial

subtle/supple *Subtle* is used for something fine or delicate: 'Many of these words have a subtle difference of meaning,' 'She has a very subtle mind' (a sensitive and perceptive one). *Supple* is used for something that bends easily, whether literally or figuratively: 'Exercise helps to keep the limbs supple,' 'She has a very supple mind' (one that responds and adapts quickly).

successfully/successively If things happen *successfully* they have success: 'The explorers reached the North Pole successfully.' If they happen *successively* they happen one after the other, in succession: 'The explorers reached the North Pole successively' (first some did, then others).

successively *see* successfully

suffocate *see* smother

suit/suite Both words are used for sets of things, but not interchangeably. A *suit* is a set of clothes or playing cards: 'He always wore a three-piece suit, with matching vest,' 'Each pack of cards has four suits: spades, hearts, clubs and diamonds.' A *suite* is a set of furniture or rooms: 'Our new three-piece suite cost $3000,' 'Many hotels have suites with a bedroom, sitting room and bathroom.'

suite *see* suit

summary/synopsis A *summary* is a brief account of something: 'The program notes gave a summary of the plot.' A *synopsis* is more a condensed account of something, especially when the original is lengthy: 'The company secretary drafted a synopsis of the annual report.'

summon/summons To *summon* somebody is to call him or her or indicate that you want him or her to come: 'He summoned me to his chair,' 'The bell summoned the children in from the playground,' 'The driver was summoned to appear before the court.' To *summons* somebody is to take out a summons against him or her, that is, to give him or her an order to attend court. The third sentence above could thus equally read: 'The driver was summonsed.'

summons *see* summon

sumptuous *see* scrumptious

supernatural/preternatural *Supernatural* relates to something divine or superhuman: 'Many local people trusted the supernatural powers of the witch doctor.' *Preternatural* relates to something that *seems supernatural* but is known not to be in reality: 'The preternatural silence of the desert was awesome,' 'Our family doctor has a preternatural gift for knowing when a patient is not telling the truth.'

supersede/surpass To *supersede* someone or something is to take his or her or its place, and often (although not always) to be superior: 'The car superseded the horse-drawn carriage as the main form of transport.' To *surpass* a person or thing is to be superior to him or her or it: 'The car surpassed the horse-drawn carriage in both speed and distance.'

supine *see* prostrate

supper *see* lunch

supple *see* subtle

supplement/complement To *supplement* something is to add to it: 'She supplemented her son's lunch with an apple or an orange.' To *complement* something is to supply something that matches or blends with what already exists so as to make a whole or a complete set: 'Emma's plaid jacket complemented her black skirt,' 'The encyclopedia was in two complementary volumes, *Places* and *People*.'

suppose/supposing *Suppose,* as the first word of a sentence, refers to an imaginary condition, so that it really means 'if': 'Suppose you won the lottery. What would you do with the money?' *Supposing* is similar, but assumes that what follows is real or at any rate possible: 'Supposing we arrive early. What shall we do then?'

supposing *see* suppose

surpass *see* supersede

susceptibility *see* sensitivity

suspect/suspicious *Suspect* is used for something that cannot be relied on and that may be false: 'I regard most of what he says as suspect.' *Suspicious* is used for someone or something that causes suspicion: 'Her behavior was suspicious, and we decided to keep watch.'

suspense/suspension *Suspense,* apart from its sense as a mental state of tenseness, means the lifting or suspending of something, so that *suspension* is the state of being so suspended. The words frequently have a figurative sense: 'After the war the government ordered the suspense of rationing' (rationing was lifted or no longer in force), 'The suspension of rationing resulted in a richer diet for many' (people ate richer food as long as there was no rationing).

suspension s*ee* suspense

suspicious *see* suspect

swelled/swollen *Swelled* is used for something that is made acceptably larger or bigger: 'The meeting was swelled by a contingent from the branch office.' *Swollen* denotes that the increase in size is greater than it should be: 'The river was swollen from the recent rain.'

swingeing *see* swinging

swinging/swingeing A *swinging* blow is one made with a swinging action: 'The heavyweight boxer dealt a swinging blow to his opponent.' A *swingeing* blow is a heavy or hard one, however dealt: 'The bouncer felled the gatecrasher with a single swingeing blow.'

swollen *see* swelled

sylph *see* nymph

sympathy/empathy *Sympathy* (literally 'feeling with') is a compassion or commiseration with someone: 'When he heard the news, he offered her his sympathy,' 'She felt a great sense of sympathy for the homeless' (she pitied them). *Empathy* (literally 'feeling into') is the ability to understand another person's feelings and to put oneself in his position: 'She felt a great sense of empathy for the homeless' (she knew what they were feeling and what it must be like).

synopsis *see* summary

T

tablet *see* pill

tack *see* track

tactile/tactual *Tactile* relates to the sense of touch, while *tactual* relates to something caused by touch: 'The tactile senses of the skin include contact, pressure, cold, warmth and pain,' 'Tactual sensations may be pleasant or unpleasant.'

tactual *see* tactile

tall/high *Tall* relates to height from bottom to top: 'He's very tall for his age,' 'The church had four tall windows,' 'One of the buildings was taller than the others' (as we looked up at it). *High* relates to height from top to bottom, that is, how far above the ground or surface something is: 'The road skirted a high hill,' 'The church had four high windows,' 'One of the buildings was higher than the others' (as we could see when looking from the top floor).

tap *see* bug

tart/pie A *tart* is often distinguished from a *pie* by not being covered over with pastry.

tasteful *see* tasty

tasty/tasteful Both adjectives are approving, although *tasty* usually applies to food and drink and *tasteful* to anything that shows good taste or is generally agreeable and attractive: 'The lunch was tasty, and the table arrangement was tasteful to go with it,' 'The band played a nice tasty number that was new to me.'

taut *see* tight

team/teem A *team* is a group of people working or playing together: 'Welcome to the new team,' 'The reserve team had a good season.' To *teem* is either to be abundant or to pour: 'The forest teemed with wild-life,' 'The rain was teeming down.' *Team* and the first *teem* (but not the second) are related words, the common link being in the collection of people or animals.

tedious *see* tiresome

teem *see* team

teeter *see* totter

temerity/timidity *Temerity* is audacity or foolhardiness: 'She had the temerity to suggest he had acted irresponsibly.' *Timidity* is fear or shyness: 'He found it hard to overcome his timidity and rarely spoke at meetings.'

temporize *see* extemporize

tenaciousness *see* persistence

tenacity *see* persistence

tendency *see* trend

tense/terse *Tense* relates to something strained: 'The situation was relatively calm but remained tense.' *Terse* relates to something brief and abrupt: 'Her answers to the questions were terse and to the point.'

tepid/insipid/vapid As applied to speech or manner, *tepid* is used for something that lacks the expected enthusiasm: 'The first act of the play met with only tepid applause.' *Insipid* means dull and boring: 'The manager introduced a rather insipid assistant,' *'Kisses, though pleasant in private, are insipid in public'* (Lord Lytton). *Vapid* means the same, but implies a lack of sharpness or 'flavor': 'The magazine contained some rather vapid articles on the subject,' 'She handed me the flowers with a vapid smile.'

terminal/terminus A *terminal* is usually the complex of buildings at the beginning or end of an airline route: 'Our flight left from Terminal Three at O'Hare.' A *terminus* is the equivalent for a rail or road route: 'Grand Central Station is the terminus for trains from the north and west of New York.'

terminus *see* terminal

terrible/terrific In their non-literal senses, both words can refer to something very great: 'I've got a terrible amount of work to do,' 'The taxi went at a terrific speed.' When expressing a judgment, however, *terrible* is disapproving and *terrific* highly approving: 'What did you think of the play? I thought it was terrible.' 'You can get a terrific view of Paris from the top of the Eiffel Tower.'

terrific *see* terrible

terse *see* tense

test *see* trial

testament/testimony There is a subtle difference. A *testament* is a thing that provides proof of something, while a *testimony* is evidence in support of something: 'The new shopping center is a testament to the skill and vision of the architect' (it shows that he is good), 'The Eiffel Tower is a testimony to the skill of its designer and constructor' (it is proof that he must have been good).

testimony *see* testament

testy *see* touchy

tetchy *see* touchy

their/they're *Their* means 'of them,' while there is short for 'they are': 'That's their house, over there, and they're in the garden right now.'

thesis *see* treatise

they're *see* their

though *see* although

thrash/thresh *Thrash* is used in all the 'beating' senses: 'My father said he would thrash me if I ever did that again,' 'The whale thrashed the water with its tail,' 'We thrashed them 15-0,' 'I think we'd better thrash this out.' *Thresh* is now used only for harvesting: 'Corn used to be threshed by hand, but now the work is done by threshing machines.'

thresh *see* thrash

thrilled/enthralled To be *thrilled* by something is to be excited or stirred by it: 'I was thrilled to hear you had passed,' 'She was thrilled to think she might see him again.' To be *enthralled* by something is to captivated or spellbound by it: 'We were enthralled by the traveler's account of his journey,' 'He was enthralled by her every movement and gesture.'

throes/throws The *throes* of something are its difficult or painful condition: 'The animal was in its death throes,' 'We were in the throes of moving.' *Throws* are several acts of throwing: 'She won after only three throws.' (Confusion between the words may sometimes arise through a subconscious association with a difficult or painful throw in sport, as in wrestling.)

throws *see* throes

thwack *see* whack

tight/taut Something *tight* is tied or fastened firmly: 'The knot was very tight, and I could hardly undo it,' 'These shoes are too tight.' Something *taut* is stretched *tight:* 'Make sure the rope is taut before you hang anything on it, 'Her mouth was taut with emotion.'

till/until *Till* is normally more formal than *until,* and is used more for a point in time than for a duration in time: 'I'll wait till you return,' 'I stayed up till midnight,' 'You ought to stay in bed until you're better,' 'Until she was married she lived in Omaha.'

timid/timorous *Timid* means shy or frightened: '"Do I go on now?" she asked, in a timid voice,' 'He made a timid offer to help.' *Timorous* means much the same, but implies a reluctance or shrinking back: 'The new tenants were too timorous to complain about the noise,' 'The dog gave a few timorous barks on first facing the porcupine.'

timidity *see* temerity

timorous *see* timid

tinged/tinted *Tinged* is used for something that has a faint or slight color, a 'hint' of its full strength: 'The sky was now tinged with red.' *Tinted* implies that the color is a delicate one, or that it has been added to another that is brighter: 'The autumn leaves were tinted with gold and red' (but they were basically green or brown). *Tinged* (but not *tinted)* is also used figuratively: 'His voice was tinged with regret' (there was a note of sorrow or apology in it).

tinted *see* tinged

tiresome/tedious If a person or thing is tiresome he or she or it is troublesome or annoying: 'The children were being increasingly tiresome,' 'Checking these accounts is a tiresome task.' If someone or something is *tedious* he or she or it is also *tiresome* but in a way that is boring, dull and overlong: 'I find his company very tedious,' 'Cricket can be a tedious game to watch.'

titillate/titivate To *titillate* is to stir the senses pleasantly, often by way of promising something exciting: 'The wine titillates the palate' (stimulating it for more), 'The lurid cover of the magazine was designed to titillate readers' (it suggested explicit sexual descriptions or pictures). To *titivate* is to smarten oneself up or make minor adjustments to one's clothes or appearance: 'Trudy was titivating herself in the bedroom when the phone rang.'

titivate *see* titillate

titled *see* entitled

titter *see* giggle

to-do/ado A *to-do* is a fuss or disturbance: 'There was a proper to-do when the pipes burst.' *Ado* is used for activity of 'doing' in general, and is mostly found in the phrase 'without further ado,' meaning immediately: 'I signed on the dotted line and the clerk handed over the keys without further ado.'

tolerance/toleration *Tolerance* implies a lenient or charitable attitude towards someone or something: 'We viewed his rudeness with some tolerance, as he was the one who was paying us.' *Toleration* implies that one has to put up with something that one dislikes or does not approve of: 'She had a low level of toleration for such selfish behavior.'

toleration *see* tolerance

tone *see* note

Tony *see* Emmy

torpid *see* turgid

torpor *see* stupor

torso *see* trunk

tortuous/torturous If something is *tortuous* it is full of twists and turns or is long and complicated: 'We climbed the tortuous path up the hill,' 'The negotiations for the release of the hostages were protracted and tortuous.' If a thing is *torturous* it relates to torture: 'Families of the trapped men waited in torturous silence for news.'

torturous *see* tortuous

totter/teeter To *totter* is to walk with faltering steps, as if about to fall: 'The toddler tottered along beside his mother.' To *teeter* is to sway from side to side, whether moving or not: 'The chimney teetered dangerously in the high wind,' 'Elaine teetered along on her high heels.'

touchy/tetchy/testy A *touchy* person is ultra sensitive or quick to take offense: 'Arthur was very touchy about his disability.' A *tetchy* person is irritable or short-tempered: 'The children knew the store-owner was inclined to be tetchy.' A *testy* person is impatient or easily provoked to anger: 'Halfway across the field we were stopped by a testy old farmer.'

Toulon/Toulouse *Toulon* is a city and port in southeast France, on the Mediterranean; *Toulouse* is a city in the south of France on the river Garonne: 'We took the coast road west from Toulon through Marseilles and Montpellier to arrive at Toulouse in the evening.'

Toulouse *see* Toulon

tour de force *see* coup de grâce

track/tack/trail A *track* is a line of motion or travel, whether literal or figurative: 'We followed the track through the wood,' 'At last we were on the right track.' A *tack* usually applies to the course of a ship, especially one distinct from a previous or future course, and figuratively is a change of direction of some kind: 'The ship passed us on the starboard tack,' 'The government changed tack to a new policy.' A *trail* is a *track* made to a specific destination or target: 'A trail of broken branches showed where the animal had run,' 'The police were hot on the trail of the arsonist.'

trail *see* track

traitorous *see* treacherous

tramp/vamp As applied to a provocative woman, a *tramp* is a prostitute or sexually promiscuous: 'She was a real tramp, known locally as "the girl who never said no."' A *vamp* is a woman who uses her charms and wiles to seduce or exploit men: 'The actress Theda Bara was known as a "vamp" because of her vampirish, man-hungry roles.'

transient *see* transitional

transitional/transitory/transient *Transitional* applies to something passing from one position or state to another: 'After a transitional period, the country will gain full independence.' *Transitory* is used for something that lasts only a short time: 'She had a transitory sensation of giddiness.' *Transient* means the same, but implies that the condition or state soon passes: 'Tony had a transient affair with a colleague.'

transitory *see* transitional

translate/transliterate To *translate* something is to give its meaning in a different language; to *transliterate* something is to write it in the alphabet of a different language: 'Angela translated the Russian text into English, taking care to transliterate all the names correctly.'

transliterate *see* translate

translucent/transparent A *translucent* material allows light to pass through but not people to see through: 'The bathroom windows were made of translucent glass.' A *transparent* material is one that allows light to pass through and objects to be seen through it, even if indistinctly: 'The food container had a transparent lid.'

transparent *see* translucent

transport/transportation *Transport* is the means of carrying things or people somewhere: 'Public transport may be just as expensive as private.' *Transportation* is the act or business of transporting: 'Retailers are requested to meet all transportation costs.'

transportation *see* transport

transverse *see* traverse

traverse/transverse A *traverse* is a way or course across something, or a sideways movement across: 'The climbers were faced with a difficult traverse.' *Transverse* is usually an adjective referring to something that goes across, although it can also be a noun denoting a crosswise piece or object, usually in a technical or scientific sense: 'The roof had transverse beams,' 'In early chain-driven automobiles the transverse was the sprocket axle.'

treacherous/traitorous *Treacherous* relates to an act of treachery or betrayal: 'It was a treacherous act to reveal such confidential information.' *Traitorous* relates to a traitor: 'The dictator knew that certain generals could easily turn traitorous.'

treatise/thesis A *treatise* is an academic study of something, especially one that explains it or sets out its principles: 'Stephen Hawking's bestseller *A Brief History of Time* is a treatise on the origin of the universe.' A *thesis* is similar, but is usually an extended account of original research that forms part of a university degree course: 'Jane's thesis on the education of gifted children took her two years to complete.'

treble/triple The two words can sometimes be used interchangeably. However, *treble* usually applies to something that has been increased three times, while *triple* usually relates to something in three parts: 'The cost of food is roughly treble what it was ten years ago,' 'Some houses have been fitted with triple glazing, not double glazing.'

trend/tendency A *trend* is a gradual drift or movement of some kind: 'There was an increasing trend towards self-employment.' A *tendency* is an inclination or disposition to move in this way: 'The growing tendency towards violence at athletic events is very worrying' (but it may be possible to limit it or even halt it).

trial/test A *trial* is usually a 'sample run' of something, to see how it works or operates: 'We took the car for a trial run' (to see how we liked it), 'Let's give it a trial.' A *test* is a formal *trial* under particular conditions, often to see whether somebody or something is working properly: 'The test pilot gave the aircraft a clear report,' 'Anyone failing the test will be unable to take it again.'

tricksy *see* tricky

tricky/tricksy A *tricky* person or thing is deceptive or needs careful handling: 'He's rather a tricky customer,' 'The situation is a tricky one.' A *tricksy* person is someone who habitually plays tricks or is known to be mischievous or crafty: 'Watch out for him and his tricksy little ways.' A *tricky* person, too, often causes concern or even fear, while a *tricksy* person invites admiration or even amusement.

triple *see* treble

trite *see* trivial

triumphal *see* triumphant

triumphant/triumphal *Triumphant* means that someone or something has triumphed: 'Torvill and Dean made a triumphant return to the ice rink after an absence of many years.' *Triumphal* relates to the triumph itself: 'The Romans built many triumphal arches to mark their victories,' 'The procession continued on its triumphal way.'

trivial/trite Something *trivial* is unimportant; something *trite* is hackneyed or dull: 'His comments were not only trivial, and hardly worth saying, but also trite and scarcely original.'

troop/troupe A *troop* is a body of people or animals: 'A large troop of schoolchildren waited at the crossing,' 'A troop of monkeys lived nearby.' A *troupe* is a group or company of performers: 'The dance troupe toured the country with great success.' *See also* trooper.

trooper/trouper A *trooper* is a soldier of low rank in a cavalry regiment: 'He swears like a trooper.' A *trouper* is a loyal or dependable person: 'She's a real trouper, and would help anyone in trouble.' *See also* troop.

troupe *see* troop

trouper *see* trooper

trunk/torso The *trunk* is the whole human body apart from head, arms and legs: 'His trunk was completely covered in spots.' A *torso* is either the *trunk* of a human statue or an idealized, statue-like body: 'The torso of an ancient statue was discovered on the island,' 'Steve stood before the mirror, admiring his rippling torso.'

tumid *see* turgid

tumult/turmoil A *tumult* is a sizable disturbance caused by a crowd of noisy people: 'We could hardly hear ourselves for the tumult in the hall,' *'The tumult and the shouting dies;/The Captains and the Kings depart'* (Kipling). A *turmoil* is a state of disorder or confusion, but not necessarily a noisy one: 'As a result of the coup, the country was in turmoil,' 'Her mind was in turmoil: how could it have happened?'

tune/melody A *tune* is a meaningful phrase or line of music: 'The tune was a lively one, and we wanted to dance,' 'Go on: give us a tune.' A *melody* is essentially the same, but the word implies a poetic or moving quality, or that the *tune* is specially memorable: 'The old Irish song had a haunting melody,' *'The song is ended (but the melody lingers on)'* (Irving Berlin).

turbid *see* turgid

turgid/tumid/turbid/torpid *Turgid* means unhealthily hard and swollen, and is used mostly for distendable objects or organs: 'The cows waited with turgid udders, long overdue for milking.' *Tumid* means almost the same, but does not necessarily imply a hardness: 'The malnourished children had tumid stomachs.' *Turbid* means opaque or muddy: 'The stream was turbid from the recent heavy rain.' *Torpid* means sluggish or lethargic, with a suggestion of drowsiness: 'The actors performed to a torpid audience.' *See also* stupor.

turmoil *see* tumult

U

unartistic *see* inartistic

unaware/unawares *Unaware* describes the state of a person who does not know something or about something: 'I was unaware you had moved,' 'He was unaware of the trouble he had caused.' *Unawares* is used for something that happens unexpectedly or as a surprise: 'You caught me unawares: I was just taking a shower,' *'Be not forgetful to entertain strangers: for thereby some have entertained angels unawares'* (Bible: Hebrews 13:1).

unconscious *see* subconscious

undertone/overtone An *undertone* is an undercurrent of some kind, often of something unpleasant; 'The discussion had an undertone of hostility about them.' An *overtone* is an additional or implied meaning to something: 'The play had fairly obvious political overtones.'

undoubtedly *see* doubtless

unexceptionable *see* unexceptional

unexceptional/unexceptionable If something is *unexceptional* it is unremarkable or ordinary: 'The weather was quite unexceptional for the time of year,' 'The milk yield that year was unexceptional and about average.' If a thing is *unexceptionable* it is quite satisfactory, and meets with no criticism: 'Maisie's work at school was unexceptionable and rarely faulted.'

uninhabitable *see* habitable

uninterested *see* disinterested

unreadable *see* illegible

unsanitary *see* insanitary

unsociable/unsocial *Unsociable* is used for someone who does not wish to be friendly or talk to others: 'He's very unsociable, and doesn't like parties.' *Unsocial* can also mean this, but more commonly refers to something that is in some sense anti-social: 'Anne's new job involves unsocial hours, so that she has to work in the evening or on weekends.'

unsocial *see* unsociable

until *see* till

unwanted/unwonted Someone or something *unwanted* is not wanted; something *unwonted* is out of the ordinary or unusual: 'What do you do with your unwanted presents?' 'All the others had left, and Frances felt unwanted,' 'That was an unwonted liberty on your part,' 'Sarah settled down to the unwonted task of designing a flag.'

unwonted *see* unwanted

upstage/downstage Technically, *upstage* is at the back of the stage (which was formerly higher than the front): 'Crowd scenes usually take place upstage.' *Downstage* is thus at the front of the stage: 'The actress moved downstage where all could see her.' Hence to *upstage* someone, by drawing attention away from him to oneself: 'The Vice-President was apparently trying to upstage the President.'

uptown *see* downtown

urban/urbane *Urban* relates to the town and its life: 'The urban population gradually decreased as people moved out to live in the country.' *Urbane* is used (sometimes derogatively) for a refined manner or smooth sophistication, supposedly like that of a town or city dweller (as distinct from a country bumpkin): 'He gave me an urbane smile.'

urbane *see* urban

Uruguay *see* Paraguay

usage *see* use

use/usage *Usage* is the regular or accepted method of making *use* of something: '*Nor thou be rageful, like a handled bee,/And lose thy life by usage of thy sting*' (Tennyson), 'The food blenders seized up as a result of improper usage,' 'The aim of this dictionary is to illustrate correct English usage.'

V

vacant/vacuous A *vacant* look is one suggesting that the person has not understood or is unintelligent: 'When I asked him if he wanted to realize his assets, he simply gave me a vacant look.' A *vacuous* look is a stupidly or dully *vacant* one: 'The man's vacuous expression was typical of someone who had undergone such terrible experiences.'

vacate/evacuate To *vacate* something is simply to leave it: 'The audience vacated their seats when the performance ended.' To *evacuate* a place is to leave it because of danger: 'The audience evacuated the theater because of a bomb scare.'

vacuous *see* vacant

vale/veil A *vale* is a poetic word for a valley, surviving in various place-names: 'We sailed forth to see the sunset from the vale,' 'They lived in the Vale of Evesham.' A *veil* is a covering of some kind: 'The bride raised her veil to kiss the groom,' 'There was a veil of mist over the valley.'

valiant/valorous/gallant A *valiant* person or deed is a brave one: 'Despite a valiant attempt, he failed to rescue the dog.' *Valorous,* as a loftier word, often connotes a successful act or deed: 'Many admired the inhabitants' valorous defense of their city.' A *gallant* person or deed is also a brave one, but the word has overtones of honor and even self-sacrifice: 'The strikers put up a gallant fight but in the end lost their claim.'

valorous *see* valiant

vamp *see* tramp

vantage *see* advantage

vapid *see* tepid

vaunt *see* flout

vegan *see* vegetarian

vegetarian/vegan A *vegetarian* eats no meat; a *vegan* does not eat or use any animal product whatsoever for any purpose: 'Felicity was happy to be a vegetarian, but did not go so far as to be a vegan.'

vehement *see* violent

veil *see* vale

venal *see* venial

venial/venal A *venial* offense is a slight or excusable one: 'Some dogs are punished for relatively venial offenses.' A *venal* offense is a serious one that involves corruption and bribery: 'The candidate committed the venal offense of bribing colleagues to vote for him.'

venturesome *see* adventurous

venturous *see* adventurous

verbiage/verbosity Although the words are largely synonymous, *verbiage* often applies to the use of too many obscure or difficult words in speech or writing, while *verbosity* is simply the use of too many words in general: 'Lawyers have to plow through the verbiage of many long and tedious documents,' 'He was basically a good speaker, but much of what he had to say was lost in sheer verbosity.'

verbosity *see* verbiage

vertex/vortex A *vertex* is the highest point or top of something: 'The vertex of a triangle is the point opposite the base.' A *vortex* is a whirling mass of something, literally or figuratively: 'The whale dived suddenly, leaving nothing but a white and green vortex in the blue of the ocean,' 'Many of the citizens were drawn against their will into the vortex of the rebellion.'

verve *see* vim

view/vista In a figurative sense, a *view* is a person's opinion or outlook: 'He expressed his views on the matter,' 'In my view, this should be stopped,' 'We should take a long-term view of all this.' A *vista* is a far-reaching *view,* especially one with many prospects and possibilities: 'The political vista was uncertain,' 'The important discovery opened up new vistas of research for the scientists.'

vigorous/rigorous *Vigorous* is used for something energetic or whole-hearted: 'Vigorous exercise in the young is not always beneficial,' 'He gave the proposal his vigorous support.' *Rigorous* is used for something strict or even harsh: 'The manufacturing process was subjected to rigorous scrutiny at every stage,' 'Only by rigorous training did the team get where they are today.'

vim/verve *Vim* means vigor: 'She tackled the job with real vim and determination,' 'Put some vim into it!' *Verve* means enthusiasm: 'The team played with real verve, often outrunning their opponents,' 'Her first novel had a verve and style that won the acclaim of many reviewers.'

violent/virulent/vehement *Violent* relates to power or strength in general: 'There was a violent storm last night,' 'The constituents wrote a violent letter of protest to their congressman about the matter.' *Virulent* has to do with something harmful or hostile: 'The police were the subject of virulent verbal attacks.' *Vehement* is used for something strong and passionate, not necessarily unpleasantly so: 'The school board issued a vehement denial of the allegations,' 'The performance was outstanding and won the vehement praises of all who saw it.'

virulent *see* violent

vista *see* view

vocation/avocation A person's *vocation* is his calling or profession: 'Nina always felt it was her vocation to be a doctor.' A person's *avocation* is also this, although the word has retained something of its former meaning, which denoted a minor occupation taken on by way of a diversion: 'Although long a teacher, Alan considered his true avocation to be that of a writer.'

vogue *see* fashion

voodoo *see* hoodoo

voracious *see* rapacious

vortex *see* vertex

vouch *see* avow

W

wages *see* salary

wait/await To *wait* for someone or something is to expect him or her or it: 'I waited for Kim to catch up with me,' 'I hate waiting for trains.' To *await* a person or thing is the same, although the verb has a formal ring: 'A warm welcomes awaits all our guests,' 'We await your reply.' Occasionally one can *wait* something directly (without 'for'): 'You'll have to wait your turn.' But often *wait* has no following noun: 'Have you been waiting for long?'

waive *see* wave

wake/awake/waken/awaken The four verbs are to an extent inter-changeable. The various senses and uses are best shown by the examples: 'The cat woke me by jumping on the bed,' 'I usually wake at seven,' 'The old lady awoke to find a burglar in her room,' 'Only much later did Sue awake to the reality of the situation,' 'The nurse was careful not to waken the baby,' 'Hazel's work with animals awakened an interest and concern that never left her,' 'I was awakened by a loud knocking at the door,' 'We awakened to find the others had already gone.'

waken *see* wake

warranty *see* guarantee

wary/chary To be *wary* of something or someone is to be cautious of it or him or her: 'I was wary of upsetting his feelings,' 'Many of us were wary of our new boss.' To be *chary* of something is to be careful or reluctant about it: 'I'm rather chary of giving money to charities,' 'The firm was chary about taking on applicants with little or no experience.'

wastage *see* waste

waste/wastage *Waste* is the useless expenditure or consumption of something: 'The city council was criticized for its waste of public money on the project,' 'What a waste of time!' *Wastage* is the loss of a part or portion of something, especially when it is expected or allowed for: 'The daily wastage of water from many reservoirs can amount to

245

hundreds of gallons,' 'The firm reduced its workforce by natural wastage, and did not hire new employees when existing ones retired or left for another job.'

wave/waive/waver To *wave* is to gesture to someone with the aim of conveying a meaning or message: 'I waved her goodbye,' 'The clerk waved the small boy aside.' To *waive* something is to give it up voluntarily although one has a right to it: 'The prisoner waived his right to appeal the sentence,' 'I waived my claim for damages as it was too much trouble.' To *waver* is to falter or hesitate: 'Her courage never wavered for an instant,' 'We couldn't make up our minds about the house, and while we were wavering someone else bought it.'

waver *see* wave

wet/whet To *wet* something is to make it damp or moist: 'You'll need to wet the clay before molding it,' 'I'm afraid Bobbie wet his bed again last night,' 'The old man told us he was off to wet his whistle at the tavern.' To *whet* something is to sharpen it or make it keener: 'These travel brochures whet my appetite for a vacation abroad.'

whack/thwack To *whack* is to hit hard: 'The angry father whacked his son,' 'The player whacked the ball over the net.' To *thwack* is also to hit hard, but with something flat: 'She thwacked the wasp with the folded newspaper.'

where/wherefore *Where* relates to the location of someone or something: 'Where are you going?' 'This is where we live.' *Wherefore* does not mean 'where' but 'why,' especially in Juliet's famous rhetorical question to Romeo: '*O Romeo, Romeo! wherefore art thou Romeo?*' (Shakespeare). (She is not asking where he is but why he should belong to the Montagues, the bitter enemies of her own Capulet family.)

wherefore *see* where

whet *see* wet

whim *see* fancy

whimsy *see* fancy

whirl *see* whirr

whirr/whirl To *whirr* is to make a buzzing or vibrating sound, as of a rapidly rotating object: 'The fan whirred softly overhead.' To *whirl* is to rotate quickly: 'The autumn leaves whirled as they fell,' 'William whirled the rope around his head.' The two words are related.

whiskey *see* whisky

whisky/whiskey *Whisky* is from Scotland, i.e., Scotch; *whiskey* is from Ireland and the United States: *'Freedom and Whisky gang thegither!'* (Robert Burns), *'Whiskey is the life of man,/Whiskey, Johnny!'* (anonymous American shanty).

who's *see* whose

whose/who's *Whose* means 'of whom': 'Whose house is that?' 'I don't know whose it is.' *Who's* means 'who is' or 'who has': 'Who's next?' 'Who's got my pen?' 'Let's see who's winning.'

wiggle *see* writhe

wince *see* flinch

wink/blink To *wink* is usually to close one eye briefly deliberately, while to *blink* is to close both eyes involuntarily: 'He winked when he saw what I was up to,' 'She blinked when she went out into the bright sunshine.'

woebegone *see* woeful

woeful/woebegone *Woeful* is used for something wretched or unhappy: 'It was a woeful tale she had to tell.' *Woebegone* is used for someone who is wretched or unhappy: 'The child had such a woebegone expression that it touched our hearts.'

woman *see* lady

worth/worthwhile *Worth* implies that the thing mentioned has a value: 'It's worth getting the clock repaired' (it's a good clock, and we shouldn't abandon it). *Worthwhile* refers more to an action: 'It's worthwhile getting the clock repaired' (it's worth taking the trouble).

worthwhile *see* worth

wrack *see* rack

wraith *see* wreath

wrapped/rapt *Wrapped* is used for something that has been enclosed or covered: 'The sandwiches were wrapped in aluminum foil,' *'Ye shall find the babe wrapped in swaddling clothes'* (Bible: Luke 2:12). *Rapt* is used for a person absorbed in something or carried away by it: 'The children watched with rapt attention.' The words are unrelated.

wreak *see* reap

wreath/wraith A *wreath* is a ring of something such as flowers, smoke or fog: 'There were wreaths of mist over the fields as the dawn broke.' A *wraith* is a ghost, or something that appears or moves like one: 'We could faintly see her moving through the trees like a wrath,' 'The wraiths of smoke then lifted to reveal the road stretching before us.'

wriggle *see* writhe

wring *see* ring

writhe/wriggle/wiggle The three verbs are in descending order. To *writhe* is to twist and turn the body, especially when in pain: 'The patient was writhing in agony.' To *wriggle* is to make quick, short twisting and turning movements: 'The children were wriggling in their seats, impatient to be released,' 'The baby was wriggling its toes.' To *wiggle* is the same, although the movements are often made with just a part of the body: 'He wiggled his finger at the baby.'

Y

yoke *see* yolk

yolk/yoke A *yolk* is the *yellow* part of en egg (the words are related): 'Take the yolks of three eggs.' A *yoke* is the piece of wood that joins the necks of two animals pulling together, and hence the word for anything oppressive or burdensome: 'The old photo showed a yoke of oxen drawing a plow,' *'It is good for a man that he bear the yoke in his youth'* (Bible: Lamentations 3:27).

your/you're *Your* means 'belongs to you': Is this your pen?' 'I won't forget your birthday.' *You're* means 'you are': 'Look out, you're spilling your drink.'

you're *see* your

Z

Zaire *see* Zambia

Zambia/Zimbabwe/Zaire *Zambia,* formerly Northern Rhodesia, and *Zimbabwe,* formerly Southern Rhodesia, are officially English-speaking countries in southeast Africa. *Zaire* (or *Zaîre),* originally the Belgian Congo, then Congo (Léopoldville), then Congo (Kinshara), is in central Africa astride the Equator: 'Zaire, Zambia and Zimbabwe run from north to south alphabetically and in gradually decreasing size.'

zenith *see* nadir

Zimbabwe *see* Zambia